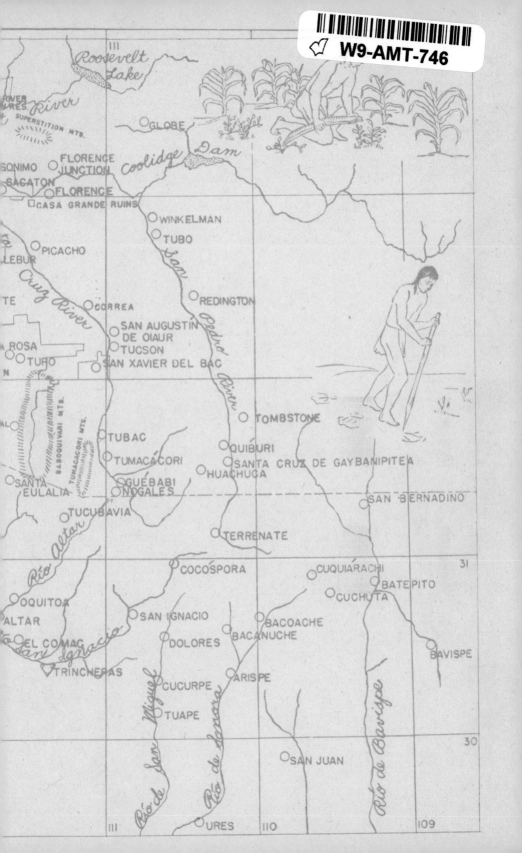

Roosevelt Lake

RIVER
URES.
SUPERSTITION MTS.
River

GLOBE

GONIMO
FLORENCE JUNCTION
Coolidge Dam

SACATON
FLORENCE
CASA GRANDE RUINS

WINKELMAN

TUBO

San

PICACHO
LEBUR

Cruz River

CORREA

REDINGTON

SAN AUGUSTIN DE OIAUR
Pedro River
TE

ROSA

TUFO
TUCSON
SAN XAVIER DEL BAC

N

BABOQUIVARI MTS.
TUMACACORI MTS.

TUBAC
TOMBSTONE

TUMACACORI
QUIBURI
SANTA CRUZ DE GAYBANIPITEA
HUACHUCA

SANTA EULALIA
GUEBABI
NOGALES

SAN BERNADINO

TUCUBAVIA

Río Altar

TERRENATE

COCOSPORA
CUQUIARACHI
31
BATEPITO

OQUITOA
CUCHUTA

ALTAR

SAN IGNACIO
BACOACHE
BACANUCHE

EL COMAC
San Ignacio
DOLORES
BAVISPE

TRINCHERAS
ARISPE

Río de San Miguel

CUCURPE

Río de Sonora

TUAPE

Río de Bavispe

30

SAN JUAN

111
URES
110
109

PIMA AND PAPAGO
INDIAN AGRICULTURE

INTER-AMERICANA SERIES

(Dealing with Latin-America and cultural relations in the
Southwest of the United States)

J. ORTEGA, *General Editor*

❖

SCHOOL OF INTER-AMERICAN AFFAIRS
THE UNIVERSITY OF NEW MEXICO

❖

Published by the University of New Mexico Press
in the following sections

SHORT PAPERS

STUDIES

DOCUMENTARY SOURCES

INTER-AMERICAN TRANSLATIONS

MISCELLANEA

INTER-AMERICANA
STUDIES I

Pima and Papago
Indian Agriculture

EDWARD F. CASTETTER

WILLIS H. BELL

THE UNIVERSITY OF NEW MEXICO PRESS
ALBUQUERQUE, N. M.
1942

C3

FOREWORD

The work of publishing this first number of our *Inter-Americana Studies* was well under way when the war broke out. *Pima and Papago Indian Agriculture* is strictly an academic study, and we are glad that it is so and that our series begins true to the spirit in which it was planned: to provide, within our unfortunately too modest means, facilities for the publication of scholarly monographs bearing on Latin America and the American Southwest.

It is one of the avowed objectives of the new School of Inter-American Affairs of The University of New Mexico to encourage research. The pursuit of knowledge for its own sake is not luxury but one of the noblest functions and responsibilities of the university. The war is rightly causing a paucity, and may cause the elimination of all that is not directed towards winning it; yet democracies have a way of keeping the printing presses running. England, for instance, has continued producing scholarly literature.

Within the established aims of the series, however, the present emergency calls for a realistic policy, and the coming issues will deal with topics closely connected with the problems of cultural relations in this region. Many intelligent Americans agree that the solution of problems of cultural adjustment between our nation and the Hispanic minorities is almost a necessary prerequisite to the establishment of human bonds between the two Americas. The coming numbers in this series will contribute, we hope, much information and guidance on the question. Our School will set in motion every resource it may command toward a rational approach to the relationship of the Anglo-Saxon and Hispanic groups within and without our borders.

Clarity from the point of view of conception, significance of content, comprehensiveness and critical range, lucidity in presentation, and reasonable standards of literary form and interest, shall be expected and looked for in the manuscripts submitted for this series.

The authors of *Pima and Papago Indian Agriculture* have had the benefit of financial assistance and individual and institutional collaboration from several sources. No more eloquent tribute than this interest on the part of others could have been paid to the efforts of Drs. Castetter and Bell. I should like to add that Dr. Alan Swallow of the English department, and Mr. Fred Harvey, director of the University Press, have rendered valuable help in the supervision of the physical make-up of the book.

JOAQUÍN ORTEGA
General Editor of the Series

PREFACE

Scattered data on the early agriculture and other aspects of the economic life of various Indian groups in the Southwest are available in the literature, but treatises covering the primitive basis of subsistence of specific Indian groups, such as Hill's *The Agricultural and Hunting Methods of the Navaho Indians* and Whiting's *Ethnobotany of the Hopi*, are rare. Wilson's *Agriculture of the Hidatsa Indians*, a Plains tribe, must be regarded as the best account of the technique of Indian agriculture yet published. It is our purpose, therefore, to issue within the next few years a series of comprehensive studies, of which this is the first, presenting the early basis of subsistence of the several Indian groups in the Southwest, with special emphasis placed on agriculture.

The material herein presented is based upon field studies made by the authors among the Pima-Papago in the fall of 1938, 1939 and 1940, supplemented by data gleaned from the relevant historical, ethnographical and archaeological literature. The field studies were made among the Pima on the Gila River Indian Reservation, centering at Sacaton, Arizona; the Papago on the Papago Indian Reservation with headquarters at Sells, Arizona; the Papago on the reservation at San Xavier; and a few Papago on the so-called Maricopa Indian Reservation at Maricopa, Arizona.

The method followed in doing the field work was for the authors to work independently, each with his own informants and interpreters, then compare notes at the end of each day.

Obviously, differences in agricultural technique exist in different parts of the Papago and Pima territories. There is always danger of over-formulating procedures, such as the method of planting, and the reader is cautioned against regarding any such operation or aspect of agriculture as stereotyped. It is realized that among both peoples sub-units exist and that among different villages, and even different individuals, variations occur. The following account of Pima and Papago agriculture and of the general basis of subsistence of these people represents a composite picture drawn from a number of informants variable in background, technical knowledge, ability to impart what they knew etc., and no one of whom would be capable of presenting all the ethnographic information herein contained. A deliberate effort has been made to present as complete a picture as possible of the early basis of Piman subsistence, indicating local or individual departures from the general situation wherever these appeared to be significant or were consistent with the limitations imposed by space.

Fortunately the Pimans, particularly the Papago, are a people among whom primitive methods of agricultural technique and of food gathering are still functional and therefore recoverable. Thus it was not difficult to find old informants, especially Papagos, whose knowledge of the old crops, techniques and procedures is extensive.

Following is a list of our main informants and interpreters. Although we have interviewed many additional Pima and Papago informants to obtain data on specific aspects of agriculture, it has not been deemed necessary to list them.

Papago Informants:
  Chico Bailey—Pisinemo
  Alvina Gerónimo—Big Fields
  Ismilio Lewis—Emika
  José Petero—Silnakya
  Bernabé López—San Pedro
  San Pablo—Santa Rosa
  Santiago Maristo—Komelik
  Mattías Hendricks—Vamori
  Mariano Domingo—Kohatk
  José Santos—San Xavier

Pima Informants:
  Manuel Lowe—near Sacaton
  Nicolas John—Sweetwater
  Lewis Nelson—Casa Blanca
  Vanico—near Sacaton
  Paul Azule—near Sacaton

Papago Interpreters:
  Peter Blaine—Sells
  Martín Maristo—Topawa
  Joe Raphael—San Xavier
  Ralph Gonzales—San Xavier
  Rev. Bonaventura Oblasser also
    kindly assisted in interpreting
    and as a medium of contact.

Pima Interpreters:
  Paul Azule—near Sacaton
  Leonard Lowe—near Sacaton
  Isaac Paul—Sweetwater

No work as extensive as this can be executed without the assistance of a number of specialists in various fields. We have found it necessary to call for help upon a number of individuals, every one of whom has responded most generously. It is, therefore, a genuine pleasure to acknowledge our obligations.

Most of all we wish to express our gratitude to the officers of the American Philosophical Society who made the field work possible by two grants. We are especially indebted to Dr. Leslie Spier, who has assisted in a number of ways, most tangible of which was a careful and critical reading of the manuscript. The manuscript has been read and criticized by Volney H. Jones of the Ethnobiological Laboratory of the University of Michigan; by C. J. King, Senior Agronomist, U. S. Field Station, Sacaton, Arizona, who has assisted also in supplying data on modern Pima agriculture; by H. A. Ireland, Agricultural Extension Agent of the Gila River Reservation; and parts of the manuscript have been checked by Dr. D. D. Brand, Professor of Anthropo-geography at the University of New Mexico. C. B. Brown, Agricultural Agent for Pima County, Arizona, has kindly furnished information on modern Papago crops. To H. V. Clotts, Assistant Director of Irrigation, Office of Indian Affairs, we are especially obligated for data on Pima and Papago irrigation and for making it possible to borrow from the Office of Indian Affairs rare copies of unpublished reports on Pima-Papago irrigation. Apart from those mentioned specifically in the footnotes to the text, we are indebted to others for definite technical information. Deserving special mention are: Dr. Forrest Shreve, Carnegie Desert Laboratory, Tucson, Arizona; Dr. Charles T. Vorhies, Economic Zoologist, University of Arizona; Dr. Lyman Benson, Assistant Professor of Botany, University of Arizona.

We are particularly obligated to T. B. Hall, who, during the time of our studies among the Papago, was Superintendent of the Papago Indian Reservation, and who was very helpful in facilitating our work among these Indians; also to

Superintendent A. E. Robinson of the Gila River Indian Reservation, who assisted in making contacts among the Pima.

To Dr. Fabian García, Experiment Station Director and Horticulturist of the New Mexico State College, we wish to express our appreciation for permission to grow our Piman crops on the Conservancy District Agricultural Experiment Substation farm near Albuquerque.

Finally, we wish to thank the General Editor of the *Inter-Americana* series, Dr. Joaquín Ortega, and the Committee on Publications of the School of Inter-American Affairs of the University of New Mexico, for sponsoring this edition, for a careful checking of the manuscript, and for rendering faithfully other editorial assistance.

A number of references are cited frequently and in the interest of brevity these are given the following designations:

Bartlett, *Narrative*—Bartlett, *Personal Narrative of Explorations and Incidents in Texas, New Mexico,* etc.

Bolton, *Anza*—Bolton, *Anza's California Expeditions.*

Bolton, *Kino*—Bolton, *Kino's Historical Memoir of Pimería Alta.*

Bryan, *Papago*—Bryan, *The Papago Country of Arizona.*

Coues, *On the Trail*—Coues, *On the Trail of a Spanish Pioneer.*

Documentos—*Documentos para la Historia de México.*

Emory, *Notes*—Emory, *Notes of a Military Reconnoissance from Fort Leavenworth, in Missouri, to San Diego, in California.*

Lumholtz, *New Trails*—Lumholtz, *New Trails in Mexico.*

Mange, *Luz*—Mange, *Luz de Tierra Incógnita,* etc.

Russell, *Pima*—Russell, *The Pima Indians.*

Spier, *Yuman Tribes*—Spier, *Yuman Tribes of the Gila River.*

Underhill, *Papago*—Underhill, *Social Organization of the Papago Indians.*

Wyllys, *Velarde's Relación*—Wyllys, *Padre Luis Velarde's Relación of Pimería Alta, 1716.*

TABLE OF CONTENTS

LIST OF ILLUSTRATIONS

CHAPTER I

THE PIMANS

The Pimans, a name applied to the whole group of Pima-Papago in both Mexico and the United States, anciently extended in irregular distribution from southern Sonora to the Gila River, occupying a slightly larger territory than at present, but living in essentially the same areas since they were first discovered. The division of these Pimans into two groups designated Pima Bajo (Lower Pima) and Pima Alto (Upper Pima) is purely geographical, not linguistic; formerly both were continuous, and in Kino's day there was intercourse between them.[1] However, the Upper Pima were culturally inferior to the lower group. The term Pima Alto did not come into use in the present sense until missionary activity extended northward to the present international boundary toward the close of the seventeenth century.

The limits of Pimería Baja (home of the Pima Bajo), the distribution of whose people appears explainable largely on the basis of a very deep intrusion of the Opata, can be determined rather closely, except in the desert toward the Seri where there were no permanent water holes and hence no settlements. The Pima Bajo, except the Yécora group, occupied warm valleys in southern Sonora, while the Pima Alto held the high basins from below the present Arizona border northward to the Gila. In general, the Lower Pima occupied the margins of the Sierra Madre Mountains between the Papigochic and upper Mayo rivers on the Chihuahua-Sonora boundary (Yécora group), where they carried on agriculture without irrigation; both sides of the middle and upper Yaqui River (Nebome group) where they had irrigated agriculture; and the flood plain of the Sonora River below

1 Alegre, *Historia de la Compañía de Jesús en Nueva España*, III 83.

1

the gorge of Ures downstream to well below Hermosillo, but also to the Nacámeri (Rayon) district on the Horcasitas River. This was the Ures group, of whom some had irrigated, others non-irrigated agriculture. Thus these Pimans appropriated the river valleys as far downstream as water was available. The Seri inhabited chiefly the coast. Between the two areas lay a hunting and gathering zone of desert which both groups penetrated, and in which they sometimes clashed.[2]

The first contact of Europeans with the Pima Bajo occured in 1533 when a Spanish expedition under the command of Diego de Guzmán, sent out to continue northward explorations by Nuño de Guzmán, encountered the Nebome group at a site which may be identified with modern Cumuripa, the lowermost Pima village on the Yaqui River.[3] Missionary activity began among the Pima Bajo in 1619, and since that time they have been gradually dying out and little is known in detail of their ancient economy. They did have canal irrigation in suitable places, and cultivated maize, beans, and agave (probably), domesticated the turkey, wove colored cotton clothing, cotton and agave fiber blankets, made deerskin garments, and practiced ceremonial drinking, utilizing among other things the juice of agave and wild grapes.[4]

Pimería Alta, occupied by Pima, Sobaipuri, Soba and Papago, extended from the San Ignacio in Sonora northward to the Gila, and from the San Pedro westward to the Gulf of California and the Colorado. Its northeastern boundary was roughly the limit of the Gila plain abutting against the hills. The upper Gila, as well as upper Salt, Valley was held by the Apache, and there is no evidence that they were ever occupied

2 Sauer and Brand, *Prehistoric Settlements of Sonora*, pp. 38-41, 83; Beals, *Comparative Ethnology of Northern Mexico*, pp. 102, 157-62.

3 Sauer, *Road to Cibola*, pp. 11-13.

4 Alegre, *op. cit.*, II, 70, 117, 124, 175, 186; Pérez de Ribas, *Historia de los Triumphos de Novestra Santa Fé*, pp. 240-41, 360, 371, 384-85; *Obregón's History of Sixteenth Century Explorations*, pp. 157-58, 160; Beals, *loc. cit.*

by Pimans. Since the Pima Alto constituted the northern
frontier of Jesuit missionary activity and outpost of Spanish
domain against those Apache north of the present international boundary, the resulting greater interest in the
nature of their life than that of tribes to the south has yielded
much more knowledge of their history.[5] Records left by
Kino, Anza, Font, Mange, Velarde and Garcés, and docu-
mented by Bolton, Coues, Bandelier, et al, have given us a
better understanding of this area than any other part of New
Spain.

Spanish missionaries first came to the Papago and Gila
Pima toward the close of the seventeenth century. Although
Pimería Alta had been entered by Fray Marcos, by Melchior
Diáz (who had been dispatched overland from Sonora by
Coronado to find Alarcón, and whose route evidently ran
through the San Miguel Valley, thence down the Magdalena
to the Altar and through Papaguería to the Cocopa country
at the mouth of the Colorado),[6] and by the main Coronado
party in 1539-41, these explorers passed only along its eastern
and western borders; it is no longer believed they went down
the Santa Cruz Valley. Sauer believes the Coronado party
went down the San Pedro River Valley inhabited by Sobaipuri, through the Arivaipa basin then through Eagle Pass
between the Pinaleño and Santa Teresa mountains to the
Gila River. In the one and one-half centuries between that
day and Kino's entrance into Pimería Alta in 1687, Arizona
had not been entered from the south by a single recorded
expedition. Moreover, so far as is known, not since 1605,
when Oñate went from the Hopi country down the Colorado
River, had any white man seen the Gila. Hence, the redis-
covery and the first interior exploration of Pimería Alta were
the work of Kino, although a few of the Upper Pima were

[5] Sauer, Distribution of Aboriginal Tribes, pp. 52-3, map; Bolton, Kino,
I, 50.
[6] Sauer, Road to Cibola, pp. 36-8.

reduced (converted and settled) earlier from the Opata missions to the south.[7]

When Kino reached the scene of his labors the frontier mission station was at Cucurpe in the valley of the San Miguel. In the east, in Nueva Vizcaya, were the already important *reales*, or mining camps, of San Juan and Bacanuche, and to the south were numerous missions, ranches and mining towns; but in Pimería Alta, beyond a line extending in an arc from a little west of Tuape to a little north of the missions Cucurpe, Bacanuche, Bacoache, Cuchuta and Batepito, almost to 31°, all was to white man untouched and unknown country. This line represented the northern frontier of settlement in 1687. Bolton[8] tells us that in Kino's day the region just north of the present international boundary, between 109° and 110°, was the military frontier, and into it were made numerous forays by Spaniards and Pimans to punish the hostile Apache. Also, that by 1694 more than 100,000 head of stock ranged at Terrenate, Batepito, San Bernardino and Janos, these regions being south of the boundary.

On the edge of this virgin country, about fifteen miles above Cucurpe, in Sonora, Kino founded the mission of Nuestra Señora de los Dolores at the Indian village of Cosari. From here he and his associates pushed the frontier of missionary endeavor and exploration across Pimería Alta to the Gila and Colorado rivers. In 1700 he founded the mission of San Xavier del Bac near Tucson, and within the next two years those of Tumacácori and Guebabi in Arizona.[9]

THE PIMA ALTO

Entering Pimería Alta in 1687, Kino found northern Sonora and the interior south of the Gila occupied by four divisions of the Pimans, who were in the main agricultural

[7] Sauer, *Aboriginal Population of Northwestern Mexico*, p. 29.
[8] Bolton, *Kino*, II, Map of Pimería Alta, 1687-1711.
[9] *Ibid.*, pp. 50-52.

people, those along the Gila, San Pedro, Santa Cruz and Altar growing crops by canal irrigation. The modern delimitation into Pima and Papago was not recognized. Kino's first division comprised the Pimans along the San Pedro, middle Santa Cruz and middle Gila rivers, who were distinguished from those farther south as Sobaipuri, now practically extinct except for traces of their blood still represented in the Pima and Papago. Of these Sobaipuri there were three groups. The first dwelt along the San Pedro from about the present town of Tombstone northward to the Gila, their most southerly settlement being Gaybanipitea; another along the middle Santa Cruz from San Xavier del Bac northward roughly to Picacho, while the middle Gila from the general vicinity of Casa Grande nearly to Gila Bend was occupied exclusively by the third group, at that time called Gila Pimas, and who now for the most part dwell on the Gila River Reservation. Because they are so well known to investigators, they are today designated as the Pima proper, but in Kino's day they were usually referred to as Sobaipuris or Soba y Jipuris.[10]

The second main Piman division, then regarded as the Pima proper, occupied the slopes of the watershed which extends irregularly westward from Huachuca Mountain to Nogales, with villages on the upper waters of the south-flowing Sonora, San Miguel and Cocospora rivers, on the west-flowing Altar down to and including Oquitoa, and down the San Ignacio some distance below the modern city of the same name; also the southern stretches of the north-flowing San Pedro and Santa Cruz. The most northerly Pima settlement on the San Pedro was the village of Huachuca, and on the Santa Cruz that of Tumacácori. (A few lived as far east as Teuricachi Valley, in the vicinity of Cuquiárichi.) Another, the third division of Pimans, early known as the Soba (a term practically equivalent to the name Piato), inhabited the middle and lower Altar, and seemingly the lower San Ignacio

10 *Ibid.*, I, 50-1, 170, 173, 193n; Bolton, *Rim of Christendom,* p. 247; Spier, *Yuman Tribes,* p. 27.

in Sonora, with their principal village at Caborca. Bolton states they also dwelt along the Gulf Coast farther west.[11] When Mange[12] visited them in 1694 he described them in the vicinity of Pitiquín and Caborca as having rich irrigated land and growing an abundance of maize, beans and pumpkins.

West of the Sobaipuri and Pimas on both sides of the international boundary was the fourth Piman division, the Papago, or Papabotes as the early Spaniards called them. They are among the tribes which to the present have been least disturbed by white man. More specifically, Papaguería, a term applied to the Papago territory only after the coming of the Spaniards, was that portion of Pimería Alta occupied by the Papago, and comprised the desert area south of the Mexican border well toward but not including the Altar or Santa Cruz valleys, and westward toward the Colorado and the Gulf. Sauer and Brand[13] have pointed out that the eastward extension of the term Papaguería to include the Altar and Santa Cruz valleys is unwarranted, and that it constituted the territory west of the permanent streams, the Sonoita being the only permanent stream in the Papago country of Sonora. Neither valley was Papago territory until after the mission period.

Gifford[14] relates that near Somerton formerly dwelt a small band of Papago who made trips to the Sonoran Gulf Coast, but who were finally exterminated by Mexicans. Maricopa informants told Spier of this group, indicating that they lived in the Yuma desert region. These are, in Spier's[15] opinion, the Sand Papago of Lumholtz,[16] who occupied the desert area east of the Colorado at the head of the Gulf of California and southward to the Rio de Sonoita. Their principal camps were at the waterholes in the Gila and Pinacate

11 Bolton, loc. cit.; Sauer, Distribution of Aboriginal Tribes, p. 53.
12 Mange, Luz, pp. 217, 225.
13 Sauer and Brand, op. cit., p. 96n.
14 Gifford, The Cocopa, p. 262.
15 Spier, op. cit., pp. 7-8.
16 Lumholtz, New Trails, pp. 329, 394, map.

ranges east and south of the desert, with headquarters at Hótu-nikat. They probably never numbered more than 150, and in the middle of the nineteenth century were attacked by an epidemic which only four families survived. These remaining families retired to other areas, and for the last sixty or seventy years the sand dune country has been practically uninhabited. Underhill[17] conjectures that these people in the sand hills were ancestors of the present very poor Sand Papago who occupy the arid region west of the Ajo Mountains, around Tinajas Altas, Tule Tanks, Papago Tanks and the vicinity of Dome. Similarly Hoover[18] writes of them occupying the forbidding arid region west of the Ajo Mountains, their very existence depending upon knowledge of natural water tanks in the mountains. Also at present several small villages of Sand Papago are located around the town of Ajo and their largest remnant is at Dome and Blaisdell. He asserts that Quitobac, the old head village for the Sonoita Valley, is Sand Papago in kinship. Descendant therefrom was the Papago village at Sonoita, the now extinct village of Tak and the nearly extinct village of Quitobaquito. The village of Sonoita was a favored site as the Sonoita River is here a permanent stream.

Papago and Pima speak the same language, with but slight variations. They are combined under one name, The People, differentiating themselves as Desert People (Papago) and River People (Pima), the designation of River People denoting their dependence upon the Gila. The Papago of Southern Arizona, known in their own language as *toxono o' otam*, Desert People, have been nicknamed *papawi o' otam*, meaning Bean People, a name at one time applied only to the westernmost Desert People living in the barren region on both sides of the present Mexican border. It was not until after the mission period that those changes were initiated which resulted in the formal demarcation of Papago from Pima.

17 Underhill, *Papago*, p. 20.
18 Hoover, *Generic Descent of the Papago Villages*, pp. 261-62.

At the time of Kino's arrival in the last decade of the seventeenth century, the agricultural settlements of eastern Pimería Alta were still undisturbed, but by the middle of the nineteenth century the distribution of its Indian peoples had changed considerably, largely because of Apache pressure. This was especially true of the northeastern frontier, where Velarde in 1716 reported the Apache established to the south as well as to the north of the Gila. Spier, Underhill, and Bandelier[19] have given some information on such shifting. In general, it may be said that Apache raids, continuing from Kino's day, gained momentum during the early eighteenth century and extended at intervals with increased fury over entire eastern Pimería Alta and far down the Gila. By the middle of the eighteenth century the San Pedro, which had been densely populated by Sobaipuri and Pima, was abandoned to the Apache, and its inhabitants settled in the next valley to the west, the Santa Cruz, which also soon became untenable. In the south, the Altar too was depopulated and agriculture almost came to a standstill. From 1790 to 1815 there was in the southern part of Papaguería a temporary period of peace with the Apache, and finally terrorism from this source was terminated when the Federal Government subdued the Apache in 1874.

As the Apache decimated the villages along these rivers, the desert Papago gradually reoccupied the valleys, particularly the Santa Cruz and the Altar, being increasingly attracted to the rich lands and stable food supply of the missions; this resulted in the present modified distribution of Papago and Pima. The Papago, who previously had come into the Piman settlements along the Altar and Santa Cruz for only short periods to labor in the harvest and receive religious instruction, gradually took over the valley land; this was almost wholly a nineteenth century infiltration. Gradually the Papago became indistinguishable from other Piman groups.

[19] Spier, *op. cit.*, pp. 7-9; Underhill, *op. cit.*, p. 23; Bandelier, *Final Report*, II, 464.

Apache pressure brought about such extensive redistribution of the peoples that today it is very difficult to consider for our purposes the Sobaipuri, Pima, Papago and Soba separately.

The Papago, originally far less numerous than the Pima to the north and east, because of their isolation survived to a much greater degree than did the latter. Sauer[20] is of the opinion that the Papago are nearly as numerous today as they were at the time their area was discovered. He indicates the following population figures for the Pimans aboriginally:

```
Pima Bajo  ..............................................  25,000
Pima Alto
    On the Mexican side
        Borders of the Opatería ....................  1,000
        Hímeri group (those living northwest of the
            Opata)  ........................  4,000
        Upper Altar ..............  ..........  2,000
    ·   Soba group  ............................  4,000
    On the American side
        Tumacacori area  ........................  1,000
        San Pedro (Sobaipuri of the east)  ..........  2,500
        Middle Santa Cruz ............  ........  4,500
        Gila River  ............................  1,000
                                            ─────
Total for Upper Pima proper ..........................  20,000
Total for Papago, perhaps ............................  10,000
```

Sauer indicates an aboriginal population of 25,000 for the Pima Bajo and a total population of 40,000 for the same area in 1920. About three-fifths of the Papago were located on the American side of the border, a ratio increased at present because of the attractions of the American reservations and the amalgamation with the Mexican population of many Papagos south of the border. Papaguería was part of Mexico until the Gadsden Purchase of 1853 brought its northern portion under the rule of the United States. A number of the Papago settlements south of the international border have been abandoned,[21] but many of the Papagos in Arizona still live in the

[20] Sauer, *Aboriginal Population of Northeastern Mexico*, pp. 5, 29, 32.
[21] In 1915 the number of Papago in Mexico was estimated at between five hundred and two thousand; Clotts, *Nomadic Papago Surveys*.

same general area, and to a large extent on the very sites they occupied in Kino's day.

Although Kino labored assiduously for some twenty-five years the missions dwindled soon after his death, and, despite the courageous but less able or forceful efforts of Garcés, showed no appreciable revival. Thus after this brief Spanish influence the Papago were left to themselves. Although they had secured horses, cattle, wheat, and a few fruits and vegetables from the Spaniards, and their houses and clothing underwent some change by adoption, their fundamental material culture suffered little disturbance and their religious and social life continued with almost no change. The Papago, dwelling in a barren, inaccessible and inhospitable country, were little visited by the whites, who had no inclination to acquire their lands. Thus they remained relatively isolated, and have retained intact to the present most of their aboriginal culture.

The Pima story is vastly different. Beginning in 1825-26 with the entrance of the Patties, the first American pioneers into Arizona, who came for the purpose of trapping beaver, followed by two military expeditions along the Gila in the 1840's and the inception of the gold rush days in 1849, the Gila Pima were subjected to increasingly intensive white influence. It was the permanent flow of water over stretches of its course that made the Gila the most practicable route from the Rocky Mountains to California across the southern desert area. When the Gadsden Purchase brought northern Pimería Alta with its Gila Pima and northern Papago under the rule of the United States, the Gila Valley was soon settled by whites; the Pima rapidly became acculturated, and their history since 1840 has been one of pronounced cultural decadence.[22]

The Gadsden Purchase, which included the Gila Valley and a stretch of desert to the south, cut Pimería Alta practically in two, the northern portion thereafter being under

22 Underhill, *Papago Calendar Record*, pp. 3, 5; Russell, *Pima*, pp. 19-20.

the control of the United States, the southern under the rule of Mexico. The desert dwellers, who formally came to be known as Papago and had always had more affiliations with the Altar Valley than with the Gila, continued their connections with the people of the Altar, and this intensified their isolation.[23] Moreover, establishment of the international boundary has decreased intercourse between the upper and lower portions of the old Pimería, with the result that at present little is known of the Sonoran Pima, now amalgamated with the Mexican population, a situation which applies in less degree to the Papago below the border.

At present the Papago in the United States are located largely on three reservations in southern Arizona—one established in 1874 just southwest of Tucson at San Xavier del Bac, formerly a Sobaipuri village (70,080 acres); another, the large desert reservation established as such in 1917 and containing 2,335,510 acres; and the third is a small area (10,240 acres) at Gila Bend, founded in 1882. Also there are some Papago, as well as a few Pima, living on the so-called Maricopa Indian Reservation just south of Maricopa, Arizona, set aside in 1912. These reservations originally comprised a total of 2,884,720 acres although some deductions were made later.[24]

The Growler Mountains actually represent the present western limit of Papago distribution, for little is known of the Areneños, or Sand Papago, just north of the Gulf of California and west of these mountains. Within Papaguería there are one hundred settlements, forty-seven of which are located near Papago fields. In addition there are several abandoned villages. The Pima dwelt for the most part along the Gila and lower Salt rivers and now are concentrated largely on the reservation at Sacaton, set aside as such in 1870.

23 Underhill, *Papago*, p. 28.
24 Clotts, *History of the Papago Indians and History of Irrigation on Indian Reservations.*

CHAPTER II

LAND, CLIMATE AND VEGETATION

Most of the Piman territory lies within the area known
as the Sonoran Desert, described by Shreve, as well as within
the Sonoran Biotic Province, delimited by Dice. The vegetation of the Mexican portion of the area has been discussed by
Brand.[1] That part of Pimería Alta falling within the scope
of our field studies on the Pima-Papago lies in southern Arizona, and is nearly coincident with the southern part of the
physiographic division designated as the Basin and Range
Province. It is an arid country with well-eroded fault block
mountains rising between broad, waste-filled, intermont
depressions. In the lower portions of these depressions, far-
thest from the mountains, sand and gravel washes traverse the
flat, silt lands, which have a surface veneer of coarser material.
As the mountains are approached, the terrain rises in long,
gentle, alluvial slopes of sandy soil which still nearer the
mountains become gravelly or stony, until rock floor finally
is exposed in the washes. The general axis of surface features is northwest to southeast. These intermont plains rise
gradually from an elevation of several hundred feet in the
west to more than 2,500 feet in the east and northeast, and
from them rise abruptly the low, narrow mountain ridges
which are most massive and elevated in the east, culminating
with the Baboquivari Range and its peak with an elevation
of 7,741 feet.[2]

Climatically the chief features of our area are the low and
erratic precipitation, averaging about ten inches on the
inhabited plains and associated with a very high rate of
evaporation; the high summer temperatures often well above

[1] Shreve, *Plant Life of the Sonoran Desert;* Dice, *The Sonoran Biotic
Province;* Brand, *Notes to Accompany a Vegetation Map of Northwest Mexico.*
[2] Hoover, *The Indian Country of Southern Arizona,* pp. 39-45.

12

100° F.; mild winters with temperatures little below freezing except in the higher levels; a pronounced daily temperature range averaging from 30° to 40°; an annual high mean of 320 to 350 days of sunshine; and a long growing season.

THE GILA BASIN AND THE PIMANS

Unlike Papago agriculture, that of the other Pimans depended upon irrigation water obtained from several rivers. Chief of these, the Gila, rises in the mountainous country of western New Mexico, changes its character markedly westward from the Buttes, east of Florence, and emerges from the mountain region of eastern Arizona. Here it enters upon the detrital plains of the Basin Range Province, and, throughout its westward course to the Colorado, except at a few places, winds over deep deposits of alluvium in broad valleys between short mountain ranges. Over its lower course it has cut a very shallow valley. The Gila is an interrupted river, that is, having a permanent flow over short distances of its entire course throughout the year, and along these stretches of perennial water there have been more or less permanent settlement and irrigation. However, its volume steadily decreases and in the lower 150 to 200 miles of its course there are long stretches of its bed which are covered with water only after heavy rains.[3] The precipitation in the middle Gila area, covering the region of the Gila River Indian Reservation, roughly is between ten and thirteen inches. Precipitation figures for stations within and adjacent to our area are: Casa Grande, 19.39 in.; Florence, 9.99 in.; Phoenix, 7.90 in.; Gila Bend, 5.95 in.; and Sacaton, 10 in. Farther to the east and north in the mountains precipitation ranges from fifteen to twenty inches or more. At Sacaton the highest rainfall occurs in July and August, the lowest in April, May and June. Here the temperature during the coldest weather seldom goes below 20° F. and the summer temperatures have been as high as 117°. The mean daily range between day and

3 Hoover, *op. cit.*, pp. 39-48; Ross, *The Lower Gila Region*, pp. 62-7.

night temperatures is about 35° F. There is a long frost-free period of about 263 days.[4]

Only a few tributaries of importance flow into the Gila River below the point where it leaves the mountains. One of these, the Santa Cruz, rising in the rather high mountains east of Nogales, is an interrupted stream constituting a more or less continuous watering place from the Mexican border to Tucson, although little water flows from it into the Gila except during floods. Anciently the Pimans carried on irrigated agriculture throughout this southern portion of the valley. North of Tucson there is no permanent watering place on the Santa Cruz much south of its junction with the Gila, the stream there being wholly intermittent, but throughout this area some flood-water irrigation has always been practiced. The San Pedro River rises in Mexico and flows in a direction a little west of north to its junction with the Gila, and, although perennial, it fluctuates greatly.[5] Here, too, the Pimans pursued irrigated agriculture.

It is advisable now to return to the Pima on the Gila, since we have more definite information on them than on the other Pimans who pursued agriculture based on river irrigation. Since about 1880 the character of the Gila has changed markedly. Prior to that time the greater low-water flow was confined to a relatively deep, narrow channel through its flood plain, overflowing only in time of heavy rains or melting snows. It was bordered by more luxuriant vegetation than at present, consisting of cottonwood, arrow-weed and tall grass, and in 1849 this permanent stream was navigable in a flatboat from the present Pima villages to the Colorado. At present the channel is a sandy waste with many winding subsidiaries, constantly shifting in position, with no low-water flow except in favored places, and sediment is

[4] Smith, *Climate of Arizona*, pp. 388-92; King, Beckett and Parker, *Agricultural Investigations*, pp. 2-3; Turnage and Mallery, *An Analysis of Rainfall in the Sonoran Desert*.

[5] Bryan, *Papago*, p. 119; Ross, *op. cit.*, pp. 63-4.

silting up the channel. The river has a perennial flow below Pima Butte, due largely to underground drainage deflected from the Salt River as well as some seepage from the Roosevelt irrigation project. As late as the seventies, and even eighties, it occupied a narrow channel and provided adequate water for Pima irrigation, while lakes or ponds were once common over the river flats. Gradually, however, the river channel has widened, grassy areas have given place to a more xerophytic vegetation, and the ponds have disappeared. The condition was aggravated by the disastrous flood of 1891, coming at the end of a series of wet years. Pima informants stated that twice since 1890 the water rose over the lower terrace and covered it up to Casa Blanca.[6]

At the lower end of the Pima Reservation there is always sufficient water in the river for irrigation, although floods wash out the dams and make diversion more difficult. The upper portions of the reservation have suffered considerably from lack of water, due to its utilization farther up the river for farms operated by the whites. This first became serious in the sixties[7] with diversion in the Florence district immediately above the reservation, and reached its climax after the construction of the Florence Canal and its dam, projected in 1886, the dam being finished in 1922. The Florence district was in turn deprived of much of its water by diversion in the upper Gila. Hence, since about 1890, the demands upon the Gila waters above the reservation have caused a definite shortage of irrigation water among the Pima. Thus, by 1904, the amount of land cultivated by these Indians was reduced from 14,000 to about 7,000 acres. In the closing years of the last century a more detailed survey[8] was made by the Federal Government to determine the feasibility of constructing res-

6 Hoover, *loc. cit.*; Ross, *op. cit.*, pp. 62-7; Bryan, *op. cit.*, p. 109.

7 *Report of the Commissioner of Indian Affairs* for 1869, p. 53; *ibid.* for 1904, pp. 7-21; Russell, *Pima*, pp. 32-3; Southworth, *History of Irrigation on the Gila River Indian Reservation*, pp. 21-4.

8 Lee, *Underground Waters of Gila Valley*, p. 68; Lippincott, *Storage of Water on Gila River*.

ervoirs to impound the waters of the Gila for the purpose of ameliorating this unsatisfactory condition. One of the specific recommendations issuing from this study was that the San Carlos (Coolidge) Dam be constructed at the point where the San Carlos River joins the Gila.

In 1924 the Federal Government authorized the construction of the Coolidge Dam on the Gila in the mountain narrows below San Carlos for the purpose of preventing floods, providing water to the Indians for irrigation, and reclaiming other lands. This was completed in 1929 and has supplied water for that portion of the reservation above the Arizona Eastern Railroad, as well as made possible the irrigation of much of the upper terrace lands on the entire reservation. In addition, the Federal Government has provided, for the use of these Indians, a number of wells from which water for irrigation is supplied. In 1904 Lee observed that the Gila Valley had a considerable underflow of water, which near Sacaton and at Gila Crossing returned to the surface and to some extent formed a surface flow; also that a small amount of the underflow returned to the surface as seepage water and was used for irrigation. He further states that experiment and computation indicated the volume of water in the Gila underflow was probably greater than the needs of the Pima, could be pumped at reasonable cost, and that the chemical nature of this water was favorable for irrigation. Although in 1929 crops were harvested from only 7,774 of the 29,530 acres of available farm land on the Gila River Reservation, in 1935 the harvested acreage was about 35,000 acres, of which 24,000 were farmed by Indians, the remainder planted to alfalfa by the Indian Service. The original survey of Pima lands in 1859 allotted them 64,000 acres to which were added 81,140 acres by another survey in 1869, and in 1876 another portion consisting of 9,000 acres in the vicinity of Blackwater was added to the eastern end of the reservation.[9]

[9] King, Beckett and Parker, *op. cit.*, p. 9; Russell, *op. cit.*, p. 32n.

The sides of a well-developed valley flat in the alluvial plain along the Gila are characterized by many terraces which parallel the river. The highest one is represented in only a few areas by small benches or tops of isolated hills. The lower terrace is well developed along the whole length of the river and is bounded by bluffs about seventy-five feet high. Below this is the flood plain with its recent deposits. On the Gila River Reservation, what is known as the upper terrace ranges to as much as twenty feet high. This is best defined on the north side of the river below Gila Butte and vanishes entirely east of Gila Butte and around Sacaton. Between Casa Blanca and Snaketown the flood plain attains its greatest width, four miles, and within this plain the river has cut an inner flat or bottomland which carries all but the heaviest floods. Here this is bounded by lower terraces varying from three to ten feet in height. The bottomlands are sandy with a considerable admixture of silt, while the lower terrace has a silty and usually heavy soil. The upper terrace is of sandy composition with a veneer of gravel.[10]

Lands under cultivation today, as well as the canals, are confined to the lower terrace; the villages are situated mainly on the edge of the upper terrace, although Sacaton, Blackwater and the villages between are not located with reference to terraces. However, before whites settled in the area there were no Pima villages in the upper end of the present reservation. Canals on the lower terrace today form a veritable network which reaches a very high development north of Casa Blanca. The main fields as well as the bulk of canals of the prehistoric inhabitants of the area (Hohokam) were situated on the lower terrace. Some of the Hohokam canals, such as the prehistoric Snaketown Canal, with an apparent total length of more than ten miles (a short distance as compared with some of the ancient canals in the Gila and Salt river valleys), ran along the upper terrace, which was evi-

[10] Hoover, loc. cit.; Bryan, op. cit., p. 108.

dently cultivated in places; none of these upper terrace lands has been utilized by the modern Pima. Since the subjugation of the Apache, the Pima have been extending their settlements gradually over the tillable lands of the lower terrace, although at the middle of the last century they were almost entirely concentrated in villages on the south side of the river from about two and one-half miles below Sacaton westward nearly to Pima Butte.[11] Irrigated lands in the vicinity of Sacaton have always been located chiefly on the south side of the Gila since the north side has less bottomland and irrigation is more difficult. A detailed history of irrigation on the Gila River Indian Reservation together with the history of the various canals and ditches is given by Southworth.[12]

THE DESERT AND THE PAPAGO

Our Papago land as delimited is an arid, forbidding, isolated desert region in which life was conditioned largely by the scarcity of water. Long ago Font tersely aired his opinion of the area thus: "In short, in all this land of Papaguería which we passed through, I did not see a single thing worthy of praise."[13] Formerly it was thinly populated throughout by Papagos who at present live almost wholly in its eastern and central portions. In 1925 Bryan[14] observed that the spacious western portion of the region, which has a rainfall of less than five inches per year and contains extremely few permanent watering places, was inhabited by a solitary white man. However, various factors have contributed toward making this western territory more accessible and habitable within recent years.

The climate of our Papago region is characterized by high temperature and low precipitation. Summer temperatures

[11] Hoover, op. cit., pp. 46-8; Haury, in Gladwin et al, Excavations at Snaketown, I, 50-8; Bartlett, Narrative, II, 233.
[12] Southworth, op. cit.
[13] Bolton, Anza, IV, 33.
[14] Bryan, op. cit., xvii.

often exceed 100° F., and at times approach 120°. The growing season is long, for example, ranging from 249 days at
Tucson to 331 at Ajo. At Yuma, killing frosts very rarely
occur except in the lower parts of the valley, while farther
east a few killing frosts occur each winter. Both daily and
seasonal range in temperature is very great.[15]

The outstanding climatic characteristic of the Papago
country is its very low precipitation; in general this increases
with altitude, although the smaller mountains seem to have
little effect on storms, and their vegetation does not indicate
any large increase in effective rainfall over that of the
adjacent plains. This is especially true of the area west of
the Growler Mountains. A most extreme desert condition is
found along the lower Colorado River, an area that may
receive from none to three or more inches of rainfall per
year, and even this may fall in a single storm. The western
portion of the area is thus a veritable desert, but to the east,
with higher elevation, the vegetation is inclined to be steppe-
like. Distance from the Gulf of California is also a governing
factor in the precipitation in this area, the amount increasing
with distance. With respect to the mean annual precipitation, Bryan distinguished three divisions in the Papago country. West of the Growler Mountains it ranges from three
and one-half to five inches (3.33 in. at Yuma) ; between the
Growler and Baboquivari mountains from five to ten inches;
east of the Baboquivari Mountains it is more than ten inches.
The belt of low precipitation, less than five inches, extends up
the Gila Valley to Gila Bend and in the interior of our Papago
area to the Growler Mountains.[16] Mallery's studies show that,
dividing his rainfall stations in the Sonoran Desert into four
groups on the basis of elevation, those below one thousand feet
had an annual average of 4.19 in.; those between one thousand and two thousand feet, 8.10 in.; those between two
thousand and three thousand feet, 11.03 in.; and those above

[15] Smith, *op. cit.;* Bryan, *op. cit.,* pp. 29-31, 79-80.
[16] Bryan, *op. cit.*

three thousand feet, 25 in. The following table lists precipitation figures as presented by Mallery and by Smith:[17]

	Altitude	Precipitation
Ajo	1770	9.88
Baboquivari	3675	17.98
Sierrita Mts.	4100	16.45
Avra Valley	2400	10.11
Soldier Camp (Santa Catalina Mts.)	7875	33.45
Pima Canyon	2600	11.00
Desert Laboratory Grounds (S. W. Corner)	2400	12.39
Tucson	2387	10.96
Sells	2500	11.62
23 Mile Hill .:.......................	2350	11.26
Growler Pass	2250	8.27
Agua Dulce	1140	6.98
Pinacate Plateau	910	4.25
Tule Tank	1115	4.13
Tinajas Altas	1050	5.47
Lechuguilla Desert	715	4.22

Distribution of rainfall in the Sonoran Desert, within which our Papago area falls, is usually concentrated in two distinct periods of the year—the winter and summer seasons.[18] Turnage and Mallery have treated the months from May to October as the summer rainy season; November to April as the winter season. They find that there is a progressive increase of summer over winter rainfall from northwest to southeast in the Sonoran Desert and adjacent territory; also that the northwestern half of the region receives more winter than summer rain. Sykes and Smith point out that for Arizona approximately 35 per cent of the total annual precipitation falls during December, January, February and March, and 45 per cent during July, August and September. The summer rains are apt to be spontaneous and of short duration, while those in winter as a rule are gentle and may continue for several days. However, the winter-summer ratio varies considerably over different parts of the state. Mallery shows that at most of his stations the summer rains were

17 Mallery, Rainfall Records for the Sonoran Desert; Smith, op. cit.
18 Turnage and Mallery, op. cit.; Smith, op. cit.; Mallery, op. cit.; Sykes, Rainfall Investigations, p. 229.

greater in amount than the winter rains, but as one went westward they tended to become more nearly equal until, in extreme southwestern Arizona, the winter rains were heavier. He refers to unpublished data of Sykes, who found that analyses of the 118 stations in Arizona show that in most sections the winter rains are greater, and that only in southeastern and southcentral Arizona and two relatively small areas in eastcentral and northeastern Arizona do the summer rains exceed winter precipitation.

Data on the total annual rainfall at any given position constitute a basic starting point for a consideration of the climate of that region. However, knowledge of the distribution, involving fluctuation in rate and amount, is more important from the standpoint of natural vegetation and agriculture than is the yearly total. The wide variation in amount and temporal distribution of rainfall, with their periods of drought and series of dry years, render the Papago country a precarious place to pursue agriculture.

VEGETATION[19]

In considering the natural vegetation of the American portion of the Pimería Alta it is desirable to begin with the watercourses that drain the southern desert; one may say that wherever deep alluvial soils have been built up and subterranean water is available, dense forests of mesquite formerly were, and to some extent still are, to be found. Such dense forests occurred on the bottomlands of the San Pedro, the flood plain of the Santa Cruz, lower and middle Gila roughly from within a few miles of Yuma as far east as the point where the Southern Pacific Railroad crosses the Gila northwest of Vahki, and the lower Colorado. Remnants of these original stands still exist along the San Pedro, notably be-

[19] This account of the vegetation of the area under consideration is based upon Nichol, *The Natural Vegetation of Arizona;* Bryan, *op. cit.;* information secured by correspondence with Dr. Forrest Shreve of the Carnegie Desert Laboratory at Tucson; and our own field observations.

tween Redington and Cascabel. Today mesquite and salt-bush *(Atriplex* and *Dondia)* bottoms characterize the Gila from a few miles east of Yuma to the railroad mentioned, as well as a few spots as one approaches Winkelman on this river. The flood plains of the Gila and upper Santa Cruz (also lower Colorado) support groves of cottonwood *(Populus Fremontii),* and associated with them less numerous black willows *(Salix nigra)* and dense thickets of arrowweed *(Pluchea sericea).* Cottonwood and willow are to be found wherever there is permanent water, as on the Arivaca and Sonoita creeks. Where the river is quite stable or the ground higher, the mesquite and saltbush encroach upon the bottom-lands; also scattering areas of such vegetation, some of considerable extent, occur in the *playas* of the Santa Cruz, Santa Rosa and, to a less extent, San Pedro valleys. In the more open stands of mesquite, squawberry *(Lycium* spp.) and saltbush are common, and sparsely intermixed with mesquite in the higher, cooler valleys of the San Pedro and Santa Cruz is the mountain hackberry *(Celtis reticulata).* Along the edges and in the openings of the forests of these two drainages, sacaton grass *(Sporobolus Wrightii)* thrives, and commonly associated shrubs are lotebush *(Zizyphus lycioides),* skunk-bush *(Rhus trilobata),* chamiso *(Hymenoclea monogyra),* desert saltbush *(Atriplex polycarpa)* and allthorn *(Koeberlinia spinosa).* Dense forests of mesquite are also to be found in the interior valleys where floods spread out thinly over the flats, and narrow strips follow up the drainage systems which arise in the washes toward the hills and desert mountains and descend to the lower levels of the desert grassland.

Along the lower, warmer watercourses of the Gila and Colorado rivers, screwbean *(Prosopis pubescens)* fringes the upper edges of the mesquite belt, on the Gila extending eastward roughly to its junction with the Salt. In these portions of the two rivers, chamiso is partially replaced by the brittle saltbush *(Atriplex Breweri)* and the burro weed *(Allenrolfea occidentalis).* The exotic salt cedar *(Tamarix gallica)* has become widely established in the saline bottoms, competing with the native arrowweed and broad-leaved broom or seep-willow *(Baccharis glutinosa).* Bermuda grass *(Cynodon dacty-lon),* too, has come in and spread extensively.

Although the vegetation of our immediate Pima area on the middle Gila has changed somewhat within the past sixty to seventy years, its general characteristics are still observable. The bottomlands continue to abound in groves of cotton-wood although not so profusely as formerly, with some mix-ture of black willow, and dense thickets of arrowweed which terminate abruptly at the lower terrace. Mesquite and salt-bushes here also occupy the higher and more stable bottom-lands. The lower terrace continues to support numerous thickets of mesquite, while on the upper terrace is found a xerophytic vegetation in which saltbushes predominate. In many places in the general vicinity of Sacaton, as around the Casa Grande ruins, where the ground water is between thirty and forty feet below the surface, the land is covered with for-ests of mesquite.

Along the permanent water courses are to be found also large trees of such species as the leatherleaf ash *(Fraxinus velutina),* western walnut *(Juglans rupestris)* and the Mexi-can elder *(Sambucus mexicana),* particularly in the Santa Cruz and Arivaca valleys. With these is often associated the Arizona sycamore *(Platanus Wrightii).* This also occurs singly or in small clumps at springs, wells and stream chan-nels along the base of the Baboquivari Mountains, as does the hackberry *(Celtis occidentalis),* which ranges as well along the foot of the Tumacácoris and in the upper Santa Cruz Valley and on Arivaca Creek.

Getting away from the watercourses, there is to be found a vegetation dominated by creosote bush *(Larrea tridentata)* and saltbush. Within the limits of the climatic factors favor-ing desert growth this association is governed by soil features.

In Arizona the areas occupied by this type in the main division of the southern desert are in general the more level terrain, the shallow valleys, mesas and the sandy soils between the desert mountain ranges. In the western part of the area, with a rainfall of rarely more than four inches, creosote bush occurs in the better-drained and sandy soil where it can utilize moisture from the winter rains. In the eastern part of the creosote bush range, where precipitation is much higher, pure stands of this plant usually occur on very shallow soil underlaid by caliche, but the species fades out in the extreme southeastern part of the Papago country.

The desert saltbush often is found in almost pure stands, representing a subtype of the creosote-Atriplex type. With it there is sometimes a scattering of *quelite salada (Dondia moquini)*, mesquite, cholla or creosote bush. This type of cover is indicative of deep, fine loam soils, highly desirable for cultivation.

The portions of the southern desert characterized by roughest terrain and highest levels are occupied by the paloverde *(Cercidium microphyllum)*-cacti type of desert. Differences in local conditions cause it to take on various expressions. In the area under consideration it is usually bordered below by the creosote bush-Atriplex association, or now and then by mesquite *bosques*. Higher it is often met by the belt of desert land grass as in much of southern Pima County. The dominant tree in this desert shrub is paloverde. From the lower San Pedro Valley this plant extends westward in the foothill cover of the desert mountains, becoming increasingly sparse, until in the vicinity of Ajo and Gila Bend it well-nigh disappears. Northward in our area it is common in the Gila and Salt drainages. Locally paloverde may give way to other trees or shrubs. Thus dense stands of sahuaro *(Carnegiea gigantea)* may dwarf the woody forest, notably on the foothills of the Santa Catalina, Tanque Verde and Tucson mountains; in the ranges bordering the Santa Rosa Valley

on the Sells Papago Reservation; along the international
boundary from Nogales west to the Gila Mountains; in the
broad desert valleys adjacent to the Gila River and its tributaries as far east as the Coolidge Dam, and in the general
vicinity of Tucson. It reaches its best expression between
altitudes of two thousand and three thousand feet. Inciden-
tally the related organ-pipe cactus *(Lemaireocereus Thurberi)* occurs in a few places, such as the Growler Mountains,
but is most abundant from a line south of Ajo to the Mexican
border in the Organ Pipe Cactus National Monument. Its
northern limit is the Ajo Valley, and Hornaday[20] observed
it from there to the eastern edge of the Pinacate lava fields on
the Sonoita River.

Next to sahuaro, extensive forests of chollas characterize
this desert shrub type. The heaviest stands, for the most part,
consist of a single species, the jumping cholla *(Opuntia fulgida)*, a plant of the mesas and valleys, while the hottest desert
hillsides are taken over by the teddy bear cactus *(O. Bigelovii)*.
Fine forests of the former species are found on the plains adjacent to the Gila, particularly in the vicinity of Florence.
In other areas various prickly pears are dominant, and in the
higher elevations covered by the desert shrub type the large-
jointed *O. Engelmannii* frequently is the important species;
in other regions *O. phaeacantha* is most abundant. Other
characteristic chollas of the paloverde belt are the vari-colored or staghorn cholla *(O. versicolor)*, tesajo, desert Christ-
mas cactus or coyote cactus *(O. leptocaulis)*, the arborescent
pencil cholla *(O. arbuscula)* and the long-jointed, dark-
spined *O. acanthocarpa*. Some of the more typical woody
members of the paloverde-cacti region, although not limited
to this zone, are various squawberries *(Lycium* spp.), ocotillo
(Fouquieria splendens), which for example is absent or nearly
so on the east side of the Baboquivari Mountains, and the
white-spined cat-claw *(Acacia constricta)*.

[20] Hornaday, *Camp-Fires on Desert and Lava*, p. 68.

As the paloverde-cacti type extends westward it can be regarded in general as gradually moving up from the foot-hill mesas and benches until confined to the higher and steeper parts of the range. As this shift occurs, *palo fierro* or ironwood *(Olneya tesota)* becomes the dominant tree in frost-free areas. This species is most abundant west of Ajo but very poorly represented in the eastern part of the region.

Desert grassland is by no means widespread throughout the area, being limited very largely to the southeastern portion of the Papago country. In the drainage washes which serve the desert grassland the prominent shrubs or trees are mesquite, cat-claw *(Acacia Greggii)*, desert hackberry *(Celtis pallida)*, lotebush, desert willow *(Chilopsis linearis)* and soapberry *(Sapindus Drummondii)*, which is found sparingly along the arroyos.

The chaparral zone is a rather limited one in our range of investigation, confined almost exclusively to the extreme eastern and southeastern portions, where with oak woodlands it occupies only higher elevations. In general the higher stretches of this chaparral belt support buckbrush *(Ceanothus Greggii)* and oak as the main species, while on the lowest, drier level adjoining the desert are thickets of jojoba or coffeeberry *(Simmondsia californica)*, with sumacs *(Rhus* spp.), *algerita (Berberis Fremontii)* and buckbrush in between.

As to the mountain areas, trees representative of the high mountains of southeastern Arizona are to be found on the Tumacácori Mountains, the westernmost wooded range in southern Arizona. The dominant trees of such mountains as the Baboquivaris and Tumacácoris are three species of oak— *Quercus oblongifolia*, common on the slopes and drier portions; *Q. arizonica;* and the sweet-acorn black oak *(Q. Emoryi)* which does best, however, in the valleys. On the Tumacácoris, oaks constitute orchard-like forests. Associated with these, although in small numbers, are the Mexican piñón

(Pinus cembroides) and the alligator-bark juniper *(J. pachyphloea)*.

Atop some of the higher mountains is to be found the western yellow pine *(Pinus ponderosa)*. It abounds in the Santa Catalinas and terminates its extreme southwestern Arizona distribution in the Baboquivaris.

CHAPTER III

EARLY BASIS OF PIMAN SUBSISTENCE

The purpose of this chapter is to present our general findings on ancient Piman agriculture as well as on early food
gathering; a detailed consideration of their agriculture
appears in succeeding chapters. Utilization of wild foods is
discussed for the reason that anciently both food gathering
and agriculture were important, and intricately interwoven
in Piman economy; thus any comprehensive treatment of
Piman agriculture must of necessity embrace food gathering.

ARCHAEOLOGICAL EVIDENCE

Looking first at the archaeology of the area, the whole
Pima-Papago territory is studded with ruins of small villages in the desert area, and of communal houses concentrated in the valleys of the large rivers—principally the Gila
and Salt but a few on the smaller Santa Cruz. These valleys
are traversed by a network of irrigation canals, the oldest
dated one extending back to approximately 800 (?) A. D.[1]

Formerly it was thought the canals and communal houses
belonged to the same culture, but more recent investigations[2]
clearly indicate the existence of two cultures—an earlier of
long duration which built the canals, designated the Red-on-
buff or Hohokam culture, and a short later one representing
a temporary, peaceful invasion from the uplands to the north,
in which were built typical pueblos in Hohokam communi-

[1] Halseth, *Prehistoric Irrigation*, p. 42; Haury, in Gladwin *et al, Excavations at Snaketown*, I, 54; Turney, *Prehistoric Irrigation;* Hodge, *Prehistoric Irrigation in Arizona.*

[2] Gladwin: *Excavations at Casa Grande; The Red-on-buff Culture of the
Gila Basin; The Eastern Range of the Red-on-Buff Culture; Excavations at
Snaketown,* I, II; Woodward, *The Grewe Site.*

ties. At about 1400 (?) A. D.[3] these later invaders, known as the Salado people, a branch of the Little Colorado Stem of Pueblo culture, left the Gila Basin after an occupancy of one hundred to one hundred fifty years. Moreover, it seems that about the year 1400 (?) cultural evolution of the original dwellers, the Hohokam, ceased, for we have no archaeologic record whatever of them after that time, nor to date has it been possible to ascertain what eventually happened to the Hohokam or what transpired in the Gila Basin between 1400 (?) and 1687, when Kino first came in contact with the Pimans. It has been postulated that the Pima are the cultural descendants of the earlier inhabitants of the same region, but the relation between the two is still a matter of controversy.

Both Gladwin and Bryan[4] have pointed out that the home of the Hohokam differed widely from that of the Pueblos in geography, climate and vegetation. Roughly, the Mogollon Rim constituted the boundary between the two, the Plateau country north of the rim with its cooler climate and Transition flora being the land of the Pueblos, the Sonoran desert country to the south, with its lower altitude, the domain of the Hohokam and the lower Colorado River tribes. The southern boundary of the Puebloan area corresponded closely to the northern limit of the Sonoran flora. In contrast to the Pueblos, the desert tribes were characterized by heavy reliance upon hunting and food gathering, and, on the Colorado and Gila rivers, by fishing, thus utilizing extensively the rather abundant food provided by the Sonoran flora. As a result, their social organization was more diffuse and their habitations less communal than those of the more sedentary Pueblos.

The Hohokam culture of the general period of 1000 (?)

[3] Dates referring to the Hohokam culture are given with some uncertainty, and in the various phases listed below are omitted. This is because we have been informed by Gladwin in personal correspondence, Jan. 22, 1942, that the Snaketown chronology is now being revised upward.

[4] Gladwin, *Excavations at Snaketown*, II, 3-4; Bryan, *Pre-Columbian Agriculture in the Southwest*, p. 221.

A. D. and that of the historic Pimas have a number of things in common, most important from our point of view being extensively irrigated agriculture, the cultivation of maize and the absence of turkey domestication. Also the wild foods utilized by the two peoples show a considerable similarity, as revealed by the animal bones and plant remains found in Hohokam sites.[5]

The animal remains found in the Snaketown excavations were identified as belonging to the following species:

Indian Dog, *Canis familiaris*
Coyote, *Canis latrans* (?) subspecies
Grey Fox, *Urocyon cinereoargenteus*
Ground Squirrel, *Citellus spilosoma* (?) subspecies
Pocket Gopher, *Thomomys cervinus*
Kangaroo Rat, *Dipodomys* sp.
Pack Rat, *Neotoma* (?) *albigula*
Muskrat, *Ondatra zibethicus pallidus*
Jackrabbit, *Lepus californicus deserticola*
Cottontail Rabbit, *Sylvilagus auduboni arizonae*
Mule Deer, *Odocoileus hemionus* (?) subspecies
Pronghorn Antelope, *Antilocapra americana* (?) subspecies
Mountain Sheep, *Ovis canadensis gaillardi*
Bison, *Bison bison*
Raven, *Corvus corax sinuatus*
Golden Eagle, *Aquila chrysaetos*
Turkey, *Meleagris gallopavo*
Sage Hen
Blue Goose
Owl
Sturgeon, *Acipenser*
Tortoise

The plant remains were:

Maize—All the material was highly carbonized and was judged by Volney H. Jones to be flour corn with smaller grains than present day flour corn. Maize was found only in the Colonial and Sedentary periods, but Haury believes it may logically be inferred that it was

5 Haury, *Roosevelt:9:6*, pp. 63, 126; Haury, in Gladwin *et al*, *Excavations at Snaketown*, I, 50, 57-8, 156-58; Woodward, *op. cit.*, pp. 14, 18-9.

grown from the beginning of the Snaketown occupa-
tion. This has been confirmed by the re-examination
of all the vegetal materials listed below.
Mesquite Beans
Screwbeans
Sahuaro fruit

Additional archaeological material from the Snaketown
site has come to light since the publication of the Snaketown
report. Through the courtesy of Gladwin, of Gila Pueblo,
and Volney H. Jones, of the Ethnobiological Laboratory of
the University of Michigan, the authors have had opportunity
to examine this material. Since nothing has been published
on this collection it seems advisable to present a somewhat
detailed statement on it, and the following findings represent the conclusions of Jones and of the authors. The first
number given is that assigned at the time of excavation, the
number in parentheses is that given by the Ethnobiological
Laboratory of the University of Michigan.

Maize:

6G:13, House 4 (1323). About one hundred charred kernels evidently representing two varieties, since some of the
grains are seven to eight mm. in width and wedge shaped, and
others are crescent shaped and about nine to ten mm. wide.
(Sacaton Phase.)

7D: House 1, floor (1327). Several masses of charred and
fused kernels and cobs. Uniform in type, fourteen rowed.
Kernels small and similar to the small ones in the preceding
collection. *(Gila Butte Phase (?).)*

Mound 29, House 1: 9E floor (1330). Several masses of
charred, and some loose, kernels, as well as cob fragments.
Apparently ten or twelve rowed. Kernels small, about eight
mm. wide. *(Snaketown Phase.)*

43229 (1332). Two charred cobs, elliptical in cross section. Apparently twelve rowed. *(General.)*

43778 (1333). A few charred grains, small (about eight
mm. wide), but crescent shaped rather than wedge shaped
as is most of the small grained corn in these collections.
(General.)

44637 (1334). Two portions of charred cobs, both twelve rowed. *(General.)*

44656; 9E: House 1 (1335). A segment of charred cob with kernels still attached. Kernels small (about eight mm. wide) and wedge shaped; twelve rowed. *(Snaketown Phase.)*

44551 (1337). Charred and fused wedge-shaped kernels which appear to be very small—apparently six to seven mm. wide. *(General.)*

45722; 4H: House 2 (1339). Small lumps of badly charred and fused kernels. Evidently quite similar to the preceding. *(Sacaton Phase.)*

45912; 6G: House 11 (1340). Fragments of charred cobs, and a few loose, charred kernels which are quite variable in size and shape—six to nine mm. wide. Ten to fourteen rowed. *(Estrella Phase.)*

45913; 6E: House 2 (1341). A quantity of masses of charred, tightly fused kernels. Appear to be mostly wedge shaped and about seven mm. wide. *(Sacaton Phase.)*

46155; 6E: House 2 (1342). Four charred kernels, one of them quite large (about eleven mm. wide) and crescent shaped; the others incomplete but much smaller. *(Sacaton Phase.)*

47555 SW—ST (1343). A very small, eight-rowed, charred cob. *(Sweetwater—Snaketown Association.)*

Beans

6G: House 8, vessel 48 (1319). Many charred beans. There is every indication they are tepary beans *(Phaseolus acutifolius). (Sacaton Phase.)*

4H: House 2, vessel 1. 2144 (1324). A handful of badly charred and broken beans. Appear clearly to be kidney beans *(Phaseolus vulgaris). (Sacaton Phase.)*

Cotton

6G: House 8 (1322). A small quantity of charred seeds and a few tufts of charred cotton lint. Presumably *Gossypium hopi. (Sacaton Phase.)*

4H: House 1 (1325). A small number of cotton seeds similar to the preceding. Probably *G. hopi. (Sacaton Phase.)*

45552; 6E: House 2 (1338). A small quantity of charred

seeds quite similar to the two preceding numbers. *(Sacaton Phase.)*

46155; 6E: House 2 (1342). Twenty charred seeds similar to the three preceding numbers. *(Sacaton Phase.)*

Wild plants

6G: House 8, vessel 48 (1319). A pint of charred seeds. Probably a species of pigweed *(Amaranthus* sp.). Size of the seeds suggests they were wild rather than cultivated. Seeds of several species of this genus were commonly used as food in the Southwest. *(Sacaton Phase.)*

4H: House 1 (1325). About two gallons of charred small seeds similar to the preceding and probably a species of *Amaranthus*. This collection of seeds contained a single kernel of corn similar to the smaller ones in 6G:13, House 4, and a single bean cotyledon which appears to be a tepary. *(Sacaton Phase.)*

7D: House 1, floor (1327). This collection contained a handful of small seeds similar to 6G: House 8, vessel 48, and apparently represents a species of *Amaranthus*. *(Gila Butte Phase* (?).)

6G: House 8, vessel 50 (1320). About a quart of charred seeds. Although there appears to be some mixture, most of the seeds seem to be a species of goosefoot *(Chenopodium* sp.). The seeds of several species of goosefoot were commonly eaten as food in the Southwest. *(Sacaton Phase.)*

3D: 2, 3 (1326). A small quantity of charred and broken mesquite beans, presumably *Prosopis chilensis. (General.)*

45416; 7J: House 3 (1336). A small quantity of charred, broken mesquite beans. Very similar to the preceding. *(Sacaton Phase.)*

If Haury's view that strong reliance upon agriculture greatly minimized hunting as a factor in Hohokam subsistence be correct, there can be no doubt that agriculture was more important among these people than with the Pimans. This conclusion also is supported by Haury's view that the maximum size and greatest scope of Hohokam irrigation canal systems was reached about 1200-1400 (?) A. D., and that after this time the systems dwindled, ending in the small but

34 PIMA AND PAPAGO INDIAN AGRICULTURE

efficient Pima systems of the seventeenth to nineteenth centuries, located largely on the south side of the river.

Pertinent to our study are the archaeological crop specimens found on the fringes of the Piman area. Thus at the Canyon Creek Ruin on a tributary of the Salt River near Roosevelt Lake, where construction started about 1278 A. D. and habitation continued until the middle of the fourteenth century, Haury[6] found the following:

Maize— (six, eight, ten, twelve and fourteen rowed) with both red and white cobs represented.
Beans—both red and white (Phaseolus vulgaris).
Pumpkins—stems and rinds of Cucurbita Pepo and C. moschata.
Cotton—cotton cloth and cord (Gossypium sp.).
Gourd—seeds, and fruits used as vessels (Lagenaria siceraria).
Pipes—neither stone nor clay pipes were found but the butts of smoked cane cigarettes appeared frequently. A partially smoked tube contained what appeared to be bits of bark.
Acorns—Quercus Emoryi.
Walnuts, black—Juglans major.
Yucca—quids.
Mule Deer (Odocoileus hemionis macrotis).
Red Fox (Vulpes fulva macroura).
Scott's Gray Fox (Urocyon cinereoargenteus scotti).
Indian Dog (Canis familiaris).
Jackrabbit (Lepus californicus texanus).
Wild Turkey (Meleagris gallapavo merriami).

Also adjacent to the Piman area is the Upper Tonto Ruin, located at the northern end of the Superstition Mountains, about five miles southeast of Roosevelt Dam. This site has a single tree-ring date of 1346 A. D. and has been classified as belonging to the Salado branch of Pueblo culture of the Pueblo IV period.[7] The cultural materials affiliate with those obtained by Haury at the Canyon Creek Ruin. Through the

[6] Haury, The Canyon Creek Ruin, pp. 59-64, ff.; pls. 47-8, 59-62, 69.
[7] Steen, The Upper Tonto Ruins.

courtesy of Volney H. Jones and the permission of Charles R. Steen it is possible to present the following unpublished data on crop specimens excavated from the ruin:

Cotton—abundant masses of lint as well as seeds, bolls, cordage and textile fragments. Probably *Gossypium hopi.*

Maize—not abundant. Husks, cobs and shanks and some kernels. Appears to be mostly ten or twelve rowed with slender cobs. Brown kernels predominate.

Pumpkins—rather common. Seeds, fruit stalks and rind of *Cucurbita moschata.* Rind fragments of the striped cushaw variety.

Beans—see section on beans in Chapter IV for discussion of the lima beans *(Phaseolus lunatus)* found and reported by Steen and Jones. Also obtained was the seed coat of a brown kidney bean *(P. vulgaris)* and a large specimen of the Jack bean *(Canavalia ensiformis).* No teparies *(P. acutifolius)* were secured.

Gourds—three or four utensils which were definitely made of fruits of *Lagenaria siceraria.* There is a single seed of this species.

Although the upper Gila River region investigated by Hough[8] is somewhat beyond the limits of the Piman area, it is close enough to be pertinent. In Tularosa Cave, on the Tularosa River, a tributary of the San Francisco, which in turn flows into the Gila, he found yellow, blue and carmine maize with eight, twelve, sixteen and eighteen rows. In addition, cobs with ten rows were found at other sites. Also found were cotton cord and cloth, gourd fruits (evidently *Lagenaria),* pumpkins (some of which from the description were doubtless the cushaw type—*Cucurbita moschata)* and a few beans (in part at least probably *Phaseolus vulgaris).*

As to Papago archaeology, Gladwin[9] tells us there is little

[8] Hough, *Culture of the Ancient Pueblos of the Upper Gila River Region,* pp. 7-11, 69, 77, 79.
[9] Gladwin, *op. cit.,* 94-5.

to be said of prehistoric remains in Papaguería, there being
no site which indicates long occupation, and the impression
one gets is that the archaeological remains are those of ven-
turesome Hohokam groups which filtered down into Papaguería, found the desert environment unfavorable and, for
the most part, withdrew. The Classic sites on the eastern
edge of Papaguería seem to be merely an overflow from the
Classic settlements along the Santa Cruz. He believes the
presence of the Papago in this region at the time Kino
arrived had no relation to the archaeological remains, but
represented a comparatively recent movement westward.

Members of the Arizona State Museum,[10] who have carried on a series of investigations on the Sells Papago Reservation, extensively excavated a site about three miles north of
Vamori, toward Kowlic. A mere handful of grinding implements, consisting of one metate and a small number of hand-
stones, was recovered here, but the site did yield a large number of mountain sheep horns and bones. These excavations
revealed a time span approximately from 800 to 1200 A. D.,
and seemingly a food-gathering culture.

At the Jackrabbit ruin, seven miles east of Sells, members of the same institution found many implements, especially for grinding, indicating an agricultural economy ranging approximately from 1200 to 1400 A. D. Traces of irrigation canals also were found on this reservation. One such
canal runs in a straight line for seventeen miles in a west by
southwest direction from Baboquivari Mountain to the vicinity of Vamori. This has been dated as being functional in the
fourteenth century. A site excavated during the winter of
1939-40 shows a short canal about a half mile long, with
strong indication of water diversion from a ditch, and this
too evidently belongs to the fourteenth century. In none of
the excavations discussed above was any trace of crop specimens found. Clotts[11] states there is evidence of prehistoric

10 Emil W. Haury, Personal conversation, April 26, 1940.
11 Clotts, *Nomadic Papago Surveys*, p. 82.

irrigation indicated by old ditches and reservoirs at Santa Rosa.

HISTORICAL AND ETHNOGRAPHICAL EVIDENCE

When Kino and Mange[12] made their first explorations in Pimería Alta, the Pima on the Gila and the Sobaipuri in the San Pedro and Santa Cruz valleys were carrying on agriculture by means of canal irrigation, and an extensive system of ditches was observed by Font and Garcés[13] among the Pima of the Casa Grande-Casa Blanca district in 1775, also along the Gila in 1846 by Emory and in 1852 by Bartlett.[14] However the historical accounts indicate the agriculture of the Gila and its tributaries was of a lower cultural level than that of the irrigated valleys of Sonora. Nevertheless, Pima and Papago were rather good farmers and developed their agriculture to a fairly high degree of efficiency—a condition which still applies, particularly to the Papago. In fact the Papago had to be efficient farmers to wrest a subsistence from so reluctant and forbidding an environment. After the period of disorganization and migration contingent upon Apache raids, which preoccupied Pima and Papago from about 1750 until the Apache were finally subdued by the Federal Government in 1874, Piman agriculture slowly revived from the severe setback which it had suffered, and, at present, irrigation is practiced in the same river valleys where the Spaniards found it, although in portions of these valleys the Indians have been displaced by whites.

The basis of Pima subsistence has become greatly modified since aboriginal times, much more so than that of the Papago, who because of their isolation as well as the limitations of their environment have remained relatively unaffected. In fact Pima economy has undergone such radical change over so long a time that it is now difficult to recon-

12 Bolton, Kino, I, 205; Mange, Luz, pp. 248-49, 256.
13 Bolton, Anza, IV, 43; Coues, On the Trail, I, 107.
14 Emory, Notes, p. 81; Bartlett, Narrative, II, 232.

struct the detailed aboriginal picture. This is attributable
to acculturation resulting from long and close contact with
the whites and the concomitant dependence upon traders'
products. Even before the arrival of white settlers in Pima
territory, the cultivation of wheat acquired from Mexico had
displaced to some extent the growing of maize by these Indians (although not by the Papago) , a condition also related
by Spier[15] for the adjacent Maricopa. Garcés[16] indicated
in 1775, before Spaniards settled in the area, the relative importance of crops thus: "In all these [Pima] pueblos they
raise large crops of wheat, some of corn, cotton, calabashes,
etc. . . ." Similarly Anza,[17] who visited the Gila Pima in 1774,
said of one of their villages that the fields of wheat were so
large that a person standing in the middle of them could not
see the ends, and that their width embraced the whole spread
of the valley on either side. In this same connection, Bartlett[18] in 1854 reported that the Pima made agriculture more
of a system than did the Colorado River tribes, the Hopi or
the Navaho, and their crops were larger and very luxuriant;
also Emory[19] in 1846 wrote of the luxuriance of Pima crops,
and in 1856 observed that these Indians were further advanced in the art of agriculture and were surrounded with
more comforts than any uncivilized tribe he had ever seen.
Some indication of the extent of Pima cultivation in 1861 is
given by Browne,[20] who records that in this year they sold the
War Department for supply at Ft. Breckenridge 300,000
pounds of wheat, 50,000 pounds of corn, 20,000 pounds of
beans and a large amount of dried and fresh pumpkins; also
that in 1862 they sold the War Department more than one
million pounds of wheat, as well as pinole, chickens, green

15 Spier, *Yuman Tribes,* pp. 48, 58-9.
16 Coues, *op. cit.,* pp. 107-08.
17 Bolton, *op. cit.,* I, 184; II, 240, 304.
18 Bartlett, *op. cit.,* pp. 262-63.
19 Emory: *op. cit.,* p. 83; *Report on the U. S. and Mexican Boundary Survey,* p. 117.
20 Browne, *Adventures in the Apache Country,* p. 110.

peas, green corn, pumpkins and melons for the entire California column.

Granting that some of the above appraisals, particularly Anza's statement, are considerably exaggerated, these historical accounts nevertheless do present a fairly accurate conception of the actual situation. One must not be misled, however, into concluding that the extent of cultivation observed in the period of Garcés, Font and Anza, and later of Emory and Bartlett, characterized aboriginal Piman agriculture. The agriculture of the Gila Basin during the eighteenth and nineteenth centuries was much more extensive and more highly developed than in the late pre-Spanish period for the following reasons: (1) The Spaniards exerted a very strong influence upon Piman agriculture as to both technique and kinds of crops cultivated. For example, the growing of winter crops such as wheat and barley, with their different technique of cultivation, had far-reaching effects. Influence was especially marked with Kino, who had an unusual gift for stimulating and encouraging cultivation and husbandry among the Indians; (2) the introduction of cattle, horses, sheep etc. which automatically required an extension of cultivation to furnish food for such domesticated animals; (3) development of the profit motive. Aboriginal agriculture was pursued purely for subsistence and the idea of growing crops for profit was unknown. When the Pimans learned they could sell or exchange excess crops, thereby securing articles of Spanish importation, a marked acceleration of cultivation resulted.

Despite the almost complete obliteration of certain aspects of aboriginal Pima economy, it is still possible to reconstruct the general scene. Pima agriculture anciently was quite extensive but somewhat uncertain, such undependability becoming rather pronounced as more extensive white settlement on the Gila decreased the available supply of water for irrigation. But even in early times the flow of the

Gila occasionally failed, and Russell[21] tells us this happened about every fifth year; this is supported by Anza, Eixarch, Font and others.[22] At times the river overflowed, destroying irrigation canals and washing out crops. Under such conditions of drought, flood or crop failure from other causes, the balance of food supply was markedly shifted in favor of the products of food gathering and hunting. In fact, in unfavorable years food was often as scarce as among the Papago, and the Pimas at such times might live with relatives whose crops had been good.

Aboriginal Pima agriculture was largely dependent upon canal irrigation from the Gila, although in places they used flood water from the washes, or water coming from the mountains in times of heavy rains and diverted by the use of temporary dikes on the flats.

Our field studies, as well as the early documentary material, reveal that the Papago, living in a very arid area with meagre agricultural possibilities, had imposed upon them a semi-nomadic life, planting and caring for their fields in the rainy period, and wandering about exploiting to the utmost the wild animal and vegetable resources of the land the rest of the year. For a period of at least three months wild plants were gathered by women; hunting was done by men, although it attained the status of a major occupation only among certain individuals. Anza[23] noted that in winter especially the Papago almost completely deserted their territory, and pictured aspects of their economy thus: "The Papago Indians who dwell in them live in greater misery and poverty than can be imagined. Seldom have they any fixed habitation, because, driven by necessity, they wander almost continually, sometimes in the sierras to maintain themselves by hunting deer, wild sheep, rats and certain roots; at other

21 Russell, *Pima*, pp. 66-7.

22 Bolton, *op. cit.*, III, 19, 353; IV, 45; *Report of the Commissioner of Indian Affairs* for 1871, p. 359; *ibid.* for 1875, p. 214; *ibid.* for 1878, pp. xxxix, 3; *ibid.* for 1904, pp. 7-21.

23 Bolton, *op. cit.*, II, 17, 260-61.

times in the arroyos to live on the bean of the mesquite, and
again in the plains, seeking the pitaya, the tuna, the sahuaro
and other wild fruits. Sometimes they go to the Colorado
River to obtain food amongst the Yumas through their skill
in their disorderly dances, and at other times down to the
missions of Pimería where, by the same means and by their
tenuous labor, they obtain a little grain, and a few pieces of
Sayal to cover the most immodest parts of their bodies." A
similar uncomplimentary characterization of the region from
Caborca to the mouth of the Colorado was given in 1764; the
author, after describing the poverty of the country, referred
to the Papago as eating "seeds of forage, herbs and wild
fruits, and even rabbits and rats." Also, "Papagos is the name
given by the Pimas to those particular Pimas who live in
the desert as far as Tucson and ... up to the Gila, living on
seeds, grass, rabbits, rats and wild fruits."[24] The same reference laments the poverty of the Papago country, stating these
Indians at times went to the villages of the other Pimans
where they worked as servants merely for their food, even
going as far as San Ignacio and Dolores; they were so fond of
meat that they ate horses and burros, and in returning to
their lands even stole and ate dogs. Pfefferkorn,[25] too, describes the inferior basis of Papago subsistence.

In the Papago country permanent sources of water in
association with tillable land are rare. This situation necessitated a compromise between sedentary life in villages and
a migratory existence which expressed itself in seasonal movement usually between two kinds of villages. Those known as
The Wells were situated at permanent sources of water in the
mountains or foothills. The other type of village, designated
The Fields, was in the open desert country adjacent to the
cultivated areas, and twenty to thirty miles distant from their
winter villages. Papago semi-nomadic life thus was not dictated primarily by the needs of hunting or agriculture but to

24 *Documentos,* 3rd ser. IV, 554, 838; *Rudo Ensayo,* pp. 189-90.
25 Pfefferkorn, *Beschreibung der Landschaft Sonora,* I, 10-12.

get actual drinking water. Even so, permanent springs were widely scattered, and the women spent more time fetching water than gathering food. Such scarcity of water also had its compensation, for it was the Papago's best defense against the plundering Apache.

During winter, families camped as near as possible to a spring, water hole or *tinaja,* as exemplified along the western foothills of the Baboquivari Mountains and at Comobabi. But even this sometimes involved a daily trip of three or four miles, occasionally as much as ten, to fetch water, chiefly by the women. One Papago informant said that as a boy he had to make a daily trip of fifteen miles on horseback to secure water, carrying two ollas, each holding about three gallons. These water holes were not only sources of drink but of game, for here it was possible to stalk deer, antelope and mountain sheep. In places, water was secured from a very small spring where an olla had to remain under the drip for as long as half an hour, and in such cases women stood in line and sometimes had to spend the night, this constituting a social occasion. A few springs were large enough to be called wells, such as Badger Well in the Comobabi Mountains. The Papago enlarged it by building fires under its rocky walls to crack off the rocks. Occasionally a water supply at these winter villages was to be had only by patient digging in the sandy washes on the mountain pediment, and then at times in very small quantities along a plane of contact between sand and stone after scraping the sand away.

Families usually did not move down to the Fields until the heavy rains had begun, so as to be certain that drinking water would be found in the depressions which had been dug near each farming village, a fact noted by Font and by Garcés.[26] Such migration between the Fields and the Wells continues today, especially in the western half of the reservation. Often there were natural water holes or pools of

26 Bolton, *Kino,* IV, 32; Coues, *op. cit.,* p. 64.

standing water of variable size along channels where flood
waters spread out over adobe flats and washes, in which case
they were known as *charcos,* usually three to five feet deep.
Dikes and ditches were sometimes constructed to assist in
trapping and impounding the surface water in such depressions. At times small earthen dams or *represas* were constructed, usually in adobe flats, to impound flood waters for
household purposes, later for the use of stock.[27] Such pools
retained water from a few days to several months and on the
whole remained available until October or November, when
the deer dance closed the agricultural season. Mange[28]
observed that the Papago at El Gubo had a small spring from
which they drank, and that the Sobaipuri at Correa on the
Santa Cruz got their drinking water from a deep well made in
the *caza* of the river, but which was at this point evidently
dry most of the time, as their agriculture was *de temporal.*
Such easy seasonal access to water freed the women for food
gathering, essentially a summer occupation. Before the time
of wheat cultivation and the digging of government wells, the
Papagos lived at their *temporales* during the summer months
only, but now, with dependable sources of water and the
necessity for sowing wheat in fall, the aboriginal situation has
been greatly modified, and the seasonal migration between
Wells and Fields has lost its importance. Formerly the village of Kaka depended wholly upon its *charco,* and when this
dried up the Indians were compelled to move or fetch water
from Moivavi, sixteen miles distant in the mountains.[29]

Obviously such natural limitations precluded permanent
homes and formal and elaborate equipment, and gave expression to a type of economy characterized by small groups of
peaceful, industrious, skilled agriculturists, meagre in equipment, and informal and decentralized in organization.

[27] Bryan, *Papago,* pp. 121, 257.
[28] Mange, *Luz,* pp. 230, 256.
[29] Hoover: *The Indian Country of Southern Arizona,* p. 52; *Generic
Descent of the Papago Villages,* p. 259.

Papago agriculture, involving no storage of water, was characteristically of the primitive but efficient *de temporal* "thunderstorm" type; that is, flood-water farming in which seed was planted in moist ground at the mouth of a wash after the first rains, which came in summer. This was reported as early as 1694 by Mange[30] at El Tupo, Tucabavia and Gubo, and there is a specific statement[31] to the effect that this was the customary method of planting by the Papago north of Casas Grandes. Kino reported the same for the Papago at San Rafael del Actúm Grande.[32] Although Gaillard[33] observed in 1894 that the Papago irrigated their crops with water drawn from natural or artificial dams, which he terms respectively *charcos* and *represos,* we have been wholly unable to confirm this practice, all our information being to the effect that such stored water was used only for domestic purposes. He gives the impression that this was the customary method of watering crops and makes no mention of flood-water farming. Bryan[34] points out that the difficulties of profitable storage of water in sufficient amounts for irrigation in the Papago country are very great. Also he has informed us in personal correspondence that he has seen no evidence that the Papago ever stored water for irrigation of fields.

To be sure, Papago agriculture was quite uncertain due to irregularity of the rainy season, then later on account of Apache raids. In years when rains were late these Indians lived entirely on wild foods without planting at all. So tenuous was Papago agriculture that Mange,[35] head of a military detachment detailed to escort Kino, in a number of places asserts that in the late seventeenth century certain *rancherías* in Papaguería had no agriculture, living entirely on wild

30 Mange, *op. cit.,* pp. 215, 229-30.
31 *Documentos,* 3rd ser., IV, 833.
32 Bolton, *op. cit.,* I, 309.
33 Gaillard, *The Papago of Arizona and Sonora,* p. 293.
34 Bryan, *op. cit.,* p. 143.
35 Mange, *op. cit.,* pp. 216, 225, 263, 286-87.

products. However, his visit may have followed a season when no crop was planted on account of late rains, such as Kino[36] cited in 1701 in the vicinity of San Rafael del Actúm Grande (in southern Arizona), where no maize had been raised by the Papago that year because of a like situation.

All our informants agreed that wild plants and animals formerly constituted a much larger, and much more dependable, fraction of the total Papago food supply than did cultivated plants. Seasonally women devoted themselves to the gathering of wild foods while men and boys hunted rabbits. When the wild foods ripened, large quantities were gathered and stored, but, just before the giant cactus harvest, food became very scarce, as indicated by one of their names for the period that would correspond to our month of May, *ko'ohk macat*, "the painful moon." One informant said that when he was a boy it was not uncommon to "be so hungry that a person became dizzy when he stood up." As in the past, so today, the Papago utilize much more wild plant and animal food than do the Pima; in fact, it is now comparatively rare to find the Pima gathering wild foods of any kind, while many Papago still utilize them to some extent as a matter of necessity, for Papago agriculture is today almost as precarious as in olden times.

Underhill[37] has well pointed out that poor as the Papago country was, its economics were those of abundance. Much the same outlook is still to be observed among the Pima, despite their deculturation. The Pimans did not hoard property; they were constantly making gifts, chiefly of food, for their food supply, meagre though it seems viewed from our standard of living, was more than sufficient for their simple needs, and anything beyond the bare necessities for sustaining life was regarded as a surplus. Papago migratory life, involving the difficulty of food storage, added to the problems of preserving food in so hot a land, greatly fostered

36 Bolton, *loc. cit.*
37 Underhill, *Papago*, pp. 90-2.

this spirit of giving. But not only was the Papago practice of giving motivated by economic considerations; generosity was a high virtue and giving was truly an investment in good will. One who secured a reputation for penury definitely lost caste in village and family life. Moreover, all gifts were returned in equal quantity and more. Such continuous exchange of goods in the form of gifts constituted the Papago equivalent for trade but only rarely attained the status of actual trade.

In addition to the extensive system of exchange of goods among themselves, some Papago made trading expeditions to the Yuma. They also journeyed to the middle Gila, the San Pedro and the Indians in the Altar Valley, then later among the Mexicans of various parts of Sonora. This was done particularly at harvest time, Papago from the northern villages traveling to the Gila where they had relatives and friends, those from the southern settlements being in closer contact with Mexico, particularly the Altar Valley. At these places they traded numerous articles and labored in return for food, in historic times chiefly wheat, but formerly maize and beans, as well as cotton. This was observed in 1740, later by Anza;[38] again in 1863-64, and in 1893 by Whittemore,[39] who also noted that when the Papago became very hungry they would journey to the Gila and present for the Pima a "Begging Dance" which had a specific form and lasted two or three nights, in return for which each Pima family was expected to contribute fifty to one hundred pounds of wheat.

In Mexico a few Papago worked as cowboys and at miscellaneous tasks, for which they were paid in money. Such contacts resulted in a more rapid deculturation and disorganization than occurred in the northern villages. Specifically these villages in the south, some of which had raised cattle since Kino's day, began about a century ago to acquire cattle in larger numbers. As a result of hire for money among the

[38] *Documentos,* 3rd ser., IV, 838; Bolton, *Anza,* II, 17.
[39] *Report of the Commissioner of Indian Affairs* for 1863, p. 384; *ibid.* for 1864, p. 153; Whittemore, in *Among the Pimas,* pp. 81-3.

Mexicans they more and more came to use Mexican goods and to pay less attention to agriculture, thus the arrangement of family geographic units was disrupted.[40]

In lean years among the desert Papago the bulk of the harvesting on Pima farms was done by the Papago, and the custom of such labor for hire has continued until quite recent times. However, desert Papago almost invariably returned to their homes later as it was very rarely that these Indians lived outside their own village except by intermarriage. In ancient times the Pima usually had a rather large and dependable crop, but Pima agriculture was given a strong stimulus beginning with gold rush days in the fifties, and by the eighties the increased penetration of whites created a demand for crop production on a commercial basis. Thus the Papago almost abandoned the northern part of their desert territory to work for the Pima during wheat harvest on the Gila. This was always a great boon to the Papago for whom this time was the leanest part of the year. Here they remained for about a month, a fourth of which was spent trading and cutting willow for making baskets. For their labor the Papago were given daily food and a share of the crop. Although May and June, the time of wheat harvest, constituted the period of greatest Papago movement to the Gila, some of these Indians returned in late fall to assist in planting, and to pick cotton.

Despite the hiring of Papagos by the Pimas, due to commercial growing of wheat by these Indians, the northern Papago villages continued to be agricultural, adding the raising of cattle to the extent of supplying the amount of meat formerly secured by hunting. Moreover, here the arrangement of family geographic units remained intact.

One must not get the impression, however, that irrigation was a culture trait characteristic of Pima, Sobaipuri and Soba, but lacking among Papago. These peoples were one in speech

40 Underhill, *op. cit.*

and general culture, the Papago simply being environmentally differentiated Pima, "desert Indians with an agricultural
heritage," who dwelt in a land where running water for irrigation was not available. Desert conditions therefore imposed upon them a different way of life in a land where agriculture could be naught else but marginal. In this connection Bryan[41] has pointed out very fittingly that the usually
clear distinction between irrigated and unirrigated farm
land breaks down in the consideration of marginal lands
irrigated by flood water, in some cases there being a complete
transition. Papago fields were situated at the mouths of
washes fed intermittently from desert mountains, and here
they utilized to the utmost, in their primitive but efficient
manner, the extremely meagre and precarious agricultural
opportunity made possible only by summer rains. Thus with
an average precipitation of less than five inches the Papago
cultivated and continue to cultivate their basin lands with an
incipient system of irrigation.

Moreover, irrigation was reported in those areas inhabited
by Papago where there were running streams. Thus at San
Marcelo de Sonoita, with its good arroyo of permanently
running water and many good springs in the vicinity, the
Papago, toward the close of the seventeenth century, were
practicing irrigation by means of ditches leading from the
arroyo, as they did at a *rancheria* near Caborca;[42] and Anza,[43]
three-quarters of a century later, noted that these Papago at
Sonoita and Quitobac were still irrigating small pieces of
land with running water from springs. The village of Sonoita
was a favored site as the Sonoita River is here a permanent
stream. Irrigation was also possible from the waters of the
large fissure spring at Quitobaquito, a veritable small oasis.
It should be explained that the Sonoita River is the only interrupted stream rising in the Papago country. Drainage

41 Bryan, *Flood-water Farming*, p. 444.
42 Mange, *op. cit.*, pp. 262, 285; Bolton, *op. cit.*, pp. 188, 225, 255.
43 Bolton, *Anza*, II, 22, 148, 150.

from the Baboquivari and Quijotoa valleys runs by a circuitous route through the Great Plain and unites with similar
ephemeral streams in Sonora to form the Sonoita.   Except
for occasional floods the channel is dry for more than twenty-
five miles to a point a short distance above Sonoita.[44] Similarly, irrigation was practiced at San Xavier by the Papago
who occupied this village after the Sobaipuri had abandoned
it within historic times.   Maps in Bryan's[45] report and those
in Hoover's paper show in parts of the Papago-Pima country
the location of fields, streams, washes, springs, tanks, *represas*
etc.

The Papago continue to the present to pursue their *de
temporal* farming much as they have always done, although
Pima agriculture has undergone marked changes.   The Federal Government, beginning in 1913, drilled wells in a number of Papago villages and such wells are now scattered
throughout Papago territory, but they are used for watering
stock and enabling residents to remain throughout the year,
and have no bearing upon the growing of crops.   In 1919[46]
the desert Papago in Arizona were reported as flood-water
farming about sixteen thousand acres of land, while those at
San Xavier had about fifteen hundred under ditch irrigation,
with water largely from wells.

Three changes in Piman life, affecting both Pima and
Papago, have been of the utmost importance in ameliorating
their economic condition, even though the concomitant white
influences have resulted in pronounced deculturation,
notably among the Pima.   The first of these was the introduction of foreign crops.   The earliest to be received, and the
most important for both peoples, was wheat.   This provided
an off-season crop, planted anywhere from mid-November to
early February, depending upon the winter rains, and harv-

44 Bryan, *Papago*, p. 119.
45 Bryan, *ibid.;* Hoover, *The Indian Country of Southern Arizona.*
46 *Report of the Commissioner of Indian Affairs* for 1919, pp. 279, 287, 289.

ested in May or early June. This also provided a more equable seasonal distribution of farm work and furnished a crop at a period of the year which heretofore had been very lean. The Papago for a long time, however, cultivated only small amounts of wheat and it has been only within the last few generations that wheat cultivation has deeply affected them. The second is the digging of government wells convenient to many of the *temporales* and farms (beginning in 1913), in some cases with a resultant development of permanent villages around them. This also has meant termination of the annual migration to the hills which had been such a potent influence in Papago life; moreover it has made possible a more sedentary life with a sanitary water supply, and the inhabitants of villages with such wells are usually more progressive and more prosperous. Important among these changes was the third factor—introduction of cattle. While this has been a boon to the Pima, it has been of more importance directly to the Papago, particularly in the eastern part of the reservation, where the stand of grass is better and the Papago now graze cattle for both home consumption and market. A pastoral economy is well suited to a scattered population such as the Papago. Cattle did not become important among the Papago, however, until the latter part of the nineteenth century. In the southern part of their area, where they had had cattle since Kino's day, several large ranches grew up, but in the north, which retained its ancient economy in a purer form, the raising of cattle was adopted more slowly. When the Jesuits left the Piman territory many of the domesticated animals went wild. Thus these Indians early had an opportunity to secure horses and cattle—a practice which began in Kino's day.[47]

By 1904 the Papago in southwestern Pima County were making their living chiefly by stock raising, while in 1908 many in Fresnal Valley were reported as having cattle, upon

[47] Mange, *op. cit.*, p. 246.

which they depended wholly for support. In 1919 it was estimated that the aggregate cattle holdings of the desert Papago were about thirty thousand head.[48] As late as 1846 the Pima were reported as having few cattle and these only for tillage.[49]

The modern Pima have profited greatly by the introduction of cattle; today they not only raise cattle for their own use, but more commonly rent their lands for pasturing cattle owned by the whites. The grazing of custom cattle by the Pima has steadily grown since November, 1932, when six hundred were secured from the Tremaine alfalfa ranch. In 1935 approximately 55,000 such cattle were on the Gila River Reservation, and during the winter months of the same year about twelve hundred sheep also were pastured there. Many of the Pimas now work for hire, as is true with the Papago at San Xavier, at Tucson and the copper mine at Ajo. Individuals of both groups eke out an existence or supplement their meagre income by cutting and marketing dead wood. Beginning in 1933 marked stimulus was given toward acculturation, particularly among the Papago, by the appropriation of emergency conservation funds. This is having far-reaching effects upon Papago as well as Pima economy and culture; it is transforming Papago economy from a gift and barter to a money basis and gradually raising their standard of living.

* * *

It would be highly desirable to present an accurate statement of the amount of land anciently cultivated per family among Pima and Papago as well as the total amount of crops and wild food used annually per family or per person. Due to cultural disturbances and distortions, however, it is now very difficult to arrive at exact figures. Moreover the ratio between cultivated and wild foods utilized fluctuated con-

48 Curtis, *The American Indian*, II, 31; *Report of the Commissioner of Indian Affairs* for 1904, p. 149; *ibid.* for 1919, p. 287.

49 Emory, *Notes*, pp. 83-5.

siderably from year to year, and the areal variability of soils and climate entered in. Thus the Papago village of Vamori was reported by Clotts[50] as having a cultivated acreage of 7.03 per person, but considerable allowance must be made for the fact that the fields there had quite poor soil. The Papago habit of seasonal movement between Wells and Fields and their migration to the Gila and the Altar to work for hire always has rendered difficult the obtaining of reliable population figures. Thus the reports of the Commissioner of Indian Affairs[51] beginning in 1863 variously recorded the Papago population of Pimería Alta as follows:

Year	Population	Year	Population
1863	7500	1885	7300
1865	5000	1895	2648
1872	6000	1903	2542
1875	6000	1911	about 5000
1883	7300		

Population on the reservation at San Xavier was reported as follows:

Year	Population	Year	Population
1865	(80 families)	1893	427
1882	250	1895	517
1883	500	1896	542
1885	250	1899	502
1887	137	1900	519
1890	363	1903	523

In 1858 Chapman's census listed the number of Pimas on the Gila as 4,117; in 1914 the number on the reservation at Sacaton was 3,796.[52] Part of the discrepancy in the above figures is due to allottees only being included in some cases, in others all the inhabitants of the reservation.

50 Clotts, *Nomadic Papago Surveys*, p. 80.

51 *Report of the Commissioner of Indian Affairs* for 1863, pp. 385, 390; *ibid.* for 1865, pp. 135, 589; Clotts, *History of the Papago Indians*, etc., pt. III.

52 *Report of the Commissioner of Indian Affairs* for 1858, pp. 554-60; *ibid.* for 1914, p. 77.

In 1878 the Papago were reported as cultivating 2,500 acres of land and as having grown six thousand bushels of wheat, five hundred of corn and three hundred of oats and barley. More directly to the point is a careful survey of 1914[53] made in an effort to determine the Papago population, and the figures presented were regarded as quite reliable. Exclusive of the San Xavier and Gila Bend reservations, the Papago population that year was reported as 5,662. This survey has particular significance for our purpose since it also reported that these desert Papago cultivated by flood-water farming 9,177 acres of land (and had from fifteen thousand to thirty thousand cattle). Clotts therein listed a large number of settlements, giving data on population and acreages; but considering only those forty-seven villages for which he presents both population and amount of land culti-vated, the average acreage per person was 1.79. The lowest per person was .02 at Copperosity, the winter home for the sum-mer village of Anegam, the former site of which was Omik-Vaxia (Salt Well); the highest, 7.03 at Vamori where the soil is of poor quality. Information given us by old Papagos indicates that in the days of their fathers and grandfathers the cultivated acreage per family in their villages ranged from one-fourth to a maximum of two acres. Chico Bailey in-formed us that, as a young man, he planted for his own fam-ily a plot of corn fifty by seventy-five yards (approximately three-fourths of an acre); José Petero stated that in his boy-hood the average family had, in addition to their corn, teparies and pumpkins, a wheat field covering about a half acre.

Our Pima informants stated that in the days of their grandfathers most families cultivated from one to five acres although a big land owner might have as much as twenty, much of which was secured by inheritance. Size of Pima farms was reported in 1871 as averaging from ten to fifteen

53 *Ibid.* for 1878, p. 298; Clotts, *Nomadic Papago Surveys,* p. 80.

acres per family (doubtless an exaggeration) ; in 1883 as from
one-fourth to two and one-half acres; and in 1887 as ten acres
which sufficed for the wants of the ordinary family.[54] Similarly, Russell observed in 1901 that Pima farms ranged from
one to five acres per family, and more recently Southworth[55]
indicated that Pima family plots varied from five to fifteen
acres, and that in 1915 on the reservation at Sacaton this was
close to ten acres, although some Indians might hold more
than one such field. The Pima around Sacaton were reported
as having cultivated about three thousand acres in 1854,[56]
and the Pima population on the Gila was listed in Chapman's
census of 1858 as 4,117. These two dates are relatively close,
and if we assume the figures to be correct we arrive at a cultivated acreage of about three-fourths of an acre per person. It
is our own judgment that in early historic times the cultivated
acreage per Pima family varied from two to five acres. Moreover, it is certain that the average size of the Pima farm
anciently was much smaller than at present.

The amount of land cultivated by the Pimas on the Gila
River Reservation in 1854 was about three thousand acres;
in 1919, 10,610 acres; in 1923, 8,965 acres, and in 1929 crops
were harvested from 7,774 acres.[57]

In a recent paper Kroeber[58] calculated a yield of fifteen to
twenty bushels of shelled corn per acre in the aboriginal
"agricultural east," the lower figure of fifteen being supported
by the work of Hinsdale[59] for Michigan. Moreover, Kroeber
concluded that the yield of one acre would be sufficient to
support one person for one year. In this connection Voe-

54 Grossmann, *The Pima Indians of Arizona*, p. 418; *Report of the Commissioner of Indian Affairs* for 1883, p. 64; *ibid.* for 1887, p. 4.
55 Russell, *Pima*, pp. 87-8; Southworth, *A History of Irrigation on the
Gila River Indian Reservation*.
56 According to Rev. C. H. Cook who began living among the Pima in
1870, Clotts, *op. cit.*
57 *Report of the Commissioner of Indian Affairs* for 1919, pp. 84, 94, 140,
160; King and Leding, *Agricultural Investigations*, p. 5; King and Loomis,
Agricultural Investigations, pp. 8-9.
58Kroeber, *Cultural and Natural Areas of Native North America*, p. 146.
59 Hinsdale, *Distribution of the Aboriginal Population of Michigan*, p. 24.

gelin[60] finds Kroeber's estimate of one acre of cultivated land per person much too high at least for the Shawnee during the eighteenth and nineteenth centuries, but does not dispute his figure of fifteen to twenty bushels of corn necessary to support one person for one year. Accepting the weight of fifty-six pounds of shelled corn per bushel (Pima-Papago corn averages three to four pounds less), Kroeber estimates that one thousand pounds of corn (in round numbers the annual yield of one acre, about eighteen bushels), or a little less than three pounds per person per day, should more than sustain the average person in a community composed of men, women and children.

Under early conditions Piman native corn yielded on the average only ten to twelve bushels of shelled corn per acre, although as grown by the U. S. Field Station on the reservation at Sacaton the same corn yields twenty to twenty-five bushels; teparies, under native conditions, five hundred to eight hundred pounds per acre—under Field Station cultivation, as high as fifteen hundred pounds; and wheat, an introduced crop, ten to twenty bushels with native culture, and forty to fifty bushels at the Station.

In our judgment the figure of 1.79 acres of cultivated land per person as derived from the data of Clotts[61] is too high when applied to the whole desert Papago area. Our most reliable figures indicate that the desert Papago, before white contact disturbed their economic pattern, cultivated from one-fourth to a maximum of two acres per family. Allowing an average of twelve bushels an acre, this means a crop of about three to twenty-four bushels of shelled corn, or its equivalent in teparies and pumpkins, per family. Assuming a family size of five, this would allow about three-fifths to five bushels per person per year. In terms of Kroeber's subsistence level (eighteen bushels per person per year),

60 Voegelin, *The Place of Agriculture in the Subsistence Economy of the Shawnee.*
61 Clotts, *op. cit.,* p. 80.

this would indicate the desert Papago cultivated food supply ranged approximately from one-thirtieth of the annual food consumption among some families to one-third of the total among others. Actually, however, the figure was somewhat less because of several factors: (1) On Papago cultivated plots not all the land was level and therefore portions of it were not tillable since they could not be flooded. This was particularly true at points where water entered fields and deposited silt; (2) Papago (and Pima) ate a large fraction of their corn crop in the roasting-ear stage and this reduced its actual yield in terms of total food value. This practice has rendered it very difficult to compute yield of maize per acre; (3) it was customary for Papago (and Pima) to gorge themselves when food was abundant, with little providence for the future. This resulted in such an inequable distribution of the crop that frequently this entire food supply was eaten up by the end of December.

On the above basis, our field and historical studies of the Pima level of economy from the standpoint of their agriculture indicate that anciently the cultivated acreage per Pima family was two to five acres. In arriving at this figure we are guided somewhat by the amount of land it was possible physically for a family to cultivate with primitive implements. Again assuming an average family size of five, we arrive at a figure of two-fifths of an acre to one and one-fifth acres per person, or five to fifteen bushels of corn or its equivalent per person per year. This would mean the cultivated crop supplied approximately from one-fourth of the total food requirements among some families to nearly the entire amount among others.

The conclusion we are forced to draw from our own field studies, as well as historical accounts as to the ancient basis of Pima subsistence, is that, before white contact radically disturbed the economic pattern, the Pima cultivated crop in average years comprised about 50 to 60 per cent of the total

food supply, wild plants and animals constituting the remainder; thus food gathering was absolutely necessary to
supplement the inadequate cultivated crop. Our estimate is
supported by Russell's[62] statement made forty years ago that
mesquite constituted nearly, if not quite, the chief native
article of Pima diet in primitive times; also by that of Whittemore[63] that mesquite beans were the principal article of Pima
food. Mesquite was a dependable food and the Pima ate it in
abundance every year. Their aboriginal crops were maize,
beans, pumpkins, cotton and gourds. In years of inadequate
water supply or crop failure from other causes they were
forced to rely even more heavily upon wild plant and animal
foods. Their strong reliance upon wild foods, chiefly mesquite and sahuaro fruit, supplemented by screwbean and
cholla buds and fruits on the plant side; plentiful jackrabbits
and less numerous deer and mountain sheep, as well as fish
(although they had less access to fish than did the Colorado
River peoples) and beaver on the animal side, bespeaks that
agriculture was not overwhelmingly their basis of food supply.
Wild plant products had a much more important place in
their diet than did game, the ratio being about three to one.
Apart from the killing of rabbits, hunting never constituted
a major occupation, but a hunter would usually get about
a half dozen rabbits in a day's hunt.

On the basis of our similar studies among the Papago, it
is possible to conclude that anciently these Indians in average
years cultivated only about one-fifth of their total food supply,
four-fifths consisting of wild plant and animal products,
supplemented by such variable amounts of cultivated foodstuffs as were secured from the Pima and their relatives in
the San Pedro and Altar valleys in exchange for labor. In
years of poor crops the balance was shifted even further in
the direction of native wild foods and reliance upon these
relatives and friends.

62 Russell, *op. cit.*, p. 74.
63 Whittemore, *op. cit.*, p. 54.

Papago utilized considerably more native plant food than wild animal life, the ratio being approximately four to one; also more deer and less rabbits than did the Pima. These native plant foods were mainly sahuaro and organ-pipe cactus fruit, cholla buds and fruit, mesquite beans, seeds of ironwood and paloverde, certain greens and sand root. Several months of every year were spent by the women gathering and preparing wild plant foods, and every family spent three or four weeks in late June and July gathering sahuaro, the women doing the gathering and preparing the fruit, the men guarding camp and hunting rabbits and rats. Among animals their reliance was upon deer, and, in diminishing order, rabbits, antelope, mountain sheep, rats and larvae. A family group formerly had no more than one or two hunters, each killing about twelve to fifteen deer per year. Many families had no hunter, so the kill was distributed among the entire economic unit with which they were affiliated, ranging usually from two to ten families.

Thus it is obvious that in normal years of crop production the Papago made much more extensive use of wild products than the Pima. In comparison with the Maricopa the Pima depended appreciably more upon cultivation and less upon wild products than did these neighbors on the Gila, to whom mesquite and screwbean are reported as more important than maize.[64] Bartlett[65] wrote in the middle of the last century that Leroux had ascertained the Pima were much better supplied with corn and every other commodity than were the Maricopa. The stronger emphasis upon agriculture by the Pima as compared with the Maricopa is attested also by the presence of extensive canal irrigation, while the Maricopa depended entirely upon the inundation of flood plains and sub-surface seepage.[66]

Although the agriculture of the Gila Pima and the Papago

[64] Spier, *Yuman Tribes,* pp. 48, 58-9.
[65] Bartlett, *Narrative,* II, 251.
[66] Spier, *loc. cit.*

was on a lower technological level than that of the irrigated valleys of Sonora, these Indians were relatively good farmers. Despite the fact that they, particularly the Papago, cultivated small acreages, they did so intensively. The supreme Piman virtue was industry. The farmer arose before sunrise, worked without cessation until near noon and rested during the hottest part of the day, then continued work until dark. The heat prevented rapid labor, hence his toil was slow and plodding but unremitting.

* * *

UTILIZATION OF NATIVE WILD PLANTS

In the Papago region certain wild staple foods grew in abundance and were extensively utilized. Highly important among these were the fruits and seeds of sahuaro *(Carnegiea gigantea)*, and, in the southern part of Pimería Alta, organpipe cactus or pitajaya[67] *(Lemaireocereus Thurberi)*. Of such value was sahuaro that each family established a permanent camp in the nearest available cactus area; its significance is further indicated by the fact that sahuaro harvest marked the beginning of the new year in the calendars of both Papago and Pima. Kino noted the extensive use of pitajayas in the Indian diet in traveling among Papagos from the Gila River to La Concepción (Caborca), as well as in the vicinity of San Luis Bertrando where he observed that the numerous pitajayas lasted the Papago until December.[68]

Another very outstanding food was cholla buds, fruits and joints, and some informants regarded cholla buds of even more importance than sahuaro fruit. Buds of the abundant *Opuntia echinocarpa* and of the jumping cholla *(O. fulgida)*, gathered in May, and the fruit, which ripened in late summer, were pit-baked and constituted staple foods, while the fruit and sometimes buds and young joints of the vari-colored

[67] Pitajaya or pitaya here refers to the fruit of either or both *Carnegiea gigantea* and *Lemaireocereus Thurberi;* sahuaro invariably refers to *Carnegiea gigantea.*

[68] Bolton, *Kino,* I, 256.

cholla *(O. versicolor)* and of the related *O. spinosior* were valued to some extent. The fruits, and to a lesser degree the joints, of prickly pear cacti of several species, especially *O. Engelmannii,* ranked high in the diet. That such fruit, known as tunas, was a staple food in Kino's day is indicated by his experience among the Papago near Santa Eulalia (in Sonora) ;[69] Anza,[70] three-quarters of a century later, observed that among the Papago at Quitobac, *"abrojos* which they scald, taking off the spines" were one of the usual foods. This was doubtless the fruit of a species of *Opuntia.*

Another Papago staple was the fruit and seed of mesquite *(Prosopis chilensis),* so plentiful in the interior valleys of the Papago country. Still to be found near all their watering places are the mortars in solid rock, known as *"pechita* holes," in which mesquite beans were ground. In this connection, Kino[71] noted that at Papago *rancherías* at Santa Viviana his party was given mesquite. Of somewhat less importance were the seeds of ironwood *(Olneya tesota)* which were ground and leached, those of Jerusalem thorn or horsebean *(Parkinsonia aculeata),* and paloverde *(Cercidium microphyllum).*

Staple root crops were the sand root *(Ammobroma sonorae),* often referred to as wild potato or wild sweet potato; *Franseria tenuifolia,* which grew on the flood plains near the villages, and to a lesser extent *Monolepis Nuttalliana.* Entire families went out with digging sticks to gather these several roots, and lived on them while they lasted. Bulbs of *covenas* or Papago blue bells *(Brodiaea capitata* var. *pauciflora)* were of less importance, usually eaten raw in early spring before other foods were available. Mange[72] wrote in 1694 that the food of Indians (doubtless Soba) at *rancheria* El Comac in Sonora was "some roots of wild sweet potatoes [probably sand root, at least in part], the pitaya in their sea-

69 *Ibid.,* p. 244.
70 Bolton, *Anza,* II, 22, 150.
71 Bolton, *Kino,* II, 207.
72 Mange, *op. cit.,* pp. 216, 225.

son and a red fruit which is given toward the sea." Also that
the Papago south of Vacpia (in Sonora), who had never
before seen Spaniards, sustained themselves with "roots or
wild sweet potatoes," mesquite and other small fruits. He
also makes mention of the importance of roots near La Luna
Eddy, at Bacapa and at Basotucán (in Sonora).[73] Likewise
Font[74] referred to sahuaro, pitaya, seeds of various grasses and
various roots similar to the sweet potato (camote), as well as
covenas among the Papago. In 1912 Lumholtz[75] wrote that
during March and April the Papago in certain areas formerly
gathered in the large barren sand hills and lived almost exclusively on sand root, also that covenas furnished the Papago
a favorite food supply.

Mescal (Agave Palmeri, A. Schottii, A. deserti and A.
americana) was used to a fair degree by those Papagos who
were within reasonable access of it or could obtain it by trade,
but was more of a delicacy. It was to be found only in the
higher mountains and not in abundance, and was often
gathered along the Mexican border and pit-baked by parties
who went to Sonora to labor. The fruit of datil (Yucca bac-
cata) furnished variety to the diet and was always gathered
in August by the men when available, but plants often failed
to fruit. Yucca was obtainable on the plains of the Papago
country only at the head of the Altar Valley.

Small greens utilized in their season were amaranth, pigweed or bledo (Amaranthus Palmeri), lambsquarter (Chenopodium spp.) and saltbush (Atriplex Wrightii). Cañaigre
(Rumex hymenosepalus) was of less importance. These, particularly pigweed, were never dried and stored but while in
season constituted the main, if not the only, article of diet.

Acorns were highly valued but neither common nor easily
accessible. Wherever those of black oak (Quercus Emoryi) or
Q. oblongifolia were available without too much effort, or

73 Ibid., pp. 263, 285, 286-87.
74 Bolton, Anza, II, 320.
75 Lumholtz, New Trails, pp. 318-19.

could be secured by trade, they too constituted an interesting adjunct to the diet, and were eaten without leaching. These were found largely in the southern part of the Papago territory, as in the Baboquivari Mountains and the orchard-like forests of oak in the Tumacácori Mountains. Velarde[76] reported the important fruits of the land were tree cactus (evidently sahuaro and pitajaya), tunas, acorns and wild nuts.

The Papago formerly utilized to a fair extent the small seeds of several species of plants, but these largely have fallen into disuse. Most valued were tansy mustard *(Sophia pinnata)*, amaranth *(Amaranthus Palmeri)*, saltbush *(Atriplex* spp., especially *A. lentiformis)* and lambsquarter *(Chenopodium murale)*. Boxthorn *(Lycium Fremontii)*, gathered in early summer, was the most highly prized of the berries.

The Sand Papago, mentioned by Gifford,[77] and the most nomadic of the Papago, lived on wild foods supplemented by vegetables obtained from the Yuma in exchange for Gulf shells. Lumholtz[78] described them as depending chiefly upon the sand root, gathered the year round, and mentions a Sand Papago hermit who lived almost entirely on this root; they also extensively utilized chia *(Salvia chia)* as well as mesquite beans, in search of which they traveled as far as Quitobaquito, Santo Domingo and the lower Sonoita River. Also of considerable importance were sahuaro, pitajaya, *palo fierro* or ironwood, and a succulent plant of the sand dunes, *hierba salada (Oenothera trichocalyx)*, which was prepared by boiling. Díaz[79] noted in his diary (1774) that the Papago (doubtless Sand Papago) living in the sierras between El Carrizal and the Gila, in extreme southwestern Arizona, maintained themselves, so far as plant food was concerned, on mesquite, screwbean, pitayas, tunas, sahuaro and certain roots. Although the Sand Papago almost completely lacked agricul-

[76] Mange, *op. cit.*, p. 309; Wyllys, *Velarde's Relación*, p. 128.
[77] Gifford, *The Cocopa*, p. 262.
[78] Lumholtz, *op. cit.*, pp. 204, 330-33.
[79] Bolton, *op. cit.*, pp. 260-61, 263.

ture, a single agricultural site is attributable to them at Suvuk, southeast of Tinajas de Emilia, in Pinacate. Here, by means of the planting stick, were sowed on a very small scale maize, beans and pumpkins. Once a year they journeyed to the Yuma and bartered baskets and sea shells for maize, teparies and pumpkins. Emory[80] observed that they subsisted principally on fish.

Our Pima informants agreed that the predominant ancient native food plant was mesquite, followed in order by sahuaro fruit and cholla buds. Garcés, in 1774, encountered Pimas from the village of Sutaquison, on the Gila, gathering sahuaro; and Font[81] a year later wrote of the Gila Pimas having an evil odor because of the mesquite flour, screwbeans and grass seed which they ate. In this same connection Bartlett[82] wrote, in 1854, that the Pima granaries were filled with mesquite beans and sahuaro fruit (in addition to wheat, corn, beans and pumpkins), and twenty years later Grossmann[83] noted the great importance of mesquite as a Pima food. Similarly Russell[84] found the most important, abundant and accessible Pima wild foods were mesquite and sahuaro; even in his day both were extensively utilized. This is supported by Whittemore's[85] statement in 1893: "The *principal* article of food was the bean of the mesquite, ..." which was gathered by large parties. Lloyd[86] also says that, up until shortly before 1903, mesquite beans and fruits of various cacti were staple articles of food. One informant, Manuel Lowe, insisted that cholla buds formerly constituted the most staple wild plant food. The jumping cholla *(O. fulgida)* was very plentiful on plains adjacent to the Gila and therefore easily accessible. However, *O. echinocarpa* thrived more in the hotter areas.

80 Emory, *Report on the U. S. and Mexican Boundary Survey*, p. 123.
81 Bolton, *op. cit.*, pp. 388; IV, 44.
82 Bartlett, *op. cit.*, p. 264.
83 Grossmann, *op. cit.*, p. 419.
84 Russell, *op. cit.*, pp. 66, 71, 74.
85 Whittemore, *op. cit.*, p. 54.
86 Lloyd, *Aw-aw-tam Indian Nights*, pp. 123-24.

The remainder of Pima native plant economy was, in general, quite similar to that described for the Papago, with only such departures as were imposed by vegetative differences of their area. Thus, the organ-pipe cactus and the sand root were not available in their region; in fact, roots of any kind except *Monolepis Nuttalliana* were little used. Mescal, because of its scarcity in the area, ordinarily was gathered only in time of famine, but was sometimes secured from the Papago in trade. On the other hand, there was a greater abundance of mesquite than among the Papago and this was of marked significance in their diet. Also the screwbean *(Prosopis pubescens)* abounded along the Gila and ranked high in Pima economy, though little known to the Papago. Acorns were secured only by trade from the Papago. Neither Pima nor Papago utilized sunflower seeds.

It should be noted here that the importance of specific wild plants in Pimería Alta varied somewhat locally, depending upon their abundance geographically and from year to year. In addition to those listed the Pimans utilized many others of less value, and these have been discussed in detail elsewhere.[87]

UTILIZATION OF NATIVE WILD ANIMALS

Wild animals constituted a valuable source of food for both tribes in early days, and the proportion of game in the diet was greater than at present. Chico Bailey said that when he was a boy the Papago in his area almost always had meat at each of their two meals (doubtless beef in part). The mule or black-tailed deer *(Odocoileus hemionus)*, formerly more abundant in Pimería Alta and hunted throughout a large part of the year, was of considerable value as a source of food and clothing for both Papago and Pima. This also is indicated for the Papago by the fact that it was the game animal around

---

[87] Castetter and Underhill, *Ethnobiology of the Papago Indians;* Russell, *op. cit.;* Hrdlicka, *Physiological and Medical Observations.*

which some of their ceremonies centered. Pima informants maintained that as a source of animal food it ranked second only to the black-tailed jackrabbit which was also emphasized in Pima ceremonials. More rarely hunted by both peoples was the Arizona white-tailed deer *(Odocoileus couesi)*, found only in the mountains. Antelope *(Antilocapra americana)* were formerly quite plentiful, as indicated by the fact that the international boundary survey of 1892-94 found antelope in every open valley along the border between Nogales and Yuma. They were sometimes stalked by both peoples, particularly in the tall grassland in the eastern part of Pimería, but did not constitute a dependable source of food and were more rarely hunted than were deer. When the Gila dried up, as it did periodically, both Papago and Pima stalked deer and antelope at water holes. Bear were not taboo, but were never hunted.

Some information on early utilization of animals was presented by Kino, who related that in 1698 Sobaipuri Indians at Quíburi, on the San Pedro, furnished him various "spoils" including buffalo and deer skins, also buckskins at San Xavier del Bac. The buffalo hides were doubtless obtained from farther east, either by trade or through hunting expeditions. Toward the end of his memoir he writes of the natives of Pimería having many deer and buffalo hides, and antelope skins.[88] Likewise Font,[89] writing in 1775, noted that the Gila Pima women covered themselves with deer skins. Velarde,[90] too, writes of the many deer in Pimería, pointing out that among the Indians to the west the hunting of deer was more common. The Soba at Pitiquín and Caborca were absent hunting deer when Mange[91] visited there in 1694, and the Soba men at El Comac were nude, only the women clothing themselves with "soft skins of hare and deer." In the

[88] Bolton, *Kino,* I, 183, 292; II, 267.
[89] Bolton, *Anza,* IV, 49.
[90] Mange, *op. cit.,* pp. 310, 312; Wyllys, *op. cit.,* pp. 129, 132.
[91] Mange, *op. cit.,* pp. 216-17, 220.

middle of the nineteenth century Audubon[92] characterized
the Papago as living on turtles and what game they could get,
and said "I have seen some elk and antelope skins dressed and
terrapin shells are everywhere. We have bought two terrapin
... some roots and the fruit of a plant like the maguey. ...
The Indians kill them (lizards) with a light wand, giving
them a dexterous tap on the head." He also described a kind
of mush made of dried grasshoppers, pounded and mixed
with meal.

Rabbits were easily secured and were very important to
both peoples for food and clothing. Three kinds occurred
in the area—the California or black-tailed jackrabbit (*Lepus
californicus eremicus* and *L. californicus deserticola*), the
antelope or white-sided jackrabbit (*L. alleni alleni*) and the
Arizona cottontail (*Sylvilagus auduboni arizonae*); the black-
tailed jackrabbits, available at all seasons, were most numerous, the white-sided ones least so. Pima informants maintained that the black-tailed jackrabbit formerly was the
most staple Pima animal food and they killed it in large
numbers, chiefly in late summer when it was fattest. Although the Papago regarded cottontail meat as sweet and that
of the other varieties poor, the black-tailed jackrabbit was
nevertheless of considerable value as food because it was both
plentiful and available at all seasons. Except for the communal drive made just before the Papago drinking ceremony,
rabbits were often shot by boys, who were expected to keep
the family supplied. Men did shoot rabbits when encountered, but made no specific search for them unless other foods
were scarce. Some indication of the early situation in this
regard is given by Kino,[93] who reported that in going from
the Gila to La Concepción (Caborca) in Sonora, the Indians
(largely Papago) in all places gave the Spaniards hares, deer,
rabbits etc., from their hunts.

Mountain sheep (*Ovis mexicana*) are now rarely seen, but

92 *Audubon's Western Journal*, pp. 148-50.
93 Bolton, *Kino*, I, 187.

anciently were fairly abundant over portions of Pimería, and a food of considerable significance in Piman diet, although the Pima ate fewer than did the Papago as distances were too great to hunt them. Papago camped seasonally near the mountain tanks or springs and lay in wait for wild sheep. Lumholtz[94] wrote in 1912 that they were still to be found in Sierra del Viejo and Sierra del Alamo, and in rare instances survived almost as far as Hermosillo; Hornaday[95] has presented in some detail the distribution of these animals in Mexico, including *O. canadensis*. They were fairly common in the Pinacate region of northwestern Sonora. Bryan[96] has listed specific points of their occurrence in southern Arizona and Sonora within the present century.

At the close of the seventeenth century Mange[97] found at Bacapa (in Sonora) eighty Papago who sustained themselves with roots, deer and mountain sheep, and noted that part of the people had gone hunting sheep. He encountered at the Pima village of Tusonimo or La Encarnación, in the vicinity of present day Blackwater, on the Gila, a large mound or hill of mountain sheep horns *(carneros cimarrones o silvestres)*, which he estimated contained more than 100,000, and this abundance of horns led him to conclude sheep must have been their common food. Similarly Anza,[98] in seeking to open a land route from Sonora to California, observed in 1774 that in extreme southwestern Arizona, at what are known as the Cabeza Prieta Tanks in the Cabeza Prieta Range, as well as other *tinajas* in the area, certain Papago always camped during the height of the dry season to hunt mountain sheep which came there to drink. In his description he states that whenever the Papago killed a sheep they were very careful to preserve its horns; these were carried to the neighborhood of the water holes and piled there to

94 Lumholtz, *op. cit.*, p. 220.
95 Hornaday, *Camp-fires on Desert and Lava*, pp. 329-44.
96 Bryan, *Papago*, p. 49.
97 Mange, *op. cit.*, pp. 253, 285.
98 Bolton, *Anza*, II, 29-30, 155.

"prevent the Air from leaving the place." Also they cautioned others against removing them because "that element would come out to molest everybody and cause them to experience great troubles." One of our Pima informants, Manuel Lowe, said mountain sheep horns had to be handled carefully and even then rainy cold spells would occur. They must never be tossed out or thrown around, but placed in a designated spot where no one would bother them lest they interfere with the winds and the rains. This was mentioned by Russell[99] for the Pima, and also has its counterpart among the Maricopa.[100] Russell states the Pima ate mountain sheep when obtainable, although even in his day they were no longer abundant, only a few remaining in the Superstition Mountains and in other high ranges on and around the reservation. His experience with a Gila Pima chief indicates these Pima regarded mountain sheep as food fit only for the Papago, who had no fields to look after. However, our Pima informants were all of the opinion that this animal was always eaten when available but that it was of much more importance anciently; and this would seem to be confirmed by Mange's experience at Tusonimo.

The peccary, *javelina* or *jabalí (Pecari angulatus)* was fairly plentiful in places although not utilized for food to any great extent. Our observation is that neither Papago nor Pima seem to have cared greatly for it, although Lumholtz[101] thought it was much relished by the former. Russell[102] noted it could not have been an important article of diet among the Pima. Nevertheless the Pima did hunt it somewhat in the desert country to the east of Sacaton.

Various rats were eaten, particularly by the Papago, the packrat (*Neotoma* sp.), most common food in the group,

99 Russell, *op. cit.,* p. 82.
100 Spier, *op. cit.,* p. 71.
101 Lumhotz, *op. cit.,* p. 169.
102 Russell, *op. cit.,* p. 80.

being rather extensively utilized. An early reference[103] characterizes the Papago as living on seeds, grass, rabbits, rats and wild fruits.

A few birds were included in Piman diet, Gambel quail *(Lophortyx gambelii)* providing the main source of supply, with the abundant western white-winged dove *(Melopelia asiatica mearnsii)* and the mourning dove *(Zenaidura macroura marginella)* also ranking high. The only eggs utilized were those of the Gambel quail. Merriam turkey *(Meleagris gallopavo merriami)* was to be found more plentifully in the mountains formerly than at present, but was hunted only occasionally and then mostly for feathers rather than food. It was not domesticated, although Velarde[104] noted this would not have been difficult. Russell makes no reference to the use of turkeys by the Pima. Velarde relates that in Pimería there were countless turkeys in the mountains. In the same connection he states: "In some places are found thousands of birds *(pavos o gansos)* which are called chickens of the Indies, large and fat and of pleasant taste."[105] These, too, unquestionably were turkeys.

Highly prized as food by both peoples, but more especially by the Papago, were the larvae of the very common lined sphinx moth *(Celerio lineata)* which is two and one-half to three inches long. These caterpillars occurred in great numbers in limited areas on any vegetation, especially amaranth *(Amaranthus Palmeri)*, during or immediately following the rainy season. With their appearance everyone dropped work to gather this great delicacy, which was dried and stored. This is what Garcés[106] referred to, when on a journey from Tubac to San Gabriel he noted the Papago ate

103 *Documentos*, 3rd ser., IV, 554; *Rudo Ensayo*, p. 190; Hrdlicka, *op. cit.*, p. 24.
104 Mange, *op. cit.*, pp. 309-10; Wyllys, *op. cit.*, pp. 129-30.
105 Mange, *loc. cit.*; Wyllys, *loc. cit.*
106 Bolton, *op. cit.*, p. 320.

and dried for storage "some yellow-green worms." It is also mentioned by Lloyd.[107]

Lumholtz[108] described the Sand Papago as depending for their animal food upon jackrabbits, which were caught by running them down in the sand; mountain sheep, mule deer and antelope, all three killed with bow and arrow; and muskrats, lizards, and fish obtained on the Gulf Coast. Similarly Díaz,[109] in 1774, observed that the Indians (doubtless Sand Papago) living in the sierras between El Carrizal and the Gila, in extreme southwestern Arizona, maintained themselves on deer, mountain sheep and rats (also mesquite, screwbean, pitajaya, sahuaro, tunas and certain roots). Only one of Underhill's informants, a Sand Papago from Sonora, had any recollection of mountain sheep hunting.

Mange's[110] account informs us of the poverty of some of the Papago as well as the utilization of certain animal foods not heretofore mentioned. Thus he referred in 1699 to a *ranchería* at an eddy, twelve leagues from the Eddy La Luna (in extreme southwestern Arizona), where there were thirty nude and poor Indians "who only sustained themselves with roots, locusts and other wild fruits." Also at Bacapa *ranchería* there were eighty Papagos, nude and poor, who "at times of the year they sustain themselves with shellfish." Likewise, at Basotucán (in Sonora) were nude and poor Papagos whose only sustenance was roots, some shellfish, locusts, and lizards which they called iguanas. One reference characterizes the Papago as not disdaining, in seasons of scarcity, "even snakes, lizards, and toads."[111]

The dog was really the only animal domesticated by either Pima or Papago. A few species of birds were kept captive for their feathers, especially the golden eagle (*Aquila chrysaetos*), the thick-billed parrot or macaw (*Rhynchopsitta pachyrhyn-*

107 Lloyd, *op. cit.*, p. 124.
108 Lumholtz, *op. cit.*, pp. 204, 330-33.
109 Bolton, *op. cit.*, pp. 260-61, 263.
110 Mange, *op. cit.*, pp. 263, 285, 286-87.
111 Bancroft, *Native Races*, I, 539.

cha), the western red-tailed hawk *(Buteo borealis calurus)* and the western white-tailed dove *(Melopelia asiatica mearnsii)*. Velarde[112] stated that at San Xavier and neighboring *rancherias* the Indians (Sobaipuri) raised many macaws for their feathers.

The Pima situation, with reference to the utilization of native animals for food, differed in only a few respects from that of the Papago. Forty years ago Russell[113] pointed out that the Pima at that time lived upon a mixed diet in which vegetable food predominated; also, that it seemed probable the proportion of meat in their diet in the past was much greater than in his day.

The main point at which native animal food in Pima diet departed widely from that of the Papago was reliance upon fish. Papago utilized fish wherever available, but, as their territory was quite devoid of permanent streams, fish were little known. When the Gila failed, the Pima had less access to fish, but in most years they caught large numbers and this constituted a staple article of diet. However, all species utilized are regarded by the whites as poor food. The only really important fish available to the Pima were two large bony hump-backed chubs, *Gila robusta* and *G. elegans,* commonly known as bony-tail, round-tail or Gila trout. Also secured from the Gila was the sucker *(Notolepidomyzon clarkii)*, the humpback sucker *(Xyrauchen texanus)*, the white salmon of the Colorado *(Ptychocheilus lucius)*, actually a minnow, and to a limited extent the small killifish *(Cyprinodon macularius)*. At times from the San Pedro were secured the suckers *Catostomus latipinnis* and *C. insignis.* Of much less importance were the quite small chubs, *Tigoma pulchella* and *Tiaroga cobitis;* the small dace, *Agosia oscula* and *A. chrysogaster;* and the desert minnow, *Meda fulgida.* In this connection, Kino[114] found in the vicinity of Casa Grande that all

112 Mange, *op. cit.,* p. 309; Wyllys, *op. cit.,* p. 129.
113 Russell, *op. cit.,* p. 66.
114 Bolton, *Kino,* I, 195.

inhabitants (Sobaipuri) extensively utilized fish throughout
the year, using many nets and other tackle. Also Velarde tells
that in the rivers of Pimería Alta there were "*bagre* and other
small fish," and Mange,[115] writing of Pima and Yuma Indians
along the Gila, observed that they sustained themselves on
the river fish caught in nets made of twisted fiber. Garcés,[116]
writing of the Gila, said: "there is found in this river no
other fish than that which they call *matalote*." As late as 1873
Grossmann[117] noted that during April and May fish were extensively eaten. The Pima had no access to sea food and
those of the Papago to whom it was available had no liking for
it.

Beavers *(Castor canadensis)*, too, although lacking in the
Papago territory, were very plentiful along the Gila and its
tributaries and were utilized to a considerable extent for food
by the Pima, who particularly relished the fat tail. The
Patties,[118] who carried on considerable trapping in the Gila
Basin at the close of the first quarter of the nineteenth century, also reported such abundance of beaver.

115 Mange, *op. cit.*, pp. 264, 309; Wyllys, *loc. cit.*
116 Coues, *On the Trail*, I, 142.
117 Grossmann, *op. cit.*, p. 419.
118 Thwaites, *Personal Narrative of James O. Pattie.*

CHAPTER IV

PIMAN CULTIVATED CROPS

Examination of the early literature reveals that Piman agriculture at the close of the seventeenth century, in harmony with the agricultural situation in the Southwest in general, centered around the maize-bean-pumpkin complex. Kino, Mange and others[1] repeatedly refer to the Papago, Pima and Sobaipuri cultivating and utilizing much maize, beans, pumpkins and in some places cotton. Although these Indians had gourds,[2] there is no specific reference to their cultivation. The early accounts do not record the growing or utilization of tobacco, and there is no indication that its culture was pre-Spanish. While *Martynia* for some time has been grown for use in basketry, it is uncertain whether it was cultivated aboriginally. Sunflowers were never cultivated nor even utilized. Although maize was the most important Piman crop, and could be utilized as food in more ways than any other, among the Papago the tepary bean approached it in value because of its tolerance of drought. As indicated by our own field studies, as well as the work of Forde, Gifford, Kroeber, Drucker and Spier,[3] there was considerable similarity between the crops and basic economy of the Pima-Papago and those of the tribes on the lower Colorado River.

With the coming of the Spaniards various Old World crops were introduced into Pimería Alta, although it is clear

[1] Mange, *Luz*, pp. 215-17, 229-30, 247-50, 256; Bolton, *Kino*, I, 187, 195, 207, 246, 255, 291; II, 207; *Documentos*, 3rd ser., IV, 838-39; Coues, *On the Trail*, I, 107.

[2] Bolton, *op. cit.*, 270; Wyllys, *Velarde's Relación*, pp. 133, 136; Mange, *op. cit.*, pp. 249, 265.

[3] Forde, *Ethnography of the Yuma Indians*, pp. 107-14; Gifford, *The Cocopa*, pp. 263-67; Kroeber, *Handbook*, pp. 735-37; Drucker, *Culture Element Distributions: XVII, Yuman-Piman*; Spier: *Yuman Tribes*, pp. 48-81; *Cultural Relations of the Gila River and Lower Colorado Tribes*.

that at least wheat, flax and watermelons had reached part of the area before Kino's arrival in 1687. In order to furnish a more stable food supply for Indians at the missions, and to give them a more secure basis of economic prosperity and independence, Kino distributed seed of wheat, chick peas, bastard chick peas, lentils, cowpeas, cabbages, lettuce, onions, leeks, garlic, anise, pepper, mustard, mint, melons, watermelons and cane, as well as grapevines, roses, lilies, and trees of pear, apple, quince, mulberry, pecan, peach, apricot, plum, pomegranate and fig.[4] Some suggestion of the extent of his industry in getting crops planted and herds of cattle established may be obtained from his observation that in April, 1687, only about a month after his arrival in Pimería Alta, the Indians in Nuestra Señora de los Remedios were very disconsolate and did not wish to be Christians, because among other things the fathers required so much labor and sowing for their churches that no opportunity was left the Indians to sow for themselves, and so many cattle were pastured that the watering places were drying up.[5]

An interesting reference was made by Mange[6] to the effect that in June, 1694, in company with Kino and Gilg, he found the Pima Indians growing flax in the vicinity of San Miguel del Tupo, which had a lake and springs of water. Kino was very skeptical of its being flax, but this was later verified and, although not as fine as that cultivated in Europe, they concluded it was of the same kind. Thus Kino's surprise at the occurrence of cultivated flax in Pimería Alta indicates that it had been introduced into Mexico from Europe and moved northward into Sonora previous to his arrival in the area. A wild blue flax *(Linum Lewisii)* does occur in mountain valleys through the Southwest into Mexico, but we have no knowledge of its having been cultivated, except ornamentally by whites.

4 Bolton, *op. cit.*, 122-23, 204, 248-49, 253, 321; II, 89, 100, 138, 165, 265.
5 Bolton, *op. cit.*, pp. 114-15.
6 Mange, *op. cit.*, p. 260; Bolton, *op. cit.*, p. 194.

As the penetration of foreign animals into Pimería became very rapid soon after Kino's arrival, he quickly established a number of stock ranches with cattle, oxen, horses, mules, burros, goats, sheep and chickens.[7] A letter written by Salvatierra to Father Leal in 1699 notes that "already there are here eight species of animals from the other side, now acclimated to Loreto [in adjacent Lower California]."[8] However, as late as 1846 Emory[9] stated that the Pima had few cattle and these were used for tillage.

There is every indication that no antagonism existed on the part of the Pima-Papago to the introduction of foreign crops by the Spaniards, in fact they received them with enthusiasm. Although these Indians had a very high regard for their own ancient crops, the mere fact that the introduced ones produced well was all the justification needed for their acceptance.

The introduced crops which proved to be of greatest significance in early Piman economy were wheat, barley, watermelons and cowpeas, and in that order; the most important domesticated animals were horses and cattle. Although maize was anciently the leading crop the introduction of wheat gradually shifted the balance, and, among the Pima, wheat rather quickly came to rank first, maize second; among the Papago, maize continued to hold first place until about a hundred years ago because of the difficulty of adjusting wheat culture to the desert habitat. A perusal of reports of the Commissioner of Indian Affairs for the last third of the nineteenth century, with their tables showing the large yields of wheat in comparison with the small yields of maize for Pima and Papago, enables one to appreciate the marked extent to which wheat replaced maize in Piman economy.

In 1863 the Pima were reported as growing wheat, maize,

[7] Bolton, op. cit., pp. 122-23, 143-44, 165-66, 204, 321, 357-58; II, 150, 166; Mange, op. cit., p. 309; Wyllys, op. cit., pp. 128-29.
[8] Bolton, op. cit., p. 223.
[9] Emory, Notes, pp. 83-5.

barley, beans, peas, melons and pumpkins.[10] In 1846 Emory found them cultivating maize, wheat, watermelons, beans, pumpkins and cotton, and in 1856 he added to the list sugar cane and peas.[11] Similarly, in 1873 Grossmann[12] said of them "Wheat, corn, beans, and above all, pumpkins and mesquite-beans are their principal food," and indicated that wheat actually was their main crop, with barley, onions and cotton of lesser importance. Whittemore[13] wrote in 1893 that more than one hundred years before that time the Pima on the middle Gila raised maize, melons, pumpkins, cotton and "a small round seed which they ground and boiled as mush"; Lloyd[14] in 1903 likewise found them growing wheat, maize, beans, pumpkins, watermelons, peppers, gourds, tobacco, and a pea which was probably the chick pea (native cotton by that time had ceased to be grown). Although he observed that perhaps even more than maize or wheat the staple food of the Pima was beans, there can be no doubt that wheat was their leading crop then as it had been for a long time. This is supported by the statement of Russell[15] that wheat was their most important crop when he worked among them in 1901-02. Wheat continued to hold this leading position with both Pima and Papago, at least until 1924, and today ranks second only to alfalfa in Pima acreage. In 1919 the main Pima crops, ranked on the basis of cultivated acreages, were wheat, cotton, alfalfa (one thousand acres, practically all Hairy Peruvian), barley, milo and beans.[16]

In 1907 the Coöperative Testing Station at Sacaton, on the Gila River Indian Reservation, was established through

10 *Report of the Commissioner of Indian Affairs* for 1863, p. 384.

11 Emory: *loc. cit.; Report on the U. S. and Mexican Boundary Survey,* p. 117.

12 Grossmann, *The Pima Indians of Arizona,* p. 419.

13 Whittemore, in *Among the Pimas,* p. 52; although one cannot be certain of the identity of this plant, it is possible it was one of the semi-cultivated grasses known to the lower Colorado River tribes and to the Maricopa.

14 Lloyd, *Aw-aw-tam Indian Nights,* pp. 58, 60.

15 Russell, *Pima,* p. 90.

16 King and Leding, *Agricultural Investigations,* pp. 5, 29.

a coöperative arrangement between the Office of Indian Affairs and the Bureau of Plant Industry of the U. S. Department of Agriculture. The station was created for the study of agricultural problems of the Southwest with special reference to those which might have value for the Indians on the Gila River Reservation. Many crops have received attention, but the bulk of experimental work has related to the breeding, improvement and culture of Egyptian cotton.[17]

In 1923 only 8,965 acres of Pima land were in cultivation because of water shortage; likewise a census of Pima farms and crops on the Gila River Reservation in 1929 revealed that, because of lack of water for irrigation, crops were harvested from only 7,774 of the 29,530 acres of farm land available. Of these, about three thousand acres were in cotton, 2,100 in wheat and sixteen hundred in alfalfa. The yields on these acreages were 1,264 bales of cotton, 29,913 bushels of wheat and 4,790 tons of alfalfa. In 1935 the harvested Pima acreage was approximately 35,000, of which 24,000 acres were farmed by Indians. Of the latter, 1,443 acres were planted to cotton (American-Egyptian and upland types), 4,188 to wheat and 2,500 to alfalfa. Grain sorghums, Sudan grass, corn and barley also were grown on a considerable acreage for feed and pasture. Truck crops, consisting of beans, corn, tomatoes, onions and melons, were also grown for home use and, to a small extent, for commercial purposes. The field station has maintained a very productive strain of yellow Bermuda onions for about thirty years and the Pima have continued an interest in growing these, particularly for home consumption. Additional land is being brought under cultivation for the Pima, with family allotments of from ten to eighty acres, and an average of thirty.[18]

In 1878 the Papago were reported[19] as cultivating 2,500

17 King, Crop Tests at the Cooperative Testing Station, pp. 1-2.
18 King and Leding, op. cit., p. 5; King and Loomis, Agricultural Investigations, pp. 8-9; King, Beckett and Parker, Agricultural Investigations, pp. 9, 11, 56.
19 Report of the Commissioner of Indian Affairs for 1878, p. 298.

acres of land and as having grown six thousand bushels of wheat, five hundred of corn and three hundred of oats and barley. Among the desert Papago the cultivated crops today are, in order of their importance, kidney beans (pinto and pink or rosa beans), Sonora and Early Baart wheat, maize (both flour and dent varieties as well as small amounts of flint corn), black-eyed beans, white and brown tepary beans, pumpkins (principally cushaw and cheese types), Anaheim chili, watermelons, muskmelons, a few varieties of lentils and small amounts of chick peas. In 1919 common pink beans were reported as a staple crop among the desert Papago, who in the previous year grew 1,800,000 pounds of beans and 300,000 pounds of maize. Most of the irrigated crops of the Papago are located at San Xavier, near Tucson. Here the chief crops were reported in 1904 and 1908 as being wheat and barley; in 1919 they were said to have raised ten thousand bushels of wheat, and 250 tons of barley hay. Today the leading crop is barley; also grown are wheat and alfalfa, as well as beans, pumpkins, maize, oats, very small amounts of cotton and tobacco, spinach, cabbage, onions, carrots, chili, a few potatoes, some apples, peaches and plums.[20]

For the past four or five years the principal Pima crops, in order of importance, with acreages, for the Gila River Indian Reservation follow:

Alfalfa (Chilean) for pasturage and hay........about 4,000 acres (1940)
    In earlier years fair amounts of Hairy Peruvian
    were grown. Alfalfa is planted chiefly in fall.
Wheat (Early Baart, Sonora, etc.) .... 2,600 acres (1940)
Cotton (American-Egyptian Pima and Acala) ...... 1,200 acres
Field Corn (Mexican June and native types) ......   800 acres
Barley (Common and Vaughn) ....   700 acres
Grain sorghums (Hegari, Yellow Milo, etc.) ....   500 acres
    Dwarf Hegari is the most popular.
Beans (Teparies, Pima-Hopi limas and common pink
    beans [frijoles]) ....   450 acres
Sudan Grass—for pasturage ....   ?
Watermelons, muskmelons, pumpkins, onions, etc... small acreage
Date palms, pecans, grapes, figs and pomegranates... small amounts

20 Ibid. for 1904, p. 148; ibid. for 1919, p. 287; Curtis, The North American Indian, II, p. 31.

The following information on the several crops is based upon numerous collections made in the field among Papago and Pima by the authors, as well as upon other field collections made by Ruth M. Underhill among the Papago. Determinations of types were made by the authors except as otherwise indicated. All lots have been deposited in the Laboratory of Biology at the University of New Mexico.

As regards maize, the following were secured:

White soft	thirty collections,	several hundred ears
Yellow soft	five collections,	fifteen ears
Purple soft	three collections	eight ears
Red soft	three collections,	nine ears
White flint	two collections,	two ears
Yellow flint	three collections,	four ears
Pop corn	two collections,	several hundred grains
Sweet corn	two collections,	several hundred grains

In the twenty collections of brown and twenty-two of white tepary beans were found occasional seeds of other tepary types. There were three lots of pinto beans, four of common pink beans, three of common red or Colorado, four common yellow kidney beans, five of lima beans, six of cowpeas; also three collections of chick peas and two of lentils.

Twenty lots of seeds of cheese pumpkin, eighteen of cushaw pumpkin and one of *Cucurbita Pepo,* as well as six of gourds, were made; also eight collections of watermelon and seven of muskmelon seeds.

As to tobacco, we have three collections of plants of *Nicotiana trigonophylla,* and one of *N. attenuata;* one of seeds of *N. tabacum* and two of seeds of *N. rustica.*

Our collections include three separate lots of *Martynia louisiana.*

MAIZE

Maize was cultivated by the Hohokam,[21] who preceded the Pimans in the Gila Basin, and there are also archaeological specimens from sites on the fringes of the Piman area, such as Tonto Cave, Canyon Creek Ruin and sites on the

21 Haury, in Gladwin *et al, Excavations at Snaketown,* I, 158.

upper Gila River (see Chapter III). Although it has been thoroughly established by documentary material, dating from the close of the seventeenth and beginning of the eighteenth century, that the Pima-Papago grew maize aboriginally,[22] neither archaeology nor the early documentary material gives any indication of the types. Thus we have only ethnographic studies, in reality tradition, to inform us as to ancient types of maize. All our informants agreed that the ancient Pima-Papago corns were of a single type, namely flour corn.

This flour corn of early times was of three distinct colors—white, yellow and blue—the white most common, yellow next. Red flour corn was occasionally seen but was not regarded as a standard sort. Ears of all four colors as grown by these Indians today are slender and only slightly tapering, rarely more than seven inches in length, and extending from about one and one-half inches in diameter at the butt to about one and one-fourth inches at the tip. The cob is regularly circular in cross section rather than elliptical as in some of the Southwestern corn, particularly archaeological specimens. Generally the ears are twelve-rowed, but occasionally ten or fourteen, and in rare cases eight, with grains wedge shaped and usually medium in size. No particular difference was observed in size of ear or grain among the several colored corns of either Papago or Pima, and all informants stated any variation was dependent upon conditions of cultivation rather than being "in the blood." For example, ears seen in Kohatk village in 1939 were of large diameter with very large grains, which the owner attributed to the abundance of water during that season. On the other hand, all ears seen at Vamori village in 1939 were quite slender and small grained, and we were informed that corn in this village is regularly small-eared because of poor soil.

A number of samples of flour maize, secured from differ-

[22] Mange, op. cit., pp. 215, 217, 230, 247, 249, 250, 256; Bolton, Kino, I, 187, 195, 246, 291; II, 207.

ent parts of the Pima and Papago reservations, were grown under irrigation on the Conservancy District Agricultural Experiment Substation farm just south of Albuquerque, in the Rio Grande Valley, during the summers of 1938 and 1939. As might be expected, when compared with each other these showed considerable variation in characteristics such as height of plant, time of flowering, time of maturity, size of ear, number of rows of kernels, color of anthers etc. In other words, different samples showed a great amount of genetic diversity and revealed that corn grown on different parts of these reservations, and even by different individuals in the same village, by no means displayed complete genetic unity.

The ears of Pima corn observed, all of which were grown under irrigation, were no larger-eared or larger-grained, on the average, than were Papago ears, nor were the largest Pima ears larger than the largest Papago ears found. This was true for the corn grown on these reservations as well as that of Pima and Papago origin grown at Albuquerque. It is interesting to note that all of this Pima and Papago corn (as well as all other Indian corn secured from the Maricopa and Colorado River tribes) planted on this plot in Albuquerque grew and gained height more rapidly than did Mexican June corn grown from certified seed on the same plot. All the Indian corn outgrew the Mexican June until mid-July when the latter began to outstrip the Indian corn in height. The above seed corn was planted May 10, 1938, and May 12, 1939.

Unless the flow of water in the Gila was abundant, often the heavy irrigation preliminary to planting was all the water that the soft native Pima varieties received. Since they flowered in from fifty to sixty days after planting, they made comparatively little demand upon irrigation water. Some of our informants spoke of "sixty-day corn." This undoubtedly had reference to time from planting to flowering rather than to time of maturity. Spier[23] wrote that the Havasupai grew

23 Spier, *Havasupai Ethnography*, p. 103.

a very small variety of starchy maize, known as Mohave corn, which yielded ears in two months, and Forde,[24] writing of the Yuma, stated "The main spring crop is yellow corn which will ripen in two months." Although the native Pima and Papago corns produce silks and tassels within fifty to sixty days after planting, our field studies consistently have failed to reveal any variety of corn among Pima, Papago, Yuma, Mohave and Cocopa which matured in this length of time. As ordinarily grown by the Pima these soft native varieties seldom yield more than ten to twelve bushels per acre; when grown by the U. S. Field Station at Sacaton they yielded twenty to twenty-five bushels. Sacaton June, a variety developed by the Field Station, yielded fifty to sixty bushels with moderate culture.

1. *White starchy maize.* Both tribes formerly grew a single variety of white corn. This was a solid white ear, both grains and cob being white, the grains having a colorless pericarp and colorless floury *(fl)*[25] endosperm.

2. *Purple starchy maize.* A single variety of purple corn was formerly grown by both tribes. This was a white-cobbed, solid purple ear with colorless pericarp and floury endosperm with purple aleurone *(A C R Pr i)*. The shade of purple varied from light blue to a blue-black, and these tribes recognized that such variation in shade may be due in part to climatic conditions and degree of maturity. However, there is also doubtless an intensifier factor *(in)* operating on this purple aleurone to give the several shades.

Neither tribe attempted to grow a mottled or speckled blue and white variety, but occasionally an ear with a few such mottled grains or even an entire mottled ear was seen.

3. *Yellow starchy maize.* The Pima and Papago grew a single variety of yellow corn. This had colorless pericarp, a yellow starchy endosperm and all ears observed had white

[24] Forde, *Ethnography of the Yuma Indians*, pp. 109-11.
[25] The symbols herein used designate hereditary factors.

cobs. It seems to have been grown less extensively than were the white and blue sorts, however. Informant Gerónimo said his grandfather grew only the white and blue varieties, never any yellow corn, and was firm in his opinion that the Papago in the Big Fields village never grew ears of solid yellow corn in that day. Occasionally a few yellow grains would appear on ears of white maize, and it was considered that this is how the yellow-grained variety originated. Several informants advised that Indians of the Altar Valley in Sonora grew this yellow variety rather commonly in the early days.

4. *Red starchy maize.* Both tribes anciently had a single type of red flour corn, a solid red ear although variable in shade, the grains having red pericarp and colorless aleurone and endosperm proper. Two Pima informants maintained that Pima red corn in early days was a deep color with no varying shades. Although red ears of maize are rarely seen on either reservation now, we have succeeded in finding a number among the Papago. The pericarp color ranges through shades from pink to dark red, seeming to represent several genes of the Pp series of alleles. Our investigations failed to reveal a single ear with red or brown aleurone. All red ears seen had white cobs.

Red corn was considered a novelty, rarely planted, and was therefore never regarded as a specific variety. Informants said it would come out of the regular white which was planted and therefore was seen only occasionally. Gerónimo said that as a boy he never saw solid ears of any shade of red corn, but that streaks of pink affecting parts of one or more rows were sometimes seen on otherwise solid ears.

Occasionally ears with variegated pericarp would appear, and were called laughing or prostitute corn. The grains of such ears were variously striped with white, cream or light yellow and shades of red or orange. Informants explained it was called laughing corn because the grains look as if they were smiling, or prostitute corn because of the bright colors of the grain. Such ears were not abundant, being found only in plantings of white flour corn; it was never planted as a separate variety.

Of the four colors of starchy corn mentioned above, only the white is seen commonly today. The next most frequent is yellow, with blue and red sorts rarely seen; this holds for both Papago and Pima.

The only satisfactory explanation found for the almost complete disappearance of some of these colored corns is that they now sell some of their corn to traders, and the only types for which there is any commercial demand are the native soft white, and American varieties which have in part supplanted the colored Indian sorts. Informants agreed that the blue and yellow corns are just as good food as the white, and can be prepared in all the ways that the white one is used, thus no explanation is forthcoming on the basis of taste preference. Nor is the explanation to be found in ceremony.

5. *Flint corn*. All our Pima and Papago informants were of the opinion that flint corn was not Indian corn, but of Mexican origin, and had come into their area comparatively recently. Both tribes grow it to some extent today and it does well. Bernabé López said that when he was a boy the Papago went down into Sonora to work for hire and brought flint corn home. Within the past forty years certain Papagos have been growing a large, flat-grained, white, flint corn, but this is recognized as of definitely Mexican origin. Also the Pima grow a hard, flinty, yellow variety now known as Santan Yellow, accepted in some quarters as an aboriginal variety.

6. *Pop corn*. The line of demarcation between flint and pop corns is not sharp. When the ears have but eight to ten rows and the endosperm is composed chiefly of hard starch they are called flints; small-seeded, multiple-rowed corn having this same type of stored starch in the grain is classed as pop.

We secured from the Papago two kinds of pop corn. The first was a mixture of grains which evidently had come from different ears. All the grains had yellow endosperm and colorless aleurone, some had colorless, others red, pericarp, while the glumes indicated part had come from ears with red, part from those with white cob. The second specimen was a somewhat smaller pop corn than the preceding, with yellow endosperm, the grains having either colorless or colored aleurone. This sample, too, apparently came from more than one ear, as the pericarps were of two kinds, red and colorless. The glumes revealed that the cobs from which the red grains came was red, that bearing the yellow grains, white.

Papago informants said the tribe has had pop corn for only about forty years and that it was originally obtained from the Mexicans.

7. *Sweet corn*. A single type of sweet corn was procured from the Papago. The sample was sent for examination to J. H. Kempton, Botanist for the Division of Cereal Crops and Diseases of the U. S. Bureau of Plant Industry. He reported that it is a many-rowed yellow true sweet *(su)* corn, restricted, to the best of his knowledge, to the Papago, and that it closely resembles one which he obtained near Sells a number of years ago. It does not compare with our modern selected sweet corns in quality, and in his opinion represents a mutation to the sugary condition that took place in a multiple-rowed flint corn. He has never seen sweet corn among the Pima, Maricopa or lower Colorado tribes. We found no sweet corn among the Pima.

All our Papago and Pima informants, save one, agreed that sweet corn was not one of the ancient Papago sorts, but that it had been introduced comparatively recently from Mexico. Several of the Papago informants had seen it grown in the Altar Valley when on expeditions to Sonora years ago. The single exception was a Papago informant, Chico Bailey, a very reliable old man at Pisinemo village, who said sweet corn was very old among the Papago—just as old as any

Papago variety. In this connection Kempton[26] informed us that when a certain Papago Indian visited in Washington, D. C., some years ago, he was pleased to see that the Bureau of Plant Industry had in its collection the sweet type of corn from his tribe, and said his father told him the Papago had always grown it.

The fact that Chico Bailey regarded sweet corn as ancient among the Papago may be understandable when we consider that, having been born in Mexico, he was often in close contact with the Papago and Soba of that region, who, for some time, have grown sweet corn; and that other informants dwelling much farther north on the reservation and not in close contact with the Indians of Mexico, had never seen or heard of it.

That sweet corn is even now rarely found among the Papago is indicated by the fact that one informant said he had never seen anything like our specimens of sweet corn, that it was not corn at all, but a freak.

Archaeological specimens of sweet corn in the Southwest, in fact in the Americas, are extremely rare, the only recorded ones for the Southwest being the Pueblo III ear secured by Morris[27] at the Aztec Ruin and a single grain obtained from the excavation of the Jemez cave,[28] both in New Mexico. Also, the writers have seen at the Arizona State Museum, in Tucson, a few grains of purple sweet corn, considered as prehistoric but not dated, secured in Cummings' excavations at Gourd Cave, Nitsie Canyon, northern Arizona. In this connection, we are indebted to Dr. Emil Haury for permission to make reference to this specimen (no. 1935).

Similarly, ethnological data on the occurrence of sweet corn in the Southwest are rare. It has been reported only for the Hopi.[29] In our own field studies it has been found at the

26 J. H. Kempton, Personal correspondence, Jan. 23, 1940.
27 Erwin, *A Rare Specimen of Zea Mays.*
28 Alexander and Reiter, *Report on the Excavation of Jemez Cave,* pp. 61-2.
29 Whiting, *Ethnobotany of the Hopi,* pp. 69-70.

Zuñi, Acoma, Laguna and San Felipe Pueblos. Although informants among each of these four Indian groups maintained that the cultivation of sweet corn was ancient, more objective evidence is needed to establish its antiquity among these pueblos.

Thus it would seem that sweet corn, commonly regarded as resulting from a mutation to the sugary endosperm from a flint corn, was not widely, if at all, cultivated in the Southwest aboriginally. Hence it is most unlikely the Pima-Papago grew it before the coming of the Spaniards, and up to the present no one has been able to ascertain when they did begin to cultivate it. The only historic mention of sweet corn among the Papago or Pima is that of Freeman.[30]

While visiting Papago villages in southern Arizona in 1910, Freeman found a number of grains of sweet corn, "wrinkled sweet grains," on ears of what he called the "true, southwestern Indian or Squaw corn [flour corn]." There were originally two types of grains of sweet corn secured from these ears. He referred to the first as flinty pop corn, with small ears and extremely hard shallow grains. The other type had larger ears, deeper grains and seemed to be sweeter than the first. Both, when grown, showed considerable variation as to type and productivity. From these, Freeman developed, by crossing and selection, a variety which he designated Papago sweet corn. However, it has not been a success in Arizona due to poor yield and low sugar content.

8. *Dent corn.* Regular dent corn, such as our commercial types, was wholly unknown to both tribes until quite recently, and many individuals have never seen it. Semidented ears were often seen but the denting was always regarded as due to immaturity of the ears.

9. *"Flathead corn,"* that is, ears that are flattened and sometimes split at the tip, when encountered in husking are laid aside to be used later. This corn is never planted. Young

---

[30] Freeman, *Papago Sweet Corn*, pp. 454-56.

people must not eat such ears, although there is no restriction upon old people doing so; if a young woman eats such
corn her next baby may be flatheaded; if a boy eats it he may
become flatheaded.

Flatheaded corn has considerable significance, and the
Papago "think something great about it." It is ground into
ceremonial meal and used only on certain occasions. In the
important Papago practice of making the ceremonial expedition to bring salt from the Gulf of Mexico, Papago men must
take some of this meal and sprinkle it in the Gulf before
removing salt or anything else produced in the water. Also,
at the harvest dance ceremonial cornmeal was sprinkled on
the ground in front of the singers. Or, it was held in the hand
as an offering when a ceremonial favor was requested.

At present the Papago grow chiefly flour and dent corns,
with small amounts of flint and sweet varieties. Twenty years
ago the best corn for growing to maturity in the Pima territory was Sacaton June, a strain of the Laguna variety developed by the Coöperative Testing Station at Sacaton; at least
as late as 1930 it continued to be superior to any of the
Pima native varieties tested. Tests made at this station
showed that Sacaton June yielded forty to fifty bushels per
acre with moderate care while the soft Pima corn yielded
about sixteen bushels. Those Pimas who had access to pump
water found Sacaton June well suited to their farming practices, since they were able to mature a crop of maize following
the harvesting of their wheat. Although some of the Pimas
who depended entirely upon summer flood water from the
Gila were able to secure good yields from Sacaton June, most
of those who did not have access to pump water planted only
native Indian varieties.[31] Recently the Indian Extension
Service has been encouraging the planting of increased
amounts of Mexican June, the acreage of native types con-

31 King and Loomis, *op. cit.*, p. 50; King, *op. cit.*, pp. 16-17.

sequently being reduced. Nevertheless, the Pima still grow from three to five hundred acres of the native types, these plantings consisting of Pima soft white, Pima soft yellow, Pima soft blue, and Santan Yellow which is a hard flinty sort. The soft Pima varieties are not only popular for domestic use but have met with favor in some of the markets of the Salt River Valley. Many of the Pimas are able to secure substantial yields of both the native Pima soft kinds and Santan Yellow flint because of the short period required for maturing and low water requirement, only one irrigation being necessary. Development for the Pima, by the Field Station, of a sweet corn with relative freedom from corn earworm damage, has proved to be quite difficult.

BEANS

Our investigations among the Pima-Papago reveal that they are now growing three species of beans: teparies *(Phaseolus acutifolius)*, kidney beans *(P. vulgaris)* and lima beans *(P. lunatus)*.[32] However, the relative antiquity of the three among these Indians is difficult to determine. Although Fewkes[33] reported finding beans (and maize) in an excavated room east of Casa Grande, an edifice occupied jointly by Hohokam and Pueblo peoples, a letter from J. E. Graf, of the Smithsonian Institution, where Fewkes' material is located, advises that neither the beans nor the maize mentioned are in the Smithsonian collections.

Kino, Mange and Velarde,[34] who visited Pimería Alta while both peoples were still on an aboriginal level, made frequent but indefinite reference to their growing *frijoles*. It is impossible to draw any conclusion regarding the kind or kinds of beans involved, and perhaps the best way to clarify

[32] For seed and vegetative differentia of the three species the reader is referred to: Bailey, *Manual of Cultivated Plants;* Hardenburg, *Bean Culture;* Piper, *American Phaseolineae;* Freeman, *Southwestern Beans and Teparies.*

[33] Fewkes, *Casa Grande,* p. 150.

[34] Bolton, *Kino,* I, 187, 195, 291; II, 207; Mange, *Luz,* pp. 217, 247-50, 256; Wyllys, *Velarde's Relación,* p. 128.

the matter is by a process of elimination. Mention of the occurrence of the lima bean appears in only one ethnographical report on Southwestern tribes—that of Whiting[35] for the Hopi—and both he and Jones[36] regard it as apparently pre-Spanish among these Indians. As to the archaeology of the lima bean, on the basis of recent investigations at the Tonto Upper Ruin, it is now certain that this bean was grown in the Southwest aboriginally. The material from this site clearly indicates that *Phaseolus lunatus* was cultivated in the Salt River region on the edge of the Piman territory as early as the fourteenth century. A poorly preserved and incomplete specimen of charred cotyledons and pod fragments from the Wupatki excavation (dated 1168-1205 A. D.), about thirty-five miles northeast of Flagstaff and overlooking the Little Colorado River, was determined by Jones with some uncertainty as *P. lunatus*. If the lima beans found by Kelly[37] in a site near Tucson prove to be authentic as to archaeological context, the lima bean in the Southwest will thereby have further support for occurrence in the late twelfth or early thirteenth century.

The early historical accounts make no reference whatever to lima beans among the Pima-Papago, and in this connection it is significant that Freeman, who in 1910-12 investigated the native beans grown by these peoples, made no mention of the occurrence of the lima bean. Thus, in the absence of any specific archaeological or historical evidence among the Pima-Papago, it seems very doubtful that these people had the lima bean aboriginally. However, if opinions secured from informants, which represent Pima and Papago tradition, may be relied upon, it would be possible to conclude that the Pima had the lima bean earlier than did the Papago. The problem, therefore, seems to resolve itself into a

35 Whiting, *Ethnobotany of the Hopi*, pp. 12, 81.

36 Steen and Jones, *Prehistoric Lima Beans in the Southwest;* Reed and Brewer, *Excavations of Room 7, Wupatki.*

37 Steen and Jones, *op. cit.*, p. 200.

question of whether the Pima-Papago had both tepary and kidney beans.

Among the references to beans by Kino, Mange and Velarde, only two are sufficiently specific to be of real value. Velarde came to Kino's mission of Nuestra Señora de los Dolores in 1702 or 1703 while the Pima-Papago were still on an essentially aboriginal level. In his *Relación,* written in 1716, he observed that "those who live here are called Papabotas, that is, Pimans who eat beans *(pimas frijoleros),* since their principal sowing is the bean called *japavi* . . .";[38] and a little further on said "The rest of the fruits of this Pimería are maize, the small bean called *tepari,* and other seeds . . ." Velarde's account here is somewhat confused and it leaves one at a loss to know whether he is writing of one or two kinds of beans being grown by the Papago. However, his reference to the "bean called *japavi* [papavi]" is evidently to the tepary bean, the Papago name for which is *pawi,* and from which these Indians received their nickname *papawi o' otam* (bean people). The name *papawi* comes from a Spanish pronunciation of the Papago phrase *t pawi,* "it is a bean." Another reason for believing Velarde's references are to the tepary bean is that the Papago name for the kidney bean is *mu:nyi.* Wyllys'[39] translation of the word *japavi* as probably meaning mesquite beans is, in our opinion, erroneous. The only other reference in the early accounts which may be interpreted as referring to the tepary is that of Mange,[40] who wrote of Indians on the Gila (Pimas and Yumas) giving his party "white beans." The absence of white kidney beans among the Papago-Pima today, and Freeman's[41] failure to encounter any when he studied the kidney beans and teparies of these tribes thirty years ago, indicate that white kidney beans at least are unlikely to be aboriginal among them and that

38 Mange, *op. cit.,* p. 309; Wyllys, *loc. cit.*
39 Wyllys, *loc. cit.*
40 Mange, *op. cit.,* p. 265.
41 Freeman, *op. cit.*

Mange was undoubtedly referring to the white tepary. More-over, the Spaniards complained that the Spanish (common or kidney) bean after being grown two or three seasons had a tendency to degenerate into the native tepary.[42] Russell[43] informs us that forty years ago the Pima were growing five kinds of beans, the first known being *tatcoa pavfi* (white bean), doubtless the white tepary, which they regarded as having been brought from the Colorado River Valley in some forgotten time. Pima and Papago informants invariably regarded the tepary bean as an aboriginal, staple crop, and Freeman[44] was definitely of the opinion that it was ancient in cultivation among these peoples. Thus the historical data show quite conclusively that the tepary was being grown by the Pimans at the time of the arrival of the Spaniards.

Archaeological evidence also amply supports the thesis that occurrence of the cultivated tepary bean antedates the coming of white man in the Southwest, but just when it began to be grown in this area is a problem that awaits solution. In addition to the archaeological teparies known from the Gila Basin, and mentioned in Chapter III, the authors have seen the following specimens from the Southwest:

(a) Well-preserved teparies, both white and brown, from Kelly Cave on the San Francisco River, Catron County, New Mexico. About ninety pounds of these beans were found in a storage basket from the Eisele collection. Antiquity uncertain.

(b) White teparies from a cave in the Mimbres River area in southwestern New Mexico. Part of a cache of seventy-five pounds found by Berry Bowen in a large basket. Dating uncertain.

(c) Some white, some black, and some red and black

[42] *Rudo Ensayo*, p. 136; *Documentos*, 3rd ser., IV, 511.
[43] Russell, *Pima*, p. 92.
[44] Freeman, *The Tepary, A New Cultivated Legume from the Southwest*, pp. 398, 400.

mottled teparies from another cave in the Mimbres country found by Berry Bowen. Age uncertain.

(d) A find of about seven quarts of what are doubtless charred teparies, secured by Cummings in 1933 from Kinishba, R 30 Gr I (no. 6742), now in Arizona State Museum at Tucson. Charcoal specimens from Kinishba Pueblo, which is situated about three miles northwest of Fort Apache, Arizona, have been studied by Baldwin, *Dates from Kinishba Pueblo*. The tree-ring dates obtained—1190-1301— indicate that the site was occupied in late Pueblo III or early Pueblo IV. Reference to this and the next specimen is made possible through the courtesy and permission of Dr. Emil W. Haury, Head, Department of Anthropology, University of Arizona.

(e) Black teparies. Cliff dweller material from Sagie Canyon, secured by Cummings in 1915. Now in Arizona State Museum. Prehistoric, but dating uncertain (no. 971).

(f) The Museum of Northern Arizona recovered charred teparies from a Pueblo III masonry pit-house, site N. A. 1814, located north of Flagstaff;[45] also another collection of charred teparies from a late Pueblo II-early Pueblo III horizon at the Winona-Ridge Ruin sites in northern Arizona dating from the late eleventh to early twelfth century. These have been described and discussed by Jones.[46]

Gray,[47] in 1852, described *Phaseolus acutifolius* from a specimen secured by Wright in 1849 in a mountain valley thirty miles east of El Paso, Texas. He also mentioned,[48] but did not name, a second variety with larger, broader leaves

[45] Dr. H. S. Colton, Director, Museum of Northern Arizona, Personal correspondence, June 28, 1935; Jones, in McGregor, *Winona and Ridge Ruin*, pt. 1, p. 298.

[46] Jones, *op. cit.*, pp. 297-98; J. C. McGregor, Museum of Northern Arizona, Personal correspondence, May 6, 1940.

[47] Gray, *Plantae Wrightianae*, I, 43-4.

[48] *Ibid.*, II, 33.

which Wright secured in a valley of Sonora in 1854. We have examined the seeds of this specimen, loaned by the Gray Herbarium, and find them to be very similar to those of the specimen from Stone Cabin Canyon mentioned below. Freeman[49] described *P. acutifolius* A. Gray var. *latifolius* from specimens which he grew from cultivated seed obtained from Papago and Pima Indians, saying that the seed color of different varieties was white, yellow, brown or bluish-black to deep violet, either self-colored or variously flecked. Also that in form the seeds were round-oval or nearly round, to strongly flattened. From his descriptions and seed measurements it is evident his variety *latifolius* is identical with that grown by the Pima-Papago today. On the basis of compared vegetative characters he concluded that Gray's unnamed variety and *P. acutifolius* A. Gray var. *latifolius* were identical.

Freeman states that later (1914) wild specimens of *P. acutifolius* var. *latifolius* were located in two places in Arizona, and describes plants from one of these localities, south of the Santa Rosa Mountains near the Mexican border, as having "small, strongly flattened gray speckled seeds." We have seen a specimen collected from the other site, in Stone Cabin Canyon in the Santa Rita Mountains, and it too has small, flattened, brownish seeds. Thus there is a vast difference between the seeds of the plants on which his description of the variety *latifolius* was based and those of the wild specimen mentioned.

Freeman[50] was of the opinion that the tepary bean was domesticated from plants growing in canyons of southwestern United States and northern Mexico by prehistoric Indian races; also that the tepary grown by Indians in the Southwest was probably domesticated from the larger, more robust, broad-leaved variety which he named *P. acutifolius* var.

[49] Freeman: *op. cit.*, pp. 396-97, 406-13; *Southwestern Beans and Teparies*, pp. 21-6.

[50] Freeman, *Southwestern Beans and Teparies*, pp. 26-8, 55.

latifolius. His view has often been quoted in the literature with approval. However, we must differ with Freeman for two reasons: the discrepancy between his conclusions and the archaeological picture, and the marked differences between the wild and cultivated teparies. As to the first point, all the known archaeological specimens, some of which date at least as far back as the eleventh century A. D., closely resemble the modern cultivated tepary, thus showing a wide departure from the wild *P. acutifolius* var. *latifolius.*

Our second reason for rejecting Freeman's conclusions is that we have seen seven different seed specimens of wild tepary beans, secured from various points in southwestern New Mexico and southern Arizona. They range in color from finely speckled light to dark brown, are quite angular and very much resemble small gravel. Four of these specimens were grown under irrigation in the nursery of the Soil Conservation Service in Albuquerque during the summer of 1940. There was no difference in size, color or shape of the seeds of this cultivated crop as compared with the wild ones from which they were grown, and none of the seed specimens mentioned resembles at all closely the cultivated tepary of the Southwest, although there is considerable similarity in vegetative characters. In fact, careful observation is necessary to see any resemblance between the seeds of the two. Moreover, Mr. Leslie N. Goodding, Associate Botanist, U. S. Indian Service, who has extensively traveled over New Mexico and Arizona and examined many specimens of teparies growing wild in these states, advises that in not a single case has he seen seeds which resemble at all closely those of the cultivated tepary. Thus, in our opinion, there is at present no evidence to support Freeman's claim for the local origin of the tepary. The answer to Gifford's[51] question, as to whether the cultivation of the tepary bean *(Phaseolus acutifolius)* in the Southwest is not merely in imitation of the

[51] Gifford, *The Cocopa,* p. 316.

cultivation of the kidney or common bean *(P. vulgaris)*, must await additional data.

Lumholtz,[52] writing of Mexico, noted he had not seen the tepary bean outside of Sonora, although Piper[53] says that in its wild form the species ranges from western Texas to Arizona and southward in Mexico to Guadalajara. It is widely distributed along the western coast of Mexico, and the Russian workers under the leadership of Vavilov have found it under cultivation in Chiapas. They regard *P. acutifolius* A. Gray var. *latifolius* Freeman as having originated in the South Mexican-Central American center.[54] However, Dr. D. D. Brand, of the Department of Anthropology of the University of New Mexico, informed us in personal conversation that he has carefully and systematically examined the markets in western Guerrero and southern and western Michoacan, and in not a single case has found any teparies. One might expect that since they are found in Sonora and in Chiapas they would be found along the entire Mexican west coast. In view of the wide distribution and varietal diversity of the wild tepary, the region where it was first brought under domestication and the wild form from which it was developed need further investigation. In the absence of proof of its origin from the wild forms of *P. acutifolius* A. Gray var. *latifolius* Freeman, perhaps its origin should be sought in varieties farther to the south. Detailed genetic and cytological studies would be of great value in solving the problem of origin.

The Papago, at least, formerly gathered and ate wild teparies. Freeman[55] stated that two old Papago women informed him thirty years ago that they remembered having gathered dark-colored wild teparies during their childhood

[52] Lumholtz, *New Trails*, p. 287.

[53] Piper, *op. cit.*, p. 693.

[54] Vavilov, *Botanical-Geographic Principles of Selection;* Bukasov, *The Cultivated Plants of Mexico, Guatemala and Colombia,* pp. 473, 485, 505.

[55] Freeman, *op. cit.*, p. 11.

in the mountains farther south, presumably in Sonora. Thornber[56] informs us that in 1914 he saw an astounding quantity of wild teparies growing near Santa Rosa, just south of the Santa Rosa Mountains on the Mexican border, and that a group of Papago women were gathering the ripe seeds. None of our own informants had any knowledge of the utilization of wild teparies.

From samples of cultivated tepary secured from the Papago and Pima, Freeman isolated and grew forty-seven distinct types, differing chiefly in flower color, and shape and color of seeds. Growth habit, foliage and pod characters of these types showed little difference, except that the white-seeded sorts had slightly smaller leaves than did those with yellow or darker colored seeds.

Both Papago and Pima had only two staple varieties of tepary—the white (really greenish white) and the brown. Black and variously speckled teparies also occurred but were rarely selected or grown as distinct varieties, and many Papagos and Pimas would pull up and discard such plants when found among crops of the white and brown ones. Informants of both tribes, with a single exception, regarded the brown as the oldest of the teparies. A present day factor which limits the growing of teparies is the commercial demand for only the white and brown varieties. The one most commonly found on the commercial market is the white, and this is often brought to trading posts for barter. Both tribes regard the white one as superior in taste and general quality to all the others.

That the kidney bean (*P. vulgaris*) was aboriginal in the Southwest is authenticated by its occurrence at a number of sites in the San Juan Basin belonging to horizons as early as Basket Maker III, such as those of Kidder and Guernsey.[57]

56 J. J. Thornber, Professor of Botany, University of Arizona, Personal conversation, Apr. 26, 1940.
57 Kidder and Guernsey, *Archeological Explorations in Northeastern Arizona*, p. 98.

Moreover kidney beans were recovered by Haury[58] at the Canyon Creek Ruin near Roosevelt Lake on the fringe of the Piman territory, and are definitely known to have been grown by the Hohokam, in the Gila Basin (see Chapter III). Although we have no specific evidence that the Pima-Papago were cultivating kidney beans before the beginning of Spanish penetration into their area, it would be reasonable to suppose that they might have done so since they were cultivated by their neighbors and predecessors.

Freeman,[59] writing thirty years ago, was of the opinion that the kidney beans grown by the Papago and Pima were probably descendants of varieties introduced by early Spanish missionaries. On the other hand, Russell,[60] who worked among the Pima in 1901-02, states: "At least one variety of the common kidney bean, pole bean, bunch bean, etc., was known to the natives before the advent of the Spaniards." Since he gives no indication of the basis for his statement, little reliance can be placed upon it. Opinions secured by the authors from Pima-Papago informants as to the antiquity of the kidney bean are conflicting, the great majority of them regarding it as post-Spanish, a few pre-Spanish. One point in this connection is highly suggestive. Dr. Ruth Underhill, who has worked a great deal among the Papago and Pima, informs us that the Papago have growing songs for the tepary but not for the kidney bean. She has never heard more laughter evoked from a Papago group than when, as she was collecting growing songs, some wit suggested a song for the kidney bean. It was unthinkable!

Freeman[61] tested twenty-three distinct varieties of P. vulgaris obtained from the Papago-Pima about thirty years ago. He found the most commonly cultivated varieties to be the common Pink or Rosa bean; the Bayou bean; the Hansen

58 Haury, The Canyon Creek Ruin, p. 59.
59 Freeman, op. cit., pp. 4, 11, 54-5.
60 Russell, op. cit., p. 76.
61 Freeman, op. cit., pp. 4-10, 15.

bean, which from his description we take to be a striped Garrapata; the Mexican Tick bean or spotted Garrapata, of which he secured two distinct true-breeding strains; the Red or Colorado bean; and "mottled Red Indian beans" or red and white calico beans, which he found as pure field cultures among both Pima and Papago, although not a common sort.

In addition to these varieties, Freeman lists a number of miscellaneous forms found among the Pima and Papago which occurred only as mixtures with other varieties and were never found cultivated as pure varieties; but these on being isolated and grown were found to breed true.

The kidney beans *(P. vulgaris)* most commonly grown by the Papago at present are, in order of importance:

1. The common Pinto bean belonging to the Garrapata group.

2. The common Pink or Rosa bean (pink *frijole*). This was a staple crop among the desert Papago at least by 1918 when they grew 1,800,000 pounds.[62]

3. The Red or Colorado bean. Freeman reported this variety was grown sparingly thirty years ago by the Indians of southern Arizona, but that it was very popular in southern Sonora, where it quite largely replaced the Bayou bean for early spring planting. Our observation is that it is now quite commonly grown by the Papago on the Sells reservation.

4. A yellow self-colored strain of the Rosa bean (evidently the Bayou variety of Freeman). Our information agrees with that of Freeman to the effect that it is and has been extensively grown in northern Sonora.

A lima bean of the Hopi type was cultivated by the Pima for many years, although evidently not aboriginally. Between 1915 and 1930 it almost disappeared from the Gila River Indian Reservation and seldom was seen at the trading posts.

[62] *Report of the Commissioner of Indian Affairs* for 1919, p. 287.

About 1930 the Coöperative Field Station at Sacaton began to select Indian lima types for adaptation to the warmer areas of the Southwest. Beginning in 1931, several color types were secured from the Hopi reservation, and the selected strains of white Hopi limas were obtained from the Agronomy Department of the University of California. In 1932 some samples of the Pima strain were secured which have been designated Pima-Hopi lima. Varying somewhat in color, this strain is typically light tan with black longitudinal markings. Selections were made from the strains and some improvement obtained in their ability to retain flowers and young pods during hot weather and to resist spotting of the young beans. The white strains show greater susceptibility to these disturbances than do the red, black and flecked ones. Nearly all the Hopi and Pima-Hopi lima strains show greater resistance to root knot nematodes than do the various common beans and teparies. Some of the vine types of limas are suitable as a summer cover crop and yield a greater tonnage of vines than do the teparies sometimes used for that purpose.[63]

The chief beans grown today by the Pima are teparies, Pima-Hopi limas and Mexican pink beans *(frijoles)*. Limas are seen in many colors but mostly brown or tan with purple longitudinal markings. These Indians occasionally try other commercial sorts but seldom have any success. The tepary continues to be a more dependable producer among the Pima and Papago than either kidney or lima beans.

PUMPKINS

That the Pima-Papago were growing pumpkins as early as the time of Kino's arrival in Pimería Alta is well authenticated. Kino and Mange[64] refer a number of times to the cultivation and utilization of pumpkins *(calabazas)* by these

---

[63] King, Beckett and Parker, *Agricultural Investigations,* p. 58.

[64] Bolton, *Kino,* I, 187, 195, 246, 291; II, 207; Mange, *Luz,* pp. 217, 249, 256.

peoples. The only other early reference is that of Velarde[65] who states that since the Spaniards had come into Pimería the Pimans grew pumpkins (calabazas) of various kinds. Complete lack of archaeological specimens of pumpkins in the area, going as far back as the Hohokam culture, renders it impossible to extend our knowledge of the existence of pumpkins among the Pima-Papago prior to Kino's day, even though all our informants regarded pumpkins as an ancient Piman crop. However, the occurrence of pumpkin remains (Cucurbita Pepo and C. moschata) in archaeological sites adjacent to the Piman area, such as the Tonto Ruin, the Canyon Creek Ruin and the upper Gila River is well established[66] (see also Chapter III).

Unfortunately the early historical accounts throw no light whatever on the kinds of pumpkins grown by the Pima-Papago. In our field studies three species were found—C. moschata, C. Pepo and C. maxima. The first was common everywhere among these tribes and consisted of several varieties, invariably regarded by informants as aboriginal. Both the buff and very dark green cheese pumpkins, usually with slender hard peduncles, were often found; these were commonly of cheese-box shape, occasionally oblong. But most abundant were the pear-shaped cushaws, with neck of varying length, in a variety of colors ranging from very dark green through yellow to netted and mottled green on a cream background. Many had corky longitudinal ridges on the neck and the peduncle was characteristically quite thick. Crookneck cushaws with strongly curved necks were seldom observed.

Although Papago and Pima informants frequently described an ancient pumpkin which gave every indication of being C. Pepo, it was only after long and diligent search that we finally found this species—at the Papago village of Big

[65] Wyllys, loc. cit.; Mange, op. cit., p. 309.

[66] Hough, Culture of the Ancient Pueblos of the Upper Gila River Region; Haury, loc. cit.

Fields, where two informants said their grandfathers had grown it; later we found it at Santa Rosa. All informants to whom it was shown regarded it as ancient. This was elongated in shape, averaging about fifteen inches in length by seven in width. The color was dark green with broad stripes of a lighter green mottled with gray. Informants said the reason it was not cultivated more widely was that it was good for roasting, but not satisfactory for drying and storing.

The third species was C. *maxima,* located among the Papago only at Big Fields, and here and there among the Pima. Informants invariably said this Banana squash at Big Fields was not a Papago type and had come into the village within the last thirty years; Pima informants also regarded varieties of this species as of recent introduction.

The above information on the three species of *Cucurbita* is in full agreement with Southwestern archaeological data in general, for numerous specimens of C. *moschata* and C. *Pepo* have been found in Southwestern excavations, but not a single archaeological specimen of C. *maxima* has ever been found in the Southwest, or for that matter in any area north of the interior of Mexico. Thus there is every indication that the Papago-Pima grew pumpkins aboriginally, both C. *moschata* and C. *Pepo* being cultivated before the coming of the white man. Russell[67] says that, according to tradition, the first Pima pumpkin (called *rsás katuk*) were obtained from the Yumas and Maricopas.

COTTON

Although investigators are not agreed that a continuity exists between the cultures of the Hohokam and their successors, the Pimans, archaeological specimens clearly show cotton was present at an early date in the Gila Basin. Fewkes found cotton at the Casa Grande ruin, and it has been reported from the Grewe site and McEwen Cave; Woodward has reported cotton seed and what appears to be impressions

67 Russell, *op. cit.,* p. 91.

of cotton textiles from a Colonial Hohokam site. Also a cotton textile was recovered from the Sacaton Phase in the Snaketown excavations, and cotton seeds and lint were found in other phases[68] (see Chapter III).

That the Pimans were growing a considerable amount of cotton when Kino arrived in Pimería Alta is amply supported. The early Spanish accounts describe the growing of cotton not only by the Gila Pima, but by the Sobaipuri on the San Pedro and at San Xavier.[69] No mention is made of cotton being grown by the desert people (Papago). Kino wrote that natives of Pimería had very good cotton fabrics, and in 1701 noted that the Sobaipuri at San Xavier had given him "many of their good fabrics and blankets of cotton"; and Velarde[70] recorded "The Sobaipuris and other Pimas of the North [evidently along the Gila] sow much cotton, which they weave, and with which they clothe themselves." He also informs us that the dress of those who lived in the north was of cotton cloth, very well woven and painted gracefully with red and yellow. Mange[71] wrote of Sobaipuri Indians at the *ranchería* Santa María de Bugota, as well as those of San Agustín de Oiaur on the Santa Cruz near present day Tucson, dressing themselves with cotton; and of the Sobaipuri Indians at Quíburi on the San Pedro gathering cotton "with which they walk dressed." He also noted that the Sobaipuri inhabitants of Arivavia, also on the San Pedro, gathered "cotton with which they weave premium mantas and painted of various colors, with which they dress and adorn themselves." The *Rudo Ensayo*, evidently written in 1763, in referring to the Gila Pima, records: "So much cotton

[68] Fewkes, *Casa Grande*, pp. 147-48; Jones, *Summary of Data on Aboriginal Cotton*, p. 5; Haury, in Gladwin *et al*, *Excavations at Snaketown*, I, 160-162.

[69] *Documentos*, 3rd ser., IV, 504, 837, 848; Sedelmayr, *Relación*, pp. 106, 108; Bolton: *Anza*, IV, 44; *Kino*, I, 291-92; II, 267; Russell, *Pima*, p. 77; Mange, *Luz*, pp. 248-50, 309; Wyllys, *Velarde's Relación*, p. 129.

[70] Mange, *op. cit.*, p. 309; Wyllys, *op. cit.*, pp. 129, 132.

[71] Mange, *op. cit.*, pp. 247-50, 256.

is raised and so wanting in covetousness is the husbandman,
that after the crop is gathered in, more remains in the fields,
than is to be had for a harvest here in Sonora—this upon the
authority of a Missionary Father who saw it with his own
eyes in the year 1757."[72] Similarly, Font,[73] who visited the
Pima along the Gila River while on his journey to Monter-
rey in 1775-76, wrote that they planted, spun and wove
cotton into fabrics, garments and blankets; this was also observed by Garcés. Whittemore[74] stated in 1893 that it was
cultivated more than a hundred years before his time. Likewise Oñate's[75] party, which made an expedition to California in 1604-05, observed that Indians along the Gila had
cotton mantas, but these were evidently the Maricopa.

Bartlett, Emory and Whipple[76] reported that a considerable amount of native cotton still was being grown and used
by the Pima between 1846 and 1850, and in 1873 Grossmann[77] found them still growing small amounts. The Pima
have grown cotton commercially for a number of years, and
as early as 1864 the Superintendent of Indian Affairs for
Arizona stated that he had furnished the Pimas with five hundred pounds of commercial cotton seed.[78]

Russell[79] pointed out forty years ago that from pre-Spanish days down to the last quarter of the nineteenth century
the Pima cultivated cotton for the fiber, as well as seeds for
food. However, cultivation of the aboriginal product gradually diminished, until by 1901-02 it had so nearly ceased that
it was only with difficulty that a sufficient amount of raw
cotton of Pima raising was secured to weave a small piece of

72 *Rudo Ensayo*, p. 128.
73 Bolton, *Anza*, IV, 44, 49; Coues, *On the Trail*, I, 107-08.
74 Whittemore, in *Among the Pimas*, p. 52.
75 Hammond, *Don Juan de Oñate*, p. 167; Bandelier, *Final Report*, I, 110.
76 Bartlett, *Narrative*, II, 223-29; Emory, *Notes*, pp. 83-5; Whipple, *Official Report*, pp. 598-99.
77 Grossmann, *The Pima Indians of Arizona*, p. 419.
78 *Report of the Commissioner of Indian Affairs* for 1864, p. 153.
79 Russell, *op. cit.*, p. 77.

cloth. Lloyd[80] found the Pima were no longer growing native cotton in 1903. We have found no trace of Pima or Papago cultivation of aboriginal cotton at the present day; in fact, it was impossible to find a single specimen of the ancient product among these Indians, and it is very doubtful whether any aboriginal cotton has been grown by the Papago-Pima for many years. Early accounts make no specific reference to the growing of cotton by the Papago, yet our informants insisted that within their memory, as well as according to tradition, the Papago grew it in favorable places in their areas with flood-water farming, the fiber for weaving and the seed for food. Moreover Lumholtz,[81] writing of the Papago in 1912, stated that native cotton was still found in use. More commonly, however, they secured their cotton by trade from the Indians of the Altar and Gila valleys.

Lewton,[82] writing in 1912, made mention of a specimen of cotton secured from the Pima at Sacaton by E. W. Hudson, which he considered as belonging to *Gossypium hopi* Lewton. Jones'[83] summary states that T. H. Kearney wrote him that little of the history of this specimen is known, aside from the fact that it was secured from the Pima and the strain has been kept from becoming extinct by making annual plantings at the Field Station at Sacaton. It is evidently seed of this specimen from which annual plantings have been made at the Sacaton Station under the name of "Sacaton Aboriginal," and which was doubtless the kind of cotton cultivated aboriginally by the Pimans. It is a strain of *G. hopi* Lewton, a species found to be very early and genetically quite heterozygous. Genetic experiments, involving interspecific crosses, are reported by Fulton[84] as confirming the evidence from morphological characters that *G. hopi* is more

80 Lloyd, *Aw-aw-tam Indian Nights*, p. 58.
81 Lumholtz, *New Trails*, p. 95.
82 Lewton, *The Cotton of the Hopi*, p. 8.
83 Jones, *op. cit.*, p. 4.
84 Fulton, *Hopi Cotton*, pp. 333, 336; Lewton, *loc. cit.*

closely related to *G. hirsutum* L. than to *G. barbadense* L. Segregation was found to be much less pronounced in the F_2 from the cross of Hopi with upland cotton *(G. hirsutum)* than from that of Hopi with Egyptian cotton *(G. barbadense)* ; also there was much less sterility in the F_2 of *hirsutum* x *hopi* than in the F_2 of *barbadense* x *hopi*.

The aboriginal cotton grown by the Papago was undoubtedly the same as that of the Pima, and the indication is that the species was a variety of *G. hopi*. Although the Arizona wild cotton plant, *Thurberia thespesioides,* is found frequently in the southwestern mountain ranges in Arizona,[85] there is little or no evidence that it was ever used by the Pimans as a source of fiber. A single Papago informant, Bernabé López, volunteered the information that it was utilized.

With work done between 1908-16 at the Coöperative Testing Station at Sacaton, the growing of Egyptian cotton in the Salt River Valley became recognized as a practicable industry. In 1912 it was shown that the Yuma variety of Egyptian cotton was suitable for this purpose, and in 1910 the Pima variety had its origin as the selection of a single plant out of a field of Yuma cotton being grown at the station. The Pima variety was not grown commercially until 1916, after the station had demonstrated it was decidedly superior in many respects to the Yuma variety, which it soon completely supplanted. The scarcity of water at a time when the cotton crop is in greatest need of irrigation has prohibited any substantial increase in cotton acreage since 1923, when the Pima crop covered 1,920 acres. The acreage is now confined largely to land regularly supplied with water from pumps in addition to the river flow. It has been ascertained that early plantings of Pima cotton are likely to be much more productive than those made after May 1, in fact the early work of the Field Station indicated that the best time

[85] Bailey, *The Wild Cotton Plant in Arizona;* Hanson, *Distribution of Arizona Wild Cotton.*

for planting cotton in the Salt River Valley in a normal season is during the first two weeks of March.[86] Browne,[87] writing in 1874, noted the Pima planted cotton when mesquite began to leaf out (late March to mid-April), and this corresponds rather well with that of the Maricopa who planted cotton in late March.[88]

GOURDS

Kino's only reference to gourds is in a letter to him from Captain Pedro de Peralta, who reported that *tecomates* (gourd vessels) and other spoils which the Apache had stolen in Saracachi had been recovered.[89] Velarde[90] makes two references in this connection. Writing of the paucity of furniture in the habitations of Pimería, he states there were some calabashes *(calabazas)* in which to carry and hold water; also that the Pimans buried the males with their quiver and arrows, some food and a little calabash *(calabazo)* of water. These were doubtless true gourds *(Lagenaria siceraria)*. Mange[91] records that in several places in Pimería the Indians gave his party food in large chocolate cups *(jícaras)*, which were possibly gourd vessels.[92] The use of gourds by the Pima was mentioned by Whittemore in 1893, and Russell,[93] who worked among the Pima forty years ago, noted that cultivated gourds had been known to the Pima for a long time. Thus, the historical evidence indicates the Pimans had and used gourds at the close of the seventeenth century, but there is no

[86] King and Leding, *Agricultural Investigations*, p. 5; King, Beckett and Parker, *Agricultural Investigations*, p. 24; King, *Crop Tests at the Cooperative Testing Station*, p. 10.

[87] Browne, *Adventures in the Apache Country*, p. 109.

[88] Spier, *Yuman Tribes*, p. 49.

[89] Bolton, *Kino*, I, 270.

[90] Wyllys, *op. cit.*, pp. 133, 136.

[91] Mange, *op. cit.*, pp. 249, 265.

[92] The academic translation of the term *jícara* is gourd. However, Dr. Lawrence B. Kiddle, Department of Spanish, Tulane University, has made a detailed study of the meaning of the word *jícara* in various parts of the New World, and he informs us that, as used in Mange's treatise, the term in all probability should be translated basket.

[93] Whittemore, in *Among the Pimas*, p. 54; Russell, *op. cit.*, p. 91.

specific reference to their cultivation. Although there are no archaeological specimens of gourds known from the Piman or Hohokam cultures, both fruits and seeds of *Lagenaria* have been recovered from the Canyon Creek Ruin[94] and from Tonto Cave which are on the edge of the Piman territory (see Chapter III).

TOBACCO

In point of time, the first tobacco smoked by the Papago and Pima was *Nicotiana trigonophylla* Dunal, known as "Coyote's tobacco." This wild species is found from the western borders of Texas to southeastern California and southward, growing in many places throughout Arizona, and in considerable abundance in northern Mexico. It is a common weed in southern Arizona desert foothills and mountains, on plains at altitudes of four to five thousand feet, on alluvial river valley soils, and is found in a number of places on the Sells Reservation. The species also occurs, although not in abundance, in central and northern Arizona at altitudes of four to five thousand feet. This is referred to by the Papago as the tobacco which Elder Brother gave them and therefore as ancient, and it is still used by them to some extent. Those Papago who could do so made expeditions to some of the mountains in southern Arizona to secure it for their own use and for trade, particularly to the Pima who used it to a lesser extent, since, in more recent times at least, they have depended largely upon cultivated tobacco. That it was not extensively used by the Pima is indicated by the fact that some of our informants had never heard of it. It was never cultivated or even semi-cultivated, and among the Papago at least the indication is that it was smoked before they grew tobacco. Both tribes regarded it as inferior in strength and quality to common tobacco *(N. Tabacum)*.

Setchell[95] refers to *N. trigonophylla* as occurring in the

[94] Haury, *The Canyon Creek Ruin*, pls. XLVII, XLVIII.
[95] Setchell, *Aboriginal Tobaccos*, p. 413 .

lower portion of the area occupied by *N. attenuata* Torr., where the latter species is the one usually employed for smoking. He also identified as *N. trigonophylla* a specimen collected by Dr. Edward Palmer, and now in the U. S. National Museum (no. 13478). Maxon[96] informs us that the notation on this specimen simply states it was collected in Arizona in 1885, gives no locality, and bears the statement "Used for tobacco by the Yuma Indians." Spier[97] writes of the Havasupai using two kinds of tobacco, both growing wild in the neighborhood and at least one of which was cultivated. The species known to these Indians as "Coyote's tobacco" was *N. trigonophylla,* but the other more commonly used one has not been identified. The Hopi smoked and semi-cultivated both *N. trigonophylla* and *N. attenuata.*[98]

The Pima and Papago smoked to some extent, but never cultivated, *N. attenuata,* which has a wide distribution in western North America and occurs on prairies and plains in central and northern Arizona at altitudes of five thousand to seventy-five hundred feet. We have seen vast areas spotted with sections practically covered with this plant. More recently, the Pima use of it has been confined to the boys when they wanted to "sneak" a smoke. A Pima informant referred to it as the "uncle" of cultivated tobacco. Russell[99] wrote of the Pima calling this species "under-the-creosote-bush tobacco," a statement which we have been unable to confirm; in fact, our Pima informants had never before heard this name. The "under-the-creosote-bush tobacco" of the Papago was *N. Tabacum.* The Maricopa[100] commonly used a wild tobacco known as "mesquite tobacco," so called because

[96] Wm. R. Maxon, Curator, Division of Plants, U. S. National Museum, Personal correspondence, Jan. 25, 1940.

[97] Spier, *Havasupai Ethnography,* pp. 105, 119.

[98] Whiting, *Ethnobotany of the Hopi,* pp. 16, 17, 40, 90; Hough, *The Hopi in Relation to Their Plant Environment,* p. 38.

[99] Russell, *op. cit.,* p. 119n.

[100] Spier, *Yuman Tribes,* p. 333.

it grew beneath mesquite trees. This name was wholly unfamiliar to our Piman informants.

A third native species, *N. Bigelovii*, designated "Coyote tobacco," was reported by Russell as having been used by the Pima for smoking. In spite of considerable effort we have been unable to confirm the use of this species by the Pima, or even to ascertain that it grows in Arizona. Thornber[101] writes that he has heard it occurs in the state, but the herbarium of the University of Arizona contains no specimens of this species from Arizona. It was smoked to some extent by the Arizona Indians, but where they secured it has not been ascertained although its distribution would indicate they may have obtained it from the Indians of southern California, just as the Maricopa[102] got tobacco by trade from the Akwa'ala in Lower California.

Both Papago and Pima are known to have cultivated the common tobacco, *N. Tabacum* L., for a number of years, although it has been impossible to ascertain when or where they first obtained it. Emory,[103] who visited the Pima in 1846, and Bartlett, there in 1852, both mentioned Pima crops but neither made any reference to the cultivation of tobacco. However, Browne[104] wrote in 1874 of its being raised by the Pimas, who planted it when the mesquite trees began to leaf out. Also the Papago at San Xavier, as well as the Pima at Sacaton, are known to have been growing *N. Tabacum* in 1903;[105] and Lumholtz,[106] writing in 1912, referred to the Papago cultivating tobacco. Gray[107] says the "Yaqui tobacco" found cultivated in Arizona by Dr. Edward Palmer, and specimens of which were grown in the Botanic Garden of

101 J. J. Thornber, Personal correspondence, Feb. 13, 1940.
102 Spier, *loc. cit.*
103 Emory, *Notes;* Bartlett, *Narrative.*
104 Browne, *Adventures in the Apache Country,* p. 109.
105 Thornber, *loc. cit.;* Lloyd, *Aw-aw-tam Indian Nights,* p. 58.
106 Lumholtz, *New Trails,* p. 52.
107 Gray, *Synoptical Flora of North America,* II, pt. 1, 241; C. A. Weatherby, Senior Curator, Gray Herbarium, Harvard University, Personal correspondence, Feb. 28, 1940.

Harvard University in 1871 from seed furnished by Palmer, probably belongs to *N. Tabacum* var. *undulata* Sendtner. Informants said the Papago had always raised tobacco, also that corn and tobacco are of equal age on the earth. However, one Papago informant, seventy-seven years of age, said that when he was a little boy his grandfather used to smoke "Coyote's tobacco" *(N. trigonophylla)*, but also had the common "Mexican tobacco" which they got from Mexico by trade for deer skins. It seems quite certain that *N. Tabacum,* north of Mexico at least, was unknown in aboriginal use.[108]

N. Tabacum, referred to by the Papago as "under-the-creosote-bush tobacco," is also spoken of as "real tobacco." It is reported as the only species cultivated, and informants said that in early days almost every family had a tobacco patch. A specimen was obtained from Bernabé López at San Pedro village under the name of "under-the-creosote-bush tobacco" and was identified by Goodspeed[109] as a pink-flowered variety of *N. Tabacum.*

Two seed samples secured from different informants were identified by Goodspeed as *N. rustica.* Informant Vanico had grown this species for many years and Manuel Lowe had grown it years ago; the latter said it was known as "Coyote's tobacco." Spier[110] reports that the Maricopa secured "real tobacco" from the Pima who cultivated it.

Leaves of the wild species of *Nicotiana,* whenever used by either tribe, were gathered, dried and stored, but generally not mixed with the cultivated tobacco. They preferred to smoke the cultivated tobacco, but when it was not available would smoke the wild species. However, when the supply of common tobacco was nearly exhausted it might be mixed with the wild species. For the most part the Pima, and to a

[108] Setchell, *op. cit.,* p. 401; T. H. Goodspeed, Professor of Botany, University of California, Personal correspondence, Jan. 30, 1940.

[109] Goodspeed, *loc. cit.*

[110] Spier, *loc. cit.*

lesser extent the Papago, now secure their tobacco from the whites and rarely grow it.

The Papago and Pima seldom smoked by itself any wild plant other than *Nicotiana,* nor did they usually mix any wild plant with tobacco to dilute it or to economize, for they liked it strong. However, a lichen known as "earth flowers," which grows on mountains in southern Arizona, was occasionally dried and a small amount mixed with the tobacco. We were unable to secure a specimen of this plant; the one secured by Underhill several years ago and seen by the authors was not in condition to make determination possible. It now seems certain from our investigations with both Papago and Pima informants that this is not the *pihol* flowers referred to by Densmore.[111] One professed to be acquainted with *piholt,* described as a desert plant which when in bloom smelled something like "earth flowers." The lichen used was described by our informants as having a strong sweet smell, being somewhat narcotic and of such magical properties that smoking a little of it mixed with tobacco would attract game while hunting. One informant said sometimes dried tepary leaves were mixed with tobacco, the smoker expressing a wish for a large crop of teparies next season.

It has been impossible for us to determine the antiquity of tobacco smoking or cultivation among the Pima-Papago. The early documentary material is strangely silent as regards both its cultivation and smoking, although it makes frequent mention that these Indians were extremely glad to receive gifts of tobacco.[112] Moreover, archaeology throws no light on the problem among the Hohokam and Piman cultures. Pertinent to the situation along the middle Gila, however, are specimens from Casa Grande National Monument. In 1935 reed pipes from this site were sent for examination to the Ethnobiological Laboratory of the University of Michi-

111 Densmore, *Papago Music,* pp. 210-11.
112 Coues, *On the Trail,* I, 106, 109; Bolton, *Anza,* III, 18, 332; IV, 44.

gan by Charles R. Steen, Ranger. Jones[113] reported that these pipes (as well as others taken from a ceremonial cave on Camelback Mountain near Phoenix) were made of reed grass *(Phragmites communis).* The pipes from Casa Grande were wrapped with cotton cloth, and both lots were stuffed with leaves of creosote bush as well as broken tobacco leaves. Jones is of the opinion that these are probably leaves of *N. attenuata.* In this same connection it is interesting to note that Fewkes[114] found large numbers of "cane cigarettes" in various rooms at the Casa Grande ruin as well as in caves near Superstition Mountain to the north of the ruin. Of special interest is the fact that he found a small dish of *N. attenuata* in one of the ruins at Casa Grande.

It is our firm belief that neither Papago nor Pima cultivated any kind of tobacco aboriginally, a situation in agreement with that for the Maricopa[115] who were adjacent to the Pima on the Gila, but that they did smoke the wild *N. trigonophylla* and *N. attenuata.*

MARTYNIA

Pima and Papago anciently utilized the pods of devil's claw or unicorn plant *(Martynia louisiana)* in basketry. Although informants asserted that the Pimans cultivated this plant a very long time ago it is impossible to establish this definitely. It is possible that aboriginally they utilized only wild plants of *Martynia,* and that its cultivation came with the commercial stimulus to increased production of baskets.

There were two kinds of devil's claw—a black-seeded variety which grew wild, and a cultivated form with longer pods and white seeds, the longer strips of epidermal tissue being more suitable for making baskets. The white-seeded variety never grew wild but often appeared as a volunteer in cultivated fields.

113 Jones, *Ceremonial Cigarettes.*
114 Fewkes, *Casa Grande,* pp. 142-43.
115 Spier, *loc. cit.*

WHEAT AND BARLEY

There is indication that wheat, which in some places had kept ahead of the frontier of Spanish settlement, had been received from the south by the Pimans of the Gila Basin before Kino's arrival in Pimería Alta in 1687.[116] Of all the Old World crops introduced among the Pimans, wheat has been of most importance in their economy. This is especially so because it came as an off-season crop, ripening in May when the fall harvest of maize, teparies and pumpkins was exhausted, and before the giant cactus harvest.

Kino himself distributed considerable wheat seed among the Pimans, and it is clear that the Pima quickly began to cultivate it in such quantity that it soon replaced maize as their leading crop. Anza,[117] writing of a Pima village on the Gila in 1774, said their fields of wheat were so large that "standing in the middle of them, one cannot see the ends, because they are so long. Their width is also great, embracing the whole width of the valley on either side . . ." Although this picture is unquestionably exaggerated, that they did grow large amounts of wheat is substantiated by Garcés. In 1858, the first year of the Overland Mail Route, a 100,000-pound surplus crop of Pima wheat was purchased by the Overland Company; in 1859, the Pima sold 250,000 pounds; in 1860, 400,000; in 1861, 300,000 pounds and in 1862 about 1,000,000 pounds to the Federal Government for use of troops operating in their territory.[118] The great quantities of wheat obtainable in the Pima country are repeatedly mentioned by the California-bound forty-niners and this was one reason for using Maricopa Wells, etc., as the jumping-off point to the Colorado. Russell[119] observed forty years ago that wheat was the principal Pima crop, in wet seasons the harvest amounting to several million pounds. In 1919 more than

[116] Bolton: *op. cit.*, I, 263; *Rim of Christendom*, p. 248.
[117] Bolton, *Anza*, I, 184; II, 240, 304; Coues, *op. cit.*, p. 107.
[118] Browne, *Adventures in the Apache Country*, p. 110.
[119] Russell, *Pima*, pp. 76, 90.

twenty-five carloads of wheat were sold by the Pima, in addition to the quantity they consumed.[120] The Papago, however, did not bring wheat into general use until they came in contact with it in Mexico several generations ago while working there seasonally for hire. One reason for this may be that, until government wells were dug, these Indians were not able to live in the flats in cool weather, when wheat should be planted. Lumholtz,[121] writing in 1912, said it was then the most important Papago crop. On the basis of acreage, wheat continued to hold the leading place among Pima and Papago crops until at least 1924. Today it ranks second among both peoples. The growing of wheat has been established for so long a time that most of our Pima and Papago informants regarded it as an aboriginal crop, and said reference to wheat appears in their creation legends.

Definite data on types of wheat grown in our area are given by Hendry,[122] who studied the vegetal content of adobe bricks from buildings erected during the mission period. He found seeds of Propo wheat (*Triticum vulgare graecum* Kcke.) and of Little Club wheat (*T. compactum Humboldtii* Kcke.) in adobe bricks at San Cayetano del Tumacácori, in southern Arizona, founded in 1701, and at San Valentín, in northwest Sonora, founded in 1706; also California Club wheat (*T. compactum erinaceum* Kcke.) at San Valentín, in southern Arizona, founded in 1706. Hendry states that Propo wheat was found at twelve of the fourteen structures examined in southern Arizona, Sonora, Lower California and California and that it seems to have been the most extensively grown variety throughout the region during the Spanish and Mexican periods. The specimens found are uniform in type and appear to be identical with the variety as known in California today. The California Club wheat found does not correspond exactly with any of the present day club varieties

120 King and Leding, *Agricultural Investigations*, pp. 5, 29.
121 Lumholtz, *New Trails*, p. 25.
122 Hendry, *The Adobe Brick as a Historical Source*.

and is thought to be the bearded, red-chaffed, club wheat reported by Davis[123] as having been grown in California at the time of the American occupation, and then known as California Club.

Russell,[124] who worked among the Pima in 1901-02, states they were then growing four varieties of wheat, Sonora and Australian being favorites. Twenty years ago the leading varieties were Early Baart, Sonora and Little Club,[125] and at present Early Baart, Sonora and Club comprise the bulk of wheat grown by the Pima. Sonora wheat is very drought resistant, although it makes an inferior bread flour because of the low percentage and poor quality of albumen. It is a beardless winter variety with round, very soft, white grains used largely in making such foods as tortillas. Club wheat resembles Sonora in that it is beardless and has soft white grains.

A few fields of black-bearded, hard wheat with amber-colored grain *(T. durum)*, and Polish wheat *(T. polonicum)*, a form with long, large spikes and kernels, locally erroneously called macaroni wheat, are to be seen at present among the Pima; the growing of these species seems to date back about thirty years. Arizona Baart, a soft, white-grained, bearded variety, covers by far the largest Pima wheat acreage, since this is the principal variety grown by the white settlers and seed is therefore readily available. As grown in the Gila and Salt river valleys, it is superior to other varieties in the same class in yield and bread making. The Sonora variety is still grown on a small acreage by the Pima; its yield is about equal to Early Baart but it is poorer in quality.

Although Sonora wheat continues to hold first place among the Papago, some individuals grow Early Baart. In exhibits at the Papago Fair, held every fall at Sells, Arizona, there is pure Sonora wheat, Early Baart, and many mixtures.

123 Davis, *California Breadstuffs*, p. 518.
124 Russell, *loc. cit.*
125 King and Leding, *op. cit.*, p. 25.

A few Indians have exhibited hard wheat *(Triticum durum)*. Neither Papago nor Pima have grown, nor grow at present, any spring wheat to speak of, although the Papago particularly are often forced to plant late in winter because of delayed winter rains, and by no means harvest a crop every year. However, yields as high as twenty-five bushels per acre have been harvested at times, and a good crop may supply sufficient wheat to last for several years. Thus Chico Bailey, a Papago informant, asserted that the best yield he ever had was one hundred sacks of wheat and twenty of barley. This fed his family for three years. Farm advisors discourage Pima plantings after mid-January. The importance of wheat in Piman economy is attributable to the fact that, in addition to being an off-season crop, it usually can be grown successfully with the moisture from the winter rains, perhaps supplemented among the Pima by one or two irrigations from river water during winter or spring freshets. Being a winter crop, wheat can often be grown successfully in the Gila Valley on soils of higher salinity than most summer crops would tolerate.

Barley, too, was cultivated by the Pimans soon after Kino's entrance into the area. In 1870 the Pima and Maricopa[126] on the Gila had issued to them ten thousand pounds of barley seed by the Federal Government. The Papago at San Xavier were reported in 1898 as very successfully growing barley for hay; in fact it was more lucrative than any other crop. Wheat and barley were the leading crops at San Xavier between 1904 and 1908. The same report for 1899-1900[127] states that barley cut for hay at this same place yielded two and one-half tons per acre, and was a more profitable crop than wheat.

Hendry[128] found in adobe bricks from the mission of San Cayetano del Tumacácori seeds of Coast barley *(Hor-*

[126] *Report of the Commissioner of Indian Affairs* for 1871, p. 359.

[127] *Ibid.* for 1898, p. 128; *ibid.* for 1899, p. 165; *ibid.* for 1904, p. 148; Curtis, *The North American Indian*, II, 31.

[128] Hendry, *op. cit.*, p. 113.

deum vulgare pallidum typica Ser.) . This is identical in type with the now widely grown variety of that name. The fact that it was found in twelve of the fourteen structures studied in Sonora, Lower California, California and southern Arizona, indicates a widespread culture in the region.

At present the Pima-Papago grow two varieties of barley, Common and Vaughn. The latter, a smooth-awned sort, is characterized by its consistently high yield and stiff straw. At the irrigated area of San Xavier the leading Papago crop is barley, harvested mostly for hay. Among the Pima and Papago barley is usually planted from November to January, although sometimes as late as February, and is grown almost entirely for pasturing cattle; this begins about six weeks after the crop is planted. Early sown barley, as well as wheat, sometimes has been reported as damaged by late frosts at San Xavier and on the Gila.

WATERMELONS AND MUSKMELONS

Of the Old World crops introduced among the Pimans, watermelons originally ranked very high in importance. That their cultivation in places preceded Kino's arrival is clearly shown by the fact that in the fall of 1698 he encountered a group of Papagos at the village of San Angelo del Bótum (present day Cocklebur) who were growing watermelons, "although never in that village or in the others of this vicinity and coast had there entered another white face or Spaniard."[129] The culture of watermelons long since has become so thoroughly established among the Pimans that all our informants regarded them as aboriginal.

The significance of watermelons in Piman economy may be attributed to two things: their extreme fondness for them, and the fact that they may be stored until well into winter. Russell,[130] in 1902, observed that watermelons were among the most important crops of the Pima, who ate them at least

129 Bolton, *Rim of Christendom,* pp. 397, 400-01.
130 Russell, *op. cit.,* p. 75.

six months of the year. Today their cultivation is general throughout our area, and even the Papago are able to grow them under flood-water farming on the desert since they have varieties which are rather drought resistant. Informants said they could not have gotten along without the watermelon.

The earliest watermelons of which the Pimans had knowledge were of two kinds, one with pinkish, the other with black, seeds. One was spherical, about eight inches in diameter, of light greenish-gray color with broad stripes of darker green. The flesh was pink. The second was an oblong melon with white skin and pink flesh. Informants also spoke of an ancient yellow-fleshed variety. The common sort today is the spherical striped one, although occasionally modern varieties are seen. The Pima are still heavy growers and consumers of watermelons, damage from aphids being the limiting factor in their production. Varieties which do well at the Coöperative Field Station are Klondike, Striped Klondike, Angeleno, Klekley Sweet, Chilian, Irish Gray, Tom Watson, Stone Mountain and Georgia Rattlesnake.[131]

Indications are that the Pimans received muskmelons at essentially the same time they did the watermelon. Mange,[132] in company with Kino, wrote in 1697 that the Indians at San Agustín de Oiaur harvested muskmelons and watermelons (*melones y sandias*); Anza[133] also reported them. However, the Pimans have never been fond of muskmelons, and this, coupled with unfavorable keeping qualities, is responsible for their lack of popularity. Some informants regarded the muskmelon as pre-Spanish, others held the opposite view. Russell[134] observed in 1902 that the Pima extensively raised muskmelons, but they are little grown by either the Pima or Papago today.

The oldest muskmelons were said to be of two sorts: an

131 King, Beckett and Parker, *Agricultural Investigations,* p. 56.
132 Mange, *Luz,* p. 256.
133 Bolton, *Anza,* II, 18, 147.
134 Russell, *op. cit.,* p. 77.

oblong fruit about twelve by eight inches, smooth skinned and not grooved. The surface was finely mottled light green, with greenish-white flesh. The other was ovoid, about twelve by six inches, smooth skinned but grooved lengthwise. The surface was a lemon yellow color, flesh rather cream colored, but not so good in flavor as the first. Both kinds were seen in Papago villages. At one village we found a third type of muskmelon unlike any we had ever seen. It was three and one-half inches long, two and three-fourths inches thick, burnt orange in color, with yellow stripes, and of excellent odor and flavor.

COWPEAS, CHICK PEAS, LENTILS AND GARDEN PEAS

Although the Papago and Pima have grown the black-eyed bean or cowpea *(Vigna sinensis)*, the chick pea or garbanzo *(Cicer arietinum)* and the lentil *(Lens esculenta)* for a long time, and many consider them as aboriginal, they are Old World crops brought in by the Spaniards by way of Mexico. All three are still in cultivation among a number of Pima and Papago families. Both the small and large forms of the cowpea were and still are grown, although both tribes obtained the small variety first. Solid black seeds of this small form without any spot sometimes occurred, but these merely appeared among the black-eyed ones and rarely were grown as a separate variety; in fact, they were usually discarded entirely even in cooking. One Papago informant said they formerly grew a cream-colored cowpea with a brownish eye. We found in cultivation among the Papago a reddish-brown cowpea with a large white spot located at one end of the seed and not around the hilum as is the case of the ordinary black-eyed pea. This is a hybrid form which breeds quite true to type. Both Pima and Papago grow the garden pea *(Pisum sativum)* on a small scale at present.

The Windsor bean *(Vicia faba)*, also known as broad, horse or Scotch bean, was not grown by either people and none of our informants had ever seen it.

CHILI

Chili *(Capsicum annuum)* was introduced among the Pimans by Kino[135] toward the close of the seventeenth century, but its cultivation was not taken over extensively. Only a few Pima grow it at present and it is cultivated by the Papago only in very favorable places. The chief variety grown is Anaheim.

Aboriginally, and even to the present, the Papago and Pima have used fairly extensively for seasoning the native, spherical, small-fruited, but very pungent, Bird Cayenne or Spur pepper *(Capsicum frutescens* var. *baccatum),* commonly known in the Southwest and in Mexico as *chiltepiquin,*[136] which grows wild in moist places in the Baboquivari Mountains and southward in Sonora. It did not occur in Pima territory but was secured by trade with the Papago. It was never cultivated by either people. Papago made expeditions to secure *chiltepiquin;* they pulled up the entire plant which they brought home for drying, then picked the fruit and stored it in a sealed olla. They always arranged to have some on hand. Its early use in Sonora was described by Pfefferkorn.[137]

[135] Bolton, *Kino,* I, 122-23, 204, 248-49, 253, 321; II, 80, 100, 138, 165, 265.
[136] Also spelled *chiltipiquin, chilepiquin, chiltepin* and *tschiltipin.*
[137] Pfefferkorn, *Beschreibung der Landschaft Sonora,* I, 62-3.

CHAPTER V

SELECTION, DEVELOPMENT AND OWNERSHIP OF LAND

SELECTION AND LOCATION OF CULTIVATED LAND

Selection of land by the Gila Pima did not present a difficult task, for the bottomlands of this river rather generally consisted of fertile soil, the main problem being to choose land which could be irrigated easily from the canals yet was not too low to drain readily. The soil at Sacaton is of uniform texture to a considerable depth, a sandy loam composed largely of fine sands and silt from the weathering of adjacent mountains. When first cleared of native vegetation it is deficient in organic material, although the large quantity of silt increases the water-holding capacity, and it responds very readily to methods of improvement. This soil is representative of considerable areas extending in narrow strips along the Gila, which are well adapted for farming when not impregnated with soluble salts.[1]

Comparatively little choice was exercised by the Pima in selecting soil either in general or for particular crops, although sandy soil was preferred for watermelons. Good land was indicated by its black color and a vigorous growth of wild plants, and these Indians, of course, knew that such soil was richer and had greater water-holding power than soils of lighter color, and that corn, for example, would have smaller ears on light, sandy soil. Practically the only additional caution to be observed in soil selection was the avoidance of land high in salinity. The Papago were little troubled with this, but the bottomlands of the Gila (and Salt) were in places heavily impregnated, a common characteristic of irrigated soils. This was observed on the Gila even in Mange's

[1] King, *Crop Tests at the Cooperative Testing Station*, pp. 7, 9.

day, for he wrote that, continuing from Casa Grande toward the west, it appeared as though the land had been strewn with salt.[2] In 1871 Grossmann[3] noted that some of the soil on the reservation was strongly impregnated with salts. However, the Pima have long coped with the problem of salinity by repeated flooding of such land with muddy water to wash out this mineral content, and, more recently, by working manure into the soil (taught by the whites). The fact that the Pima have irrigated the bottomlands of the Gila for centuries, without finding it necessary to abandon any large sections of land due to accumulation of salts, bespeaks their ancient knowledge of how to manage the fields from this standpoint. Informants recognized saline soil by: (1) The appearance of a white incrustation on the surface; (2) tasting the soil; (3) a growth of saltbush *(Atriplex);* (4) the sticky nature of such soil when wet, and (5) that such soil creaked when one walked on it. They also knew that deposits of salts are more abundant on high spots than in lower portions of a field; that their native crops and wheat would not do well but that muskmelons would do better on saline soil than many other crops. Seeds of various crops would germinate in such soil and grow for a time, but would either die before reaching maturity or not yield a harvest. As wheat is a winter crop in the Pima area, consequently requiring less irrigation, it often can be grown successfully on soils of higher salinity than most summer crops would tolerate.

Tests at the Coöperative Field Station[4] recently have shown that the alluvial soil in the vicinity of Sacaton is adapted to many kinds of truck crops, provided the concentration of salts is not too great. Also, that by turning under heavy applications of farmyard manure and cover crops, followed by growing alfalfa on the land for two or three years, it is possible to reduce the salinity to a large extent. The

2 Mange, *Luz,* p. 253.
3 Grossmann, *The Pima Indians of Arizona,* p. 418.
4 King and Loomis, *Agricultural Investigations,* p. 59.

organic matter and deeply growing roots of alfalfa result in looser structure and texture of the soil, making it more permeable to water and thus permitting leaching of the salts to lower levels.

The Gila Valley contains large areas covered with white incrustations of salts deposited by the evaporation of water reaching the surface from beneath. A comparison of the total salt content of surface flow with that of the underflow indicates the former contains salts varying from 39.4 to 120.2 parts per 100,000 of water, with an average of 96.3; the salt content of the underflow varies from 68 to 160 parts in 100,000 with an average of 126.6. Nevertheless the underground water at Sacaton is regarded as better for irrigation than the average surface water of the river. Examples of successful irrigation by waters more saline than the Gila underflow are numerous.[5]

A Papago village was invariably a settlement of kin, and others entered it only by invitation or marriage. The three Papago reservations comprise eleven village units, the location of which has changed very little since Kino first visited them.[6] The determinant reason is ecological, for they were located in spots which were then, as now, the most suitable for cultivation. Usually the main villages are situated in the north-to-south valleys, their daughter villages extending along the valley in both directions, and their Wells, or winter villages, located in the foothills on either side of the valley.

Soil in the Papago country is principally adobe, ranging from hard compact stretches, resulting from the first decomposition of lava near the mountains, to finer deposits mixed with decomposed vegetable matter on the floor of the broad valleys. With few exceptions, such as near meridian 112 at the Mexican line, where there is light, loose sand, the soil of the valley bottoms is fairly rich.[7]

5 Lee, *Underground Waters of Gila Valley*, pp. 61-2.
6 Underhill, *Papago*, p. 58.
7 Clotts, *Nomadic Papago Surveys*, p. 3.

Papago farming plots were almost without exception located at the mouths of washes,[8] where they could be watered by flood water of the summer rains, and groups of relatives camped for generations at the same washes. In the Papago country every suitable plot of ground of this kind was utilized, and in many cases the plantings were necessarily very small. These pieces of alluvial land had few or no stones, and any found there were carried away in baskets to the edge of the field. They were not very particular as to type of soil, unless it contained considerable salts, for the deciding factor was the ease with which the land might be flooded during rains. Nevertheless these Indians knew that a good growth of weeds or the presence of large mesquite or paloverde trees indicated a good soil.

CLEARING THE LAND AND LAND OWNERSHIP

Since Papago land was selected primarily on the basis of its being subject to inundation by flood water, and tended to have a sparse cover of grass, it did not have heavy stands of trees or shrubs. With primitive implements it was extremely difficult for either Pima or Papago to clear land of heavy growths of vegetation. Brush was first trampled, then allowed to dry, and burned, after which the roots were grubbed out with the planting stick and weeding hoe. Burning of any vegetative matter was thought to improve the fertility of the soil. Trees were known to interfere with the growth of cultivated plants because of their shade and extensive root systems, and were killed by burning brush in a shallow trench dug around the butt, never girdled mechanically. Dead trees might be allowed to stand in the cultivated fields, but usually were completely destroyed by continued burning.

Clearing new ground or old plots of weeds and debris in preparation for planting was men's work, in which women of

8 As used here a wash means a broad alluvial area over which the water, flowing down from the mountains in periods of rain, loses its momentum and spreads out.

neither tribe participated. There were no community fields, but families worked reciprocally. Among the Papago, these family enterprises were under the leadership of a patriarchal chief chosen by the people for life, there being but one chief to each village. The Pima agricultural unit also was the village, and, as Hill[9] points out, the necessity of communal endeavor in irrigation and for protection against alien tribes tended to solidify these village units. They were under the control of a village headman whose office was inherited and who was responsible only to the chief of the tribe and to public opinion.

Pima habitations were not then scattered as now. Families lived close together on high ground for protection, particularly after Apache raids became serious, and daily went out to work their plots as much as six to eight miles distant. During planting and hoeing periods they returned each night to their homes, but at harvest time camped at the fields.

Bringing a new tract of Pima land under cultivation and irrigation required coöperation of the men in the one or more districts which were to be benefitted, so as to arrange, dispose and dig the ditches. Under leadership of the headmen of the villages affected, meetings were held to plan the work. Hill[10] has pointed out that Pima land assignments under native custom were accomplished in two ways. When a large tract was to be developed it involved the coöperative efforts of individuals from one to three villages. Qualified men first selected the land and located the course of the canal. Then the community, under the direction of the headmen, constructed the canal from the river to the selected area. This completed, the men who had participated chose or were assigned plots of land under the supervision of the headmen assisted by an advisory body, but not all participants shared equally. The second type of assignment concerned a single individual. A man applied to the village headman, and a

9 Hill, *Notes on Pima Land Law and Tenure.*
10 *Ibid.*

plot was designated for him. In both cases assigned land became inalienable property of the assignee and his heirs. Use of the land was under the direction of the patriarchal head of the family, whose influence was partly inherited and partly due to experience and personal magnetism, and whose only coercive force was public opinion.

Our information indicates that, despite the above, any individual who wanted to and could develop a piece of idle, unclaimed land could do so without specific allotment. The situation seems to be that aboriginally land was secured by inheritance or selected individually, and only more recently has allotment been practiced. Spier[11] is probably right in suspecting that distribution by allotment, similar to the Maricopa practice, dates from the time the Pima were located on the reservations.

Pima and Papago lands were considered as belonging to the tribe, although held individually. A person had the right to loan land in case he was not using it himself, but sale and, among the Papago, trade of land was unknown. In case of a loan no charge was made, and quarrels over the ownership or right to use a piece of land were settled by two men who knew the land and parties involved. Hill[12] has discussed the Pima procedure regarding the rental of lands. Neither Pima nor Papago ever resorted to pushing contests, tugs of war or stick fights to settle disputed boundaries, as did the Mohave. Difficulties over the limits of a Papago's land resulting from the washing away of the stones or stakes which marked the corners of his field were always adjudicated amicably by conference.

Personal ownership of land has been somewhat modified since post-Spanish concepts have disturbed the original situation. Anciently, however, title to the land was vested in men, and land was inherited essentially in the male line, although all members of the family had a right to its use and products.

11 Spier, *Yuman Tribes*, p. 59n.
12 Hill, *op. cit.*

If a Pima died, his land was theoretically inherited by his immediate family—the widow, sons and daughters; practically, it remained intact so long as the widow lived, the rest of the family caring for it with the eldest son in charge. At her death the land was divided among the sons (although an unmarried daughter could claim her share), since it was expected the husbands of married daughters would inherit or develop land of their own. However, if a daughter and her husband were not doing well a piece of land might be given them. Sons were regarded as being under the jurisdiction of the father until his death. Upon the death of both parents, leaving a single young son, a relative took over the care of both boy and land until he was old enough to assume the responsibility himself. Women might own land, but this ordinarily applied only to widows who had no male members in their immediate families to cultivate it, and in such case it was planted for them by the nearest relatives. This was noted by Grossmann[13] in 1873. If a man and his wife should leave no children, their land was divided among the nearest relatives of both.

A newcomer among the Pima found it difficult to secure land, his best opportunity being to farm a piece not being used at the time by the owner. Regardless of how long he used it, however, the original owner could claim it at any time as it was still his property. If a man left the district temporarily, a relative, never a newcomer, would assume its care during his absence; if he left permanently, a relative took over the land.

Underhill[14] has shown that the center of the Papago economic system was the patriarchal family, rather than the individual, and must be regarded as the unit of property holding and of the extensive system of exchange of goods by gift, the Papago equivalent for trade. Of property there was indeed little; apart from land and dwelling the food pro-

13 Grossmann, *op. cit.*, p. 415.
14 Underhill, *op. cit.*, pp. 43-4, 90, 94-7.

duced on the land constituted almost the entire family capital. An indication of spheres of authority is seen in that the husband disposed of gifts of meat and cultivated crops; the wife, of cooked food and wild crops. The chief interest of a family was in its land. An agricultural settlement, known as the Fields, had usually been discovered and settled by a family group, and was situated on a flat plain where a wash coming down from the mountain side spread its water over the level land for as much as a square mile or more. Here the group of relatives distributed the land among themselves under the direction of some man chosen as the leader, the allotments, if possible, being as much as two acres. Tillable land was to be found only in small patches, but each family had such a field. Brothers worked together under their father during his lifetime, often living in the same house and bringing their wives home to share it. On the death of the father, sons built for themselves separate houses, but often continued to share the land, and if the land were divided, it was done very informally and the brothers continued to act together in many ways as an economic unit. The eldest son sometimes farmed his father's land, or he might turn it over to a brother and develop a new plot himself. In some cases several sons kept their land together, one being the hunter, the others doing the farming. Under special circumstances a woman brought her husband to live in the family group, where he was placed on a par with the sons and given a piece of land, this being assigned to him and not his wife. However, it was rare for a Papago to live outside of his own village, except by intermarriage. Sons usually helped enlarge the father's field if land were available, and remained with him. But as the population of a family group increased, plots within walking distance might no longer be available and one of the younger men would move. Because of fear of enemies and the necessity for reciprocal help in cultivation, he often sought among his relatives for others who needed land, and together they would settle in a new and, if possible, adjacent area. No permission was needed to develop and farm a new piece of land.

There was no private ownership of wild plants on either cultivated or undeveloped land. In developing a new piece of ground, mesquite or sahuaro trees, because of their fruit, were never removed, but such trees were regarded as common property and any person might pick the fruit.

DESTRUCTION OF PROPERTY AT DEATH

Unlike Mohave, the Pima, and especially Papago, could not afford to destroy all their property and goods on the occasion of death in the family; nevertheless, a considerable amount of Pima and Papago property was so destroyed. Usually the Papago house, excepting posts, was burned and most, if not all, of the individual's personal equipment buried with him. Cattle and crops, regarded as family property, were distributed among the children. Occasionally families died out, whereupon the Council, on request, reassigned their land. In the case of a number of successive deaths, the surviving members of a family group often deserted the land to prevent it, like the house, from being visited by ghosts. Since ghosts influenced only relatives, other persons might take over the land, but only by permission of the family, who always retained the right to reoccupy it if desired.[15] Our Pima informants asserted that in historic times when a man died and left a crop standing in the field, word was passed around to the neighbors to turn their horses into it. The reason was that the dead man's relatives wanted to see everything he possessed or had accomplished in his lifetime go with him. In this connection Grossmann[16] wrote, in 1871, that the Pima custom of destroying all the property of the husband at his death impoverished the widow and children.

15 Underhill, *op. cit.*, pp. 90-1.
16 Grossmann, *loc. cit.*

FENCING

Font[17] referred to the Pima fields being fenced in with poles and laid off in divisions, but this was, of course, long after the entrance of the first Europeans into the area. Similarly, in 1846 Emory[18] noted the fences were of sticks, wattled with willow and mesquite, and Bartlett,[19] a few years later, said their fields were generally fenced with crooked stakes, wattled with brush, chiefly mesquite, although he saw, at long distances from any village, large patches of wheat which were not enclosed. Aboriginally, Piman fields were never enclosed since there were no domesticated animals other than the dog. When a Papago patriarchal family developed a new agricultural settlement, each family head secured a field to care for himself and his sons, marking its corners with large stones or stakes. The first Pima fences were of interwoven willow, mesquite or other branches, supported by cottonwood, mesquite or willow poles, and these surrounded the land of a whole community rather than individual plots. Each family knew its own lands by their characteristic borders and ditches. At present, Pima, and to a less extent Papago, fields are enclosed with barbed wire. Pima fields were generally rectangular and arranged according to the supplying irrigation canal, and each family received a plot of the same width but varying in length. Formerly the land of either a Pima or a Papago was ordinarily in one continuous strip rather than in scattered patches, although this has become modified, particularly among the Pima, due to trade and sale of land among the Indians themselves. There are a few recorded instances, however, in which a Papago family anciently owned land at two different Fields. Pima plots were contiguous. there being no vacant land between farms unless a piece were too high for irrigation or unsuitable because of soluble salts. Since floods

17 Bolton, *Anza*, I, 263; IV, 43.
18 Emory, *Notes*, p. 83.
19 Bartlett, *Narrative*, II, 233.

on the Gila, with its low gradient and adjacent plains, were ordinarily mild and not devastating, there was little or no difficulty involved in the relocation of fields.

SIZE OF CULTIVATED PLOTS

It is certain that the average amount of land cultivated per person among the Pima and Papago is now considerably higher than formerly. Advent of the whites and introduction of the motive for growing a surplus for profit greatly stimulated development of additional acreages; aboriginal farming was purely for subsistence. Also, with Spanish contact the Pimans secured farm animals and this called for the cultivation of appreciably increased crops, made possible chiefly by the availability of improved Spanish implements as well as new and different crops, especially wheat and barley. Work for wages, with its concomitant extensive trade at stores by cash and barter, has so greatly distorted the original economic picture that it is now very difficult to reconstruct the ancient situation regarding land utilization; this applies particularly to the Pima. Knowledge of our informants in this respect was quite fragmentary.

Anciently, each Pima family had its own plot of ground and planted all the crops it could take care of, for then as now these Indians had a surplus of agricultural land above subsistence needs. Its size bore no close relation to size of the family but depended rather upon the amount of land immediately available, the man's industry in farming and whether or not he hunted much game. In early historic times the average cultivated acreage for the Pima family was two to five acres; for the Papago family, one-fourth to two acres (for a detailed discussion of this subject see Chapter III).

DIVISION OF LABOR

The sharp division of labor between male and female among the Papago kept the two sexes in separate groups during daylight hours. Season and age also entered into the arrangement, heavy labor invariably being done by the young, supervised by their elders. This has been discussed in some detail by Underhill.[20]

Among both Papago and Pima, farm work such as planting, cultivating and irrigating was accepted as man's work, and was exclusively his responsibility, but gathering the harvest was woman's acknowledged task and she took over completely the job of caring for the resultant crops, although she might be assisted by men, old men particularly. In 1871 Grossmann[21] wrote that Pima women did all the work in the field except plowing and sowing. In summer the older men worked skin clothing, wove, and did the farming, assisted with the planting by young men; in winter they made rope, tools and weapons, and built houses if needed. The younger men built or repaired ditches and houses, and, in winter, fought enemies or hunted, especially deer. In some cases one man of a family was the hunter, the others caring for the land, as deer hunting involved the development of a specialized technique entailing a long apprenticeship begun in boyhood. The modern counterpart of the deer hunter is the cowboy who cares for the cattle belonging to the family. During the summer an important feminine task was gathering and preparing wild foods for storage, and seasonally women would be away from home all day securing such foodstuffs. Throughout the year, older women cooked and worked basketry, plaited mats or made netting, while the young ground corn and carried wood and water. Only the old practiced the special crafts. Relation of the sexes to the several phases of agricultural work is treated separately in the appropriate section.

20 Underhill, *loc. cit.*
21 Grossmann, *loc. cit.*

CHAPTER VI

AGRICULTURAL IMPLEMENTS

Piman agricultural tools were few and simple, and fortunately it is still possible to find informants who carried on agriculture entirely with these primitive implements in their early manhood, thus it has not been difficult to secure accurate descriptions.

The most important of these aboriginal tools was the digging or planting stick. It was preferably of the heartwood of ironwood *(Olneya tesota)*, but might be of mesquite, screwbean or southwestern jujube *(Zizyphus lycioides)*, depending somewhat upon what hardwoods were readily available. The aboriginal type usually was made from the branch of a large tree, but might be from a shrub. The bark was first peeled off, then at the digging end all the sapwood was removed on two sides to produce the chisel-like edge, while at the handle only sufficient of the sapwood was removed to make it convenient for grasping with the hand. The finished tool was about four feet long depending somewhat upon the height of the man who used it. It tapered slightly from the handle, about one and one-half inches in diameter, to about two and one-half inches at the digging end which was sharpened to a somewhat flared wedge or chisel-like edge, with slightly rounded corners; these soon became more rounded by use (fig. 1a). It was thus fashioned by rubbing with a rough stone, and the edge was never fire-shaped or fire-hardened since the wood selected was itself very hard. There was no foot rest on their planting sticks, nor did these tribes ever have one forked like a crutch.

This implement is very similar, except in length, to those found by Hough[1] in Tularosa Cave, on the Tularosa River,

[1] Hough, *Culture of the Ancient Pueblos of the Upper Gila River Region*, pp. 62-3.

a tributary of the San Francisco, which in turn flows into the upper Gila River.

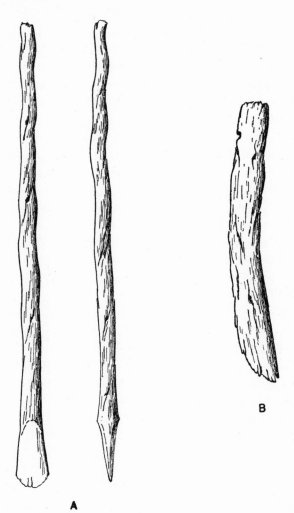

A   **B**

Fig. 1. Piman agricultural implements: (a) planting stick; (b) weeding hoe.

One Papago informant, Mattías Hendricks, maintained that, in his area, planting sticks used for wheat were made of paloverde *(Cercidium microphyllum)*, a rather soft wood, and that these were about nine inches wide at the blade and four feet long. This was obviously a post-Spanish development.

Another aboriginal farming tool was the weeding hoe, made of the heartwood of some hardwood tree, preferably ironwood, but, on occasion, mesquite or screwbean. A specimen secured from José Petero, at Silnakya, was unearthed by him in the neighborhood of that village. This was a thin-bladed, hard, heavy, sabre-shaped structure—a somewhat curved slab of the heartwood of an ironwood tree, approximately thirty-three inches long, and about five-eighths of an inch thick. It gradually extended from a width of two and seven-eighths inches at the upper end to its maximum of three and one-half inches near the knife-like edge of the convex cutting end (fig. 1b). The fashioning evidently was done with a rough stone, and the implement showed no signs of having been fire-hardened or fire-shaped. Bone, horn or stone planting or hoeing implements were unknown to both Pima and Papago.

This weeding hoe combined the functions of spade and hoe and was used for cutting weeds off below the ground line, loosening soil around cultivated plants, in preparing irrigation ditches or in digging water holes. Its length was such as to preclude a man's using it except with a sidewise scraping motion while in a kneeling or sitting position.

Russell[2] found a single specimen among the Pima, and Papago Indians offered to sell to Lumholtz,[3] who explored southwestern Arizona in 1909-10, such an ironwood "hoe," reported to have been found in a mound in the Santa Rosa Valley. Later he secured additional specimens. He also found among the Papago a simpler form of the same implement, smaller in size and consisting of a flat, oblong piece of wood with edge sharpened in a similar way, which was said to have been used by the women. That the former type of

2 Russell, Pima, p. 97.
3 Lumholtz, New Trails, pp. 68-9.

implement was used quite early is indicated by the fact that Fewkes[4] described and figured similar ironwood implements recovered in excavations at Casa Grande.

Russell[5] described and figured a type of wooden shovel (made of either cottonwood or mesquite) , which he regarded as aboriginal and as very probably making possible the digging of not only the Piman but the ancient Hohokam irrigation canals. All our information, obtained from Piman informants, is at variance with Russell's opinion. They maintained that their shovel, almost invariably made of cottonwood, was a post-Spanish implement; moreover this agrees with the ethnological and archaeological information for Southwestern tribes in general. Informants said that, anciently in digging irrigation ditches, the dirt was loosened with the planting stick and weeding hoe, then removed in baskets. The Pima shovel of historic times was a one-piece tool of heartwood, from a cottonwood tree, felled by burning, then shaped roughly by further burning, and finally by fashioning the heated blade with a rough stone. The first shovels were shaped much like a tennis racquet, the blade, about eight inches wide, following the natural curve of the tree trunk from which it came. That crude shovels were used at an early date in the Gila Basin, however, is indicated by Fewkes'[6] finds at Casa Grande; here he recovered flat, slate implements, sharp on one edge and blunt on the opposite, identified as shovels and hoes. One or more of them were shaped like spades, an extension on one side serving evidently for attachment of a handle; others were elongate, circular or semicircular. The handle on his figure 39, however, has evidently been attached purely for the purpose of illustration. Turney[7] also wrote of the ancient extensive use of stone hoes in the Gila Basin.

[4] Fewkes, *Casa Grande,* p. 146.
[5] Russell, *loc. cit.*
[6] Fewkes, *op. cit.,* pp. 131-32, pls. 70, 71, fig. 39.
[7] Turney, *The Land of the Stone Hoe.*

Another early post-contact Piman implement was the dibble, obtained from across the border. It might be described as the digging stick equipped with an iron blade, intermediate between the ancient planting stick and the modern long-handled steel shovel. The reader is referred to Russell's figure 10d.

Still another implement introduced among the Pima after the coming of the Spaniards was the rake. This was a primitive wooden tool about three and one-half feet long, made of a three-forked mesquite branch. The tines were strengthened by a cross-piece, then heated over a fire and their ends bent downward by fastening in the crotch of a tree, after which they were cut to a suitable length. When the rake had cooled, the cross-piece was removed. Sometimes a hay fork was made in similar manner, except that the tines were not bent and the cross-piece constituted a permanent part of the implement.

Of comparatively recent introduction into the Piman area is the wooden plow. The first Papago plow was made of a mesquite tree and its main root. This is shown in figure 2. Such plows were not common among the desert Papago as these Indians had little share in this early stage of cultivation by plow. They are extremely rare today. The plow was drawn by two rawhide strips passing back from the animal and fastened to a mesquite pin inserted through a slot in the share. The earliest Pima plow was fashioned a little more elaborately. The plow itself, consisting of share and single handle, was a piece of mesquite or ironwood to which was attached a cottonwood tongue fastened to the ox yoke; this in turn was tied to the horns of the oxen by leather thongs. The base and single handle were of one piece of wood, the latter being a branch of the tree trunk from which the base of the plow was fashioned, the share being about three by three by twenty-four inches and sharpened on the lower side. The lower side of the proximal end of the tongue was beveled to an edge, which fitted into a transverse notch at the base of the

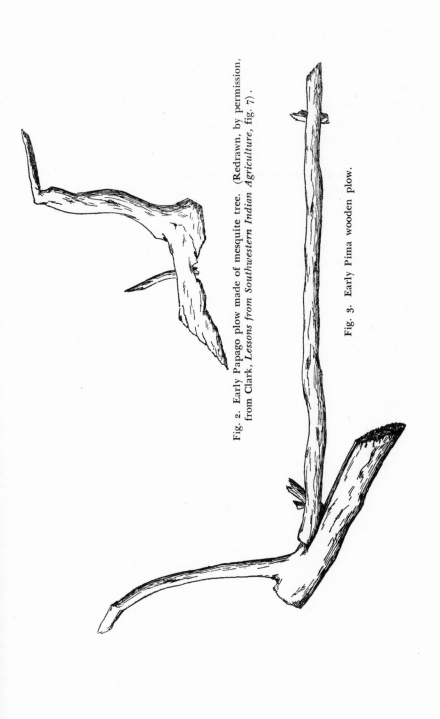

Fig. 2. Early Papago plow made of mesquite tree. (Redrawn, by permission, from Clark, *Lessons from Southwestern Indian Agriculture*, fig. 7).

Fig. 3. Early Pima wooden plow.

handle, then the tongue was attached to the share by a mesquite pin passing through both and kept tight by two wooden
wedges. On some plows a sheet of iron or steel faced the
cutting surface of the share. The plow base was oriented at a
rather sharp angle, approximately fifty degrees, allowing just
the point to come in contact with the soil, thus permitting
only very shallow plowing, a condition necessitated by the
limited strength of the plow itself. Such a Pima plow was
described in 1893 by Whittemore[8] and later figured by
Russell.[9] (See fig. 3.)

[8] Whittemore, in *Among the Pimas*, pp. 87-8.
[9] Russell, *op. cit.*, fig. 11.

Chapter VII

PLANTING, IRRIGATION AND CULTIVATION

The Piman Calendar

The Piman calendar is associated with seasonal weather and the appearance and characteristics of plants and animals. The calendar month (moon) is the lunar month, thus there are twelve such periods, although their duration evidently is not precisely designated. Our information agrees with that of Underhill,[1] that there existed no standard names for months but descriptive terms for each period between one "death of the moon" and the next. Informants said the periods, or moons, began two nights before the appearance of the new moon. The Piman year began in July with the ripening of giant cactus, which was also the beginning of the rainy season and regarded as the best time of the year. The number of periods or moons in the calendar was identical with the typical number of tail feathers in the song bird—twelve.

We were fortunate in securing the names and order for the Papago moons as Chico Bailey was fairly well informed on such matters. In this we were ably assisted by Father Bonaventura Oblasser, who was especially helpful in ironing out difficulties of interpretation, since he, too, had some knowledge of the calendar and also spoke Papago. A specific attempt was made to secure precise calendric sequence in relation to its bearing upon the agricultural picture. It was impossible to secure the Pima calendar, for our informants knew little about it, the extent of their knowledge being the names for two or three moons. Although our calendar does not equate fully with either of those given by Russell[2]

---

[1] Underhill, *Papago*, p. 124.
[2] Russell, *Pima*, p. 36.

for the Pima or with the Papago calendar of Lumholtz,[3] it
does correspond very closely with that of Underhill.

The Papago Calendar

1. Sahuaro-harvest or rainy moon. Corresponds to very
   late June and much of July. This is the period when
   the bulk of the planting was done.
2. Short-planting moon (Late Planting). Planting might
   also be done as late as this if the ground were moist, but
   it meant a short growing season and the risk that crops
   might not ripen before frost. Equates partly with
   August.
3. Dry-grass moon. The time when grass becomes dry.
   September.
4. Frost moon. The harvest season. October.
5. Small, slight or pleasant winter. Weather beginning to
   get cold. Games were now held. November.
6. Big-winter or big-cold moon. The coldest period of the
   year. December.
7. No-more-fat moon. Deer and other game begin to get
   thin. Equates approximately with January.
8. Smell moon. Deer in the mountains mating and begin
   to smell because in heat. Also known as gray moon, because the vegetation is without leaves and has a grayish
   color. Late January and early February.[4]
9. Green moon. The season when native vegetation begins
   to get green. Approximately equivalent to March.
10. Yellow moon. Called thus because many plants now are
    in yellow bloom, particularly the white brittlebush
    (*Encelia farinosa*), creosote bush and paloverde. April.

[3] Lumholtz, *New Trails*, p. 76.

[4] A. A. Nichol, Leader, Federal Aid Division, Arizona Game and Fish
Commission, has informed us in personal correspondence, Aug. 5, 1941, that
the bulk of the breeding in both Arizona whitetail and desert mule deer comes
in late January and early February. There is a twenty to twenty-three day
spread between the climactic periods, the first not coming until after the
first week in January. Thus the major portion of the rut would come early
in February. Farther north in Arizona the rutting season is known to occur
considerably earlier. The role of temperature in the development and main-
tenance of the rut in red deer has been discussed by Darling in his book, *A
Herd of Red Deer*, pp. 166-67.

11. Painful or hunger-hurting moon. Another name some-
    times used was "mesquite in flower." Crops were now
    exhausted and wild foods not yet available. This was be-
    fore they grew wheat. May.
12. Black-seeds moon. Seeds of certain native plants were
    now ripe and black. June.

The Pimans had no great store of star lore but a few constellations were recognized. We found it difficult to ascertain
much about such knowledge among the Pima, since informants had only fragmentary bits of information; it is much
better preserved among the Papago. Observation of celestial
movements in relation to their bearing upon planting time
seems to have been the function of delegated individuals.
Anciently, among the Pima, the headmen called the men together about six days before it was time to plant the several
crops, and the individual in charge of calendric sequence told
the people the time had arrived to begin planting.

Roughly the Pleiades (known as The Travelers) are used
to indicate the seasons, calculations being made from their
position at dawn. We can do no better than present Underhill's statement of seasonal sequence in this connection:

> "Pleiades rising in summer, start planting.
> At the zenith at dawn, too late to plant more.
>   Past the zenith, time for corn harvest.
> One quarter down from the zenith, time for deer
>   hunting.
> Setting, time for the harvest feast."[5]

Days were known to be of different lengths. The winter
solstice—an accepted sacred period of four days—was observed
and began with the first day on which the Pleiades had set at
dawn.

The Papago paid little attention to relative positions of
the sun, and, like Underhill,[6] we were unable to learn of any
devices for such observations. The Pima depended on the

[5] Underhill, *op. cit.*, p. 125.
[6] *Ibid.*

relation of the sun to the gap of the Sierra Estrella, the chief
purpose being to determine the latest period at which it was
possible to plant crops and have them mature before frost.
Chico Bailey said his grandfather relied upon the position of
the rising sun with reference to a certain point on Baboquivari Mountain to determine when it was too late to plant;
also that the Papagos at Pisinemo used a similar spot in the
Ajo Mountains for the same purpose.

Tribal Papago traditions were passed on by word of
mouth from official narrators to the youths. While these tales
might be told at any time upon request, particularly in winter
months, the creation myth was always formally and officially
related during the sacred four-day solstice period. Pima and
Papago annals, in reality records of important events, were
kept on a stick variously notched or carved to designate special happenings.[7]

PLANTING

Time and Number of Plantings

Wherever any group of Pimans anciently pursued agriculture based upon irrigation from more or less permanently
running streams or springs, planting was begun as soon as
possible after danger of frost had passed, contingent upon an
available supply of water at such time. But among all those
Pimans who were dependent upon flood water from the
washes the time of the single planting was governed entirely
by the occurrence of summer rains, which usually began at
any time from late June to mid-July. Aboriginally, groups
having a rather constant supply of running water usually
made two plantings, the first when danger of frost was past
and the ground warm enough for seed germination, the second sometime after sahuaro harvest, depending upon the
availability of water for irrigation, but rarely any later than
mid-August because of danger from early frosts. Thus, in

[7] Ibid., pp. 125-36; Underhill, A Papago Calendar Record; Russell, op.
cit., pp. 34-66.

addition to being limited by water supply, the time of the
first planting was governed by late, the second by early,
frosts, these dates varying somewhat in different parts of the
Piman area. In this connection, Smith[8] tells us that a correla-
tion of altitude and length of growing season, with corrections
for latitude, shows that, on the average, an increase of forty-
five feet in altitude decreases the average length of the growing season by one day, an increase of one thousand feet thus
shortening the season about three weeks. At Sacaton, on the
Gila River Reservation, with an elevation of 1,280 feet, a
twenty-one-year record showed the average date of the last
killing frost in spring as March 3, the latest known date
April 22; the average date of first killing frost in autumn,
November 15, the earliest date of killing frost, October 28.
This gives the mean length of growing season as about 263
days.[9]

All Piman groups whose agriculture anciently depended
upon flood water from washes made but a single planting,
the time of which was in no way governed by a frost-free date
since planting had to await the beginning of summer rains,
from late June to mid-July, and thus corresponding with the
end of sahuaro harvest. Such was the general Papago situation, since with very few exceptions, notably San Marcelo de
Sonoita and Quitobac, their agriculture was pursued without
irrigation from running streams and was therefore styled
de temporal or "thunderstorm." A number of reports of Indian agents at San Xavier in the closing years of the last, and
beginning of the present, century refer to the "so-called second
crop" of these Indians. By this was meant that the wheat and
barley, planted any time from November to January, was
designated as the first crop; the maize, beans and pumpkins
planted after the first summer rains, the second. But anciently
only a single crop was planted at San Xavier. Although this
village had running springs, the Santa Cruz River, upon

8 Smith, *The Climate of Arizona*, pp. 380, 383.
9 *Ibid.*; King, *Crop Tests at the Cooperative Testing Station*, p. 9.

which these people also depended, was dry for a very large part of the year, beginning to flow only with the onset of summer rains.

In addition to Pima planting seasons being governed by frost-free dates in spring and fall, they were limited as well by the availability of water in the Gila. Although the flow of this river at present is regulated by storage behind Coolidge Dam, the long-time monthly averages of the normal flow measured at a point above the Coolidge Dam are approximately as follows:[10]

January	50,000 acre-feet	July	24,000 acre-feet
February	52,000 " "	August	39,000 " "
March	56,000 " "	September	26,000 " "
April	36,000 " "	October	24,000 " "
May	12,000 " "	November	17,000 " "
June	3,000 " "	December	34,000 " "

To the above amounts should be added, as benefiting the area of the Gila River Reservation, the unregulated average flow from the San Pedro River of about seventy thousand acre-feet per year, most of which comes during July, August and September.

The Gila waters are thus seen to be highest at two periods, one during January to March, a second in August. However, this represents the mean taken over a number of years and it must be recognized that from year to year the monthly average fluctuated considerably. Only in flood season was the flow adequate to permit irrigation. It was not uncommon for the water in the Gila to fail completely, especially in winter but occasionally in summer as well. Russell[11] reports this happened about every fifth year, and is supported by comments of Anza, Eixarch, Font and others.[12] Such failure

10 L. J. Booher, Assistant Agricultural Engineer, University of Arizona, Personal correspondence, May 8, 1941.

11 Russell, *op. cit.*, pp. 66-7.

12 Bolton, *Anza*, III, 19, 353; IV, 45; *Report of the Commissioner of Indian Affairs* for 1871, p. 359; *ibid.* for 1875, p. 214; *ibid.* for 1878, pp. xxxix, 3.

either delayed or eliminated one or both of the plantings. Moreover, occasional floods resulted in a similar situation, or even washed out plantings that had been made. It is thus seen that although historic and traditional accounts refer to two plantings among the Pima, such, of necessity, was not an invariable procedure.[13]

Aboriginally the first Pima planting, ordinarily not limited by shortage of water in the Gila, was made after danger of frost had passed, and the frost-free period in spring was recognized as being coincident with leafing of the cottonwood and mesquite trees, as well as the appearance of the first western white-winged dove *(Melopelia asiatica mearnsii)*.[14] Cottonwoods came into leaf in southern Arizona varying from late February to about mid-March depending upon local and seasonal conditions. Mesquite never began to leaf out before the end of March, and more commonly toward the end of April, this depending upon location and seasonal conditions, being earlier on hills than flood plains. The leafing of mesquite was regarded as a more conservative and safer indication that danger from frost had passed than was the leafing of cottonwood. Hence maize was usually planted when the cottonwoods started to leaf; pumpkins, teparies, cotton and gourds when the mesquite began to turn green. That such an early planting was made in Kino's day is indicated by the fact that he wrote on April 8, 1701: ". . . after a sixteen leagues' journey, passing by three other *rancherias*, we arrived at that of El Tupo [about thirty miles west of Tucson], all those places also being very poorly supplied with water [evidently from

[13] Browne, *Adventures in the Apache Country*, p. 107; Russell, *op. cit.*, p. 90.

[14] Johnson A. Neff, Assistant Biologist of the Federal Fish and Wildlife Service, informs us by personal correspondence, Aug. 2, 1941, that the migratory movements of this dove are somewhat erratic and influenced by weather conditions, the spring migration being somewhat more regular than the late summer one. By late April stray individuals appear on the Pima Reservation at Sacaton and in the Salt River Valley.

springs], although the natives had already planted their crops of maize, beans and pumpkins."[15]

The first Pima planting included maize, teparies, pumpkins, gourds and cotton (a single planting). Cotton was planted in late March or early April, although unusually late frosts sometimes necessitated a replanting. They knew that common beans could be nipped by frost yet leaf out again. Browne,[16] writing in 1874, tells us the Pima planted tobacco and cotton when the mesquite leaves put forth. The second planting was not made until the first had been harvested, and was sowed on the land from which the first had been removed. In this sowing, immediately after the sahuaro harvest in July, were maize, teparies and pumpkins (cushaw type only). This schedule was modified considerably with the introduction of new crops by the Spaniards. For many decades the Pima have sowed their first crop to wheat and barley from late November to early January, and this was harvested in late May or June. Then, after the sahuaro harvest in July, the second planting, consisting chiefly of maize and teparies, was made on the same land, and this crop ripened in October or November. Usually a portion of the land was sowed from late March to early April to pumpkins, muskmelons, watermelons and cowpeas, and in some cases a second sowing of these was made after sahuaro harvest. However, there were single plantings of kidney beans, lima beans and chili when the mesquite began to leaf out. A single planting of chick peas was made from early November to mid-December and one of garden peas in January.

Today the native Pima varieties of maize planted as late as August 15 will mature, but introduced sorts usually are put out from June 15 to July 15. The wheat cultivated at present continues to be of the winter type, and is put out from November to January. Pima farm advisors today discourage plantings after mid-January, although these Indians often

15 Bolton, *Kino,* I, 291.
16 Browne, *op. cit.,* p. 109.

delay and very hot weather at time of maturity reduces the crop. Barley, however, is sometimes sowed as late as February. Early plantings of winter barley and wheat at San Xavier and on the Gila were, and are, infrequently damaged by late frosts coming the latter part of March and early in April. The best yields of Pima cotton have been obtained from plantings made before May 1.[17]

The agricultural picture for those Pimans (chiefly Papago) who pursued *de temporal* farming follows: During winter, families camped as near as possible to a permanent source of water in the foothills and moved down to their fields only after the heavy rains had begun so as to be certain that drinking water would be available. It very rarely rained before sahuaro harvest, but if rains did come during this period they caused the ripe fruit to spoil on the trees. At the onset of rains the Papago stopped gathering the fruit and began planting. Also, if it rained during the sahuaro harvest drinking ceremony this ritual was terminated, as its purpose had been accomplished.

The season in Papaguería was concentrated in July and August, when almost all of the meagre annual rainfall occurred. Sporadic showers began toward the end of June, and by mid-July there were heavy thunderstorms if the season were good. It was immediately after the ground had been moistened by these rains that the Papagos did their *de temporal* planting, which was thus governed by the rains rather than season or temperature. As these rains might be local, some variation occurred in the planting season in different areas. Both Papago and Pima maintained that in early days there was always more rainfall than in recent years, the main reasons being that "the earth was younger and had greater powers and the Indians more carefully observed the rituals in those days."

July was known as the "Month of Rains," and August as the "Month of Short Planting." Plantings could be made up

17 King, Beckett and Parker, *Agricultural Investigations*, p. 24.

to the middle of the latter period and still mature, but if the heavy rains were delayed beyond this the Papagos sometimes did not plant at all since the growing season would be too short before frost. The latest safe date for sowing maize is now regarded as about August 17; for teparies, August 20-25. Under especially favorable moisture conditions two sowings of teparies might be made, the early one after the first summer rains, the second as "short planting" in mid-August. At present this late planting period is regarded as much more desirable for common pink beans and limas, since they go mostly to stems and leaves if planted early. If no planting were done, this changed their whole plan of life. Sometimes they ate their seed corn and beans, and spent the rest of the summer food gathering; then in winter worked for the Pimas in Sonora or on the Gila, earning their food and seeds for the next year. Due to the erratic rainfall, a crop often had to be reseeded, and even then there might be no harvest. In 1927 the tepary crop had to be planted three times on some parts of the reservation.

After the first heavy rains all Papagos hastened to plant their crops in order to get them up before the soil again became dry, always beginning with maize. Ordinarily only one planting of each crop was made, but, in the event of another period of rainfall within two or three weeks, a second planting might be made if land were available.

These Indians rarely planted anything before the rains started; a few individuals might plant small patches of corn, never any other crop, in the hope that the rains would soon begin and thus give them an early source of food. This could not be risked on any large scale, however, both on account of the uncertainty of the rainy season and the possibility of floods washing out the planting.

Since the fairly widespread cultivation of wheat within the past few generations, the Papago have modified their program to the extent of sowing wheat any time from late November to February, depending upon the rains, although they much preferred to have it in by the first of January. If sowed late the plants were short and the grains small, due to the effect of high temperature, or plants might be damaged by late frosts at the time of heading. In no case did they make more than one planting. Otherwise they continue to pursue their "thunderstorm" planting as they have always done, living at the *temporales* during the summer months only.

Method of Planting

In the main, Pima pursued irrigated agriculture and customarily did their planting after first heavily irrigating the land and allowing it to dry out for about a week. Unless water from the Gila were available, it often happened that this one irrigation constituted all the moisture that crops received. Papago farming however was of the flood-water type, the seed being planted in moist ground at the mouth of a wash after it had been flooded by the first summer rains. The washes, usually dry for the rest of the year, were at that time filled for several hours with a torrent of muddy water which sometimes covered the flood plain to a depth of two or three inches. Here they put in their crops, knowing that even with very low rainfall a crop would mature if the rains were not too long delayed and surface run-off or sub-surface flow favorable.

Pima-Papago sowing aboriginally was done entirely with the planting stick; this continued well into modern times and several of our old informants, both Papago and Pima, have had considerable personal experience in its use. In this connection Díaz, writing in 1774 of the extensive cultivation of wheat, maize etc. by the Pimas, noted that all their fields were cultivated "with no more oxen and no more implements than a wooden stick, with which they make holes in the ground and go slowly burying the seed."[18] Informants invariably regarded ancient farming with the planting stick as superior to modern methods.

[18] Bolton, *Anza*, II, 304.

Planting among both peoples was a family enterprise done chiefly by the man, assisted by the older children; the wife might help if she were not otherwise engaged. Often this was handled reciprocally, families helping each other, a practice rarely followed today. Díaz[19] stated that the Pima planted in common. He doubtless meant that fields were worked in common under a coöperative plan, not that fields were communally owned.

Aboriginally all crops were planted in hills, never in rows or broadcast. The planter stood in a somewhat stooped position to make holes for the seeds, thrusting the stick forcefully into the moist earth one or more times, depending upon the condition of the ground, and each time pried and jiggled with the stick to loosen the dirt. The surface soil at each hill was never scraped off before digging the hole, as was done regularly by some tribes. Hills were about six inches in diameter and into the center of each he next thrust the stick perpendicularly, turning it in a wide circle to provide a hole for inserting seed. Holes for maize were four to six inches deep regardless of the type of soil, and this same depth was used for several crops. There was no deliberate attempt to loosen soil in the hill to a depth greater than necessary for planting the seeds. When planting corn, the planter, if right handed, next took one step with his left foot and made another hill just like the first at the end of his foot, making the hills about thirty inches apart. After thus digging a number of holes the planter stopped to put in the seeds, which he carried in a leather or woven cloth sack tied around the waist, meanwhile carrying the planting stick in the other hand. Some individuals dug and planted one hole at a time. In any case only a few holes were dug at a time as they dried out quickly. When two persons worked together, one dug the hills, the other dropped and covered the seeds. The planter stooped to about a foot from the ground to drop the seed, making no effort to arrange them in the hole, and im-

19 *Ibid.*

mediately covered the seeds by scraping dirt over the hole with his foot. The surface was left flush with the ground, the soil not pressed down. Informants stated that, using the digging stick, a man could plant about a half acre of corn or teparies per day.

There was no device for making certain the hills would be in straight rows, as one learned by experience how to gauge this with the eye. When tree stumps were encountered no special effort was made to keep rows straight and the hills were staggered around them. All crops were planted with the hills in adjacent rows alternating, and in no case was the soil between the hills worked at planting time. Since no attempt was made to locate hills in the same spots year after year, this was conducive to maintaining soil fertility.

Maize was planted four to six inches deep; teparies, kidney beans, lima beans, pumpkins, gourds, black-eyed beans, chick peas, watermelons, muskmelons and cotton about three inches, since, unlike corn and pumpkins, they could not push up from a greater depth of soil; lentils were planted about one to one and one-half inches and chili merely pressed into the soil, while tobacco was blown from the hand and the surface soil then scratched with a branch. Two informants said for watermelons, pumpkins and muskmelons holes were made about six inches deep, the seed covered shallowly, leaving a depression, and the hole gradually filled in as the plants grew.

Hills and rows for the last three were located six to eight feet apart; teparies, kidney beans, black-eyed beans, chick peas and cotton, one and one-half to two feet; lima beans about three feet, and lentils about twelve inches. Maize rows were thirty inches apart; teparies, kidney beans, black-eyed beans and cotton about two feet.

The Piman ritual number was four, and, theoretically, four seeds of any crop were to be planted to each hill; practically, this has long been ignored. Maize, teparies, kidney beans, black-eyed beans, lima beans, chick peas, cotton, gourds, melons and pumpkins were planted three to five seeds per hill. These people knew by experience how many seeds of each crop should be planted per hill, for if plants came up too thick they did not produce well.

Gourds were planted differently from other crops. Among the Pima, about four hills, each three feet in diameter, were located and prepared near an irrigation ditch and close to a tree or bush if possible so the plants could climb; otherwise a forked pole was placed in the hill for support. Four seeds were placed in each hill at a depth of two to three inches, and the hills walled to retain water. When water in the ditch was high, it was conducted to the hill and walled in; when low, the channel connecting the ditch and hill was left open, allowing water to move to the hill at will. It was woman's responsibility to cultivate and care for gourds, as they were rather looked upon as her pet crop and easy to grow. The Papago planted gourds around the base of a small mesquite tree and fenced them with mesquite poles or sahuaro ribs to keep out jackrabbits. The vines climbed on the tree and fence. Occasionally water was carried to them for they required lots of moisture. They grew quite slowly and were cultivated twice. Informants said the signs of a well-grown gourd plant were that it had a thick stem even when very young and had wide leaves. Gourds were not planted by everyone every year, but as need dictated.

Chili required more frequent irrigation than maize. Informants knew that, although it needed considerable moisture, it would die if the ground were continually wet. Hence it was not planted on flat ground but on the sides of borders[20] about eight inches apart. A pinch of seed was merely pushed shallowly into the soil with the thumb, then the plants thinned out as desired. At present, plants for setting out are usually purchased by the Pima at a greenhouse.

[20] In irrigated areas the term border is used to designate a unit of land enclosed by a continuous ridge of earth erected to facilitate irrigation; also at times to designate the ridge itself.

Fig. 4. Papago field of Baart wheat planted in hills and harvested by hand sickle June 2, 1926. Grown by flood-water farming near San Miguel. (Photograph furnished by C. J. King, U. S. Field Station, Sacaton, Ariz.)

When the Pimans first used wheat it was planted in hills like maize as this was the only method they knew. Hills were dug with the planting stick about six inches apart, the rows spaced the same distance and manner as described for corn, and the ground between hills was not disturbed. One person dug the holes, another put in and covered the grains. Seed was planted two inches deep, about four or five grains per hill, and the soil in the hill left loose. Informants said such a planted field of wheat looked much as though it had been plowed. Later it was planted about fifteen inches apart in furrows made with a spatula-like wooden implement about four feet long and nine inches wide at the blade. Not until the introduction of the wooden plow was wheat broadcast, and when this was done some individuals mixed the seed with wood ashes and scattered the two together. However, some Papago, in flood-water farming, still plant wheat in hills (fig. 4).

Some soaked their seeds before planting. One cannot be certain, however, that this was an aboriginal practice. This was done particularly with flint corn and black-eyed beans, occasionally chili. The practice was resorted to especially when the first sowing did not come up, or was destroyed soon after germination by rabbits, floods etc. Some informants said when maize was soaked before planting its chief purpose was to wash off the corn odor so that the small ants which often ate young seedlings would not be attracted. Maize was known to germinate even though the soil was not very moist, but teparies, pumpkins and cotton required more moisture.

Pimans invariably planted the several crops separately in different plots and never mixed them either in the hill or plot, and any modification of this was a later development. Even brown and white teparies and the several varieties of pumpkins were planted in separate hills and plots, as were the different colors of maize in order to retain their purity.

There was no ritual planting by direction as among the Pueblo Indians.

IRRIGATION

When Kino and Mange,[21] in 1687, made their first explorations in Pimería Alta, the Pima on the Gila and the Sobaipuri in the San Pedro and Santa Cruz valleys were carrying on agriculture by means of irrigation from canals and ditches, a fact later noted by Anza (1774), Díaz (1774), Font (1775), Garcés (1776), Emory (1846) and Bartlett[22] (1848-62) for the Gila Pima.

Haury[23] reports that the Hohokam, who preceded the Pimans in the Gila Basin, are known to have practiced canal irrigation as early as 800 (?) A. D. His excavation of a portion of the Snaketown Canal reveals the superposition of three canals, number two having been dug in part out of the sediments filling the first canal, the third channel being excavated into the silt of the second.

Testimony of the early explorers indicates that the Piman canals formed a veritable network and were much larger and more extensive than required. Nevertheless, Haury states the maximum size and greatest scope of systems of the Hohokam canals was rather definitely reached about 1200-1400 (?) A. D. After this the systems dwindled, ending in the comparatively small but efficient Pima ones seen by the explorers of the seventeenth to nineteenth centuries cited above. These were very largely on the south side of the river. When Kino and Mange[24] first encountered the Pima on the Gila and the Sobaipuri on the San Pedro and Santa Cruz, they were carrying on agriculture by means of canal irrigation; Font and Garcés,[25] in 1775, referred to an extensive system of ditches among the Pima of the Casa Grande-Casa Blanca region, and Emory,[26] in 1846, was "impressed with the beauty, order and

21 Bolton, *Kino*, I, 205; Mange, *Luz*, pp. 248-49, 256.

22 Bolton, *Anza*, II, 19, 303; IV, 43; Coues, *On the Trail*, I, 107-08; Emory, *Notes*, p. 83; Bartlett, *Narrative*, II, 232.

23 Haury, in Gladwin *et al*, *Excavations at Snaketown*, I, 57-8.

24 Bolton, *Kino*, I, 205; Mange, *loc. cit.*

25 Bolton, *Anza*, IV, 43; Coues, *op. cit.*, p. 107.

26 Emory, *loc. cit.*

disposition of the arrangements for irrigation and draining the land." There seems to be no doubt that irrigation on the middle Gila anciently centered around what are now the Casa Blanca and Sweetwater villages. Nor is there doubt that the irrigated tracts were formerly distributed over a much larger territory and involved considerably more land than at the time of the coming of the Spaniards, this retraction of the inhabited and cultivated area becoming more accentuated with Apache pressure. Forbes[27] estimated, on the basis of Mexican tradition and an old map in the office of the assessor of Pima County, that about two thousand acres of land (not including Indian lands) were under irrigation in all of Arizona in 1854. Also, according to Rev. C. H. Cook, who began living among the Pimas in 1870, this tribe was irrigating about three thousand acres on the Gila below Sacaton in 1854. Recent reclamation projects again have brought large and intricate canal networks to the Pima area, some of which conduct water to land never before cultivated by the Indian. Haury's[28] map shows, for part of the Gila River Indian Reservation, the extensive system of irrigation canals now in use by the Pima (which are particularly striking north of Casa Blanca), old canals formerly used by the Pima, and the prehistoric Snaketown Canal; also the maps of Turney and of Forbes[29] show the distribution of prehistoric canals in the Salt River Valley. The more general aspects of Pima irrigation are covered in Chapter II of this book, and a detailed treatment of the subject is given in Southworth's[30] paper. Also, considerable information bearing on the history of irrigation among the Papago is given by Clotts and others.[31]

In the vicinity of the Gila River Reservation the gradient

[27] Forbes, *Irrigation and Agricultural Practice*, p. 12, fig. 2.
[28] Haury, *op. cit.*, fig. 16.
[29] Turney, *The Land of the Stone Hoe;* Forbes, *loc. cit.*
[30] Southworth, *A History of Irrigation on the Gila Indian Reservation.*
[31] Clotts: *Nomadic Papago Surveys; History of the Papago Indians,* etc.; Olberg and Schanck, *Special Report on Irrigation.*

of the Gila is between seven and eight feet per mile. The main canal of the irrigation project, which diverts at Ashurst-Hayden Dam, on the Gila, has a capacity of twelve hundred second feet and a grade of .00037 feet per mile. The main branch of this lateral which goes to the Gila River Reservation has a capacity of about 450 second feet and has a slope of .0004 feet per mile, except for three miles of concrete-lined section which has a grade of .0045. Smaller canals on the reservation have gradients varying from .0005 to .00065.[32]

Pima and Hohokam canals were built at the expense of tremendous effort, and this is all the more striking when we realize that the dirt removed in making these ditches had to be loosened with planting sticks, weeders and flat, stone, spade-like blades (see Chapter VI), then carried away in baskets.

Ancient Pima agriculture in general was based upon canal irrigation from the river, although in places these Indians also utilized flood water from the washes, or diverted water coming from the mountains in times of heavy rains by the use of temporary dikes on the flats. Thus Bandelier,[33] writing in 1890-92, states the Pimas formerly irrigated in two ways: from the Gila by ditches; and in sections where the fertile spots lay at some distance from the watercourses or at the foot of steep mountains they dug channels from arroyos to their fields to lead the torrents coming from showers, this latter being especially true in the vicinity of Casa Blanca and toward Sierra Maricopa. Russell[34] informs us that one Pima village located southwest of Maricopa Wells depended entirely upon flood water.

The river was customarily dammed in places by the Pima to turn the water into the irrigation canals. In times of abundant flow, which occurred only following heavy rains in

[32] L. J. Booher, Assistant Agricultural Engineer, University of Arizona, Personal correspondence, May 8, 1941; C. J. Moody, Project Engineer, Personal correspondence, May 16, 1941.
[33] Bandelier, *Final Report of Investigations*, I, 254; II, 17.
[34] Russell, *Pima*, p. 88.

the mountains, a diagonal wing was built across the entire width of the river, a fact noted for the Gila Pimas by Font[35] in 1775. For this purpose a place was selected at a bend in a narrow part of the river to secure greater force in the flow.

In either case the dam was made by first driving pilings of thick mesquite poles into the river bed in zigzag arrangement. For the diagonal diversion dam, mesquite branches were merely arranged among the poles, but for the cross dam, willow branches were first tied among the pilings, then arrow-weed bushes were tied into bundles with mesquite or willow bark and floated against the pilings. Rocks, too, might be piled against these bundles. Tree trunks, when available, were placed in the river with stones and brush piled against them to serve as a dam.[36] Grossmann[37] stated in 1871 that, in order to force the water into their acequias, the Pima dammed the Gila at convenient spots "by means of poles tied together with bark and rawhide and stakes driven into the bed of the river. Small crevices were filled with bundles of willow branches, reeds and a weed called 'gatuna'." They rarely stood longer than a year, at times being carried away when the river rose suddenly.

Irrigation canals might run a long distance and often were as much as ten feet deep at the point where they left the river. From the several main canals branched many laterals. Grossmann[38] observed that the canals were usually ten feet deep at the dam and averaged four to six feet in width. An effort was always made to arrange ditches so that land could be irrigated on both sides of them, and ditches could be closed at the end when a higher head of water was desired. Head gates in canals were unknown. As late as 1891, it was reported[39] the Pima had no head gates and brush dams were used to stop the flow of water in the canals and ditches.

[35] Bolton, op. cit., I, 263; IV, 43.
[36] Report of the Commissioner of Indian Affairs for 1891, p. 217.
[37] Grossmann, The Pima Indians of Arizona, p. 418.
[38] Ibid.
[39] Report of the Commissioner of Indian Affairs, loc. cit.

Curtis[40] tells that the Pima, from their earliest history, have grown crops by irrigation, conveying water from the river in canals; also that they did not flood the land directly from the canals, but dipped water out of the canals and carried it to the crops. It is his opinion that irrigation by flooding was learned by the Pima after the coming of the Spaniards. However, our studies indicate that flooding fields by the use of ditches and borders was definitely aboriginal; this is supported by Haury's[41] observation that on one of the terraces of the middle Gila are seen old canals and low earth ridges of the borders in areas now covered with large mesquite trees, testifying to cultivation by the Pima within early historic times. In 1846 Emory[42] observed that the Pima fields were subdivided, by ridges of earth, into rectangles of about two hundred by one hundred feet for the convenience of irrigating.

The main canals were considered as communally owned and were cleaned and kept up by all the men in a district working together. There were a number of these districts in the Pima area each under the rule of a headman, and when a dam was to be constructed the men of the districts benefited worked together to build it. In the spring, residents of each district, after an address of exhortation by the subchief or foreman, cleaned and repaired their part of the main canal, cutting off the brush along its banks and removing debris; in this several districts often worked reciprocally. In this connection, Grossmann[43] wrote in 1871 that each Pima village elected two or three old men who decided everything pertaining to the digging of canals and construction of dams and regulated the distribution of water for irrigation. Landholders were responsible individually for the lateral which irrigated their fields. Ditch work was recognized as men's responsibility, although women might help in constructing

[40] Curtis, *The American Indian*, II, 5.
[41] Haury, *op. cit.*, I, 53.
[42] Emory, *loc. cit.*
[43] Grossmann, *loc. cit.*

ditches by carrying baskets of dirt, a fact noted by Whitte-more[44] for the Pima in 1893.

The Pima leveled their fields by carrying baskets of soil from high spots to fill the low ones. Small irregularities were often leveled by flooding the fields when the river was carrying a heavy deposit of sediment.

Over a period of time the Federal Government has supplemented the supply of irrigation water among the Pima by drilling wells on the Gila River Reservation, the first experimental pumping plant having been installed at the Sacaton School Farm in 1904. The Pima do not regard this as very successful since the well water carries a fair amount of salts, and lacks the soil-enriching sediments carried by the silty flood water of the Gila which also improves sandy areas although it penetrates poorly. Despite the fact that the average salt content of the Gila underflow is greater than that of the surface flow, the underground water at Sacaton is regarded as better for irrigation than the average surface water of the Gila.[45] Pumped irrigation water has the advantages of being free of noxious weed seeds, soaks in more deeply and carries out the salts more effectively. The rather clear stored water would be preferable to both except for carrying weed seeds.

Canal Irrigation Among the Papago

One must not suppose that irrigation was a Pima-Sobaipuri trait lacking among the Papago, and that flood-water farming was characteristic of the Papago and not found among the Pima and Sobaipuri. These peoples were one in speech and general culture, the Papago simply being environmentally differentiated Pima whose desert land presented no opportunity for river irrigation. Thus all Pimans who dwelt in areas remote from the rivers necessarily pursued flood-water farming. Moreover, as pointed out in Chapter III, in

[44] Whittemore, in *Among the Pimas*, p. 53
[45] Lee, *Underground Waters of Gila Valley*, pp. 61-2.

those Papago areas where there were running streams ditch irrigation was practiced, and that this was done aboriginally is clearly shown by Haury,[46] who found traces of ancient canals on the Sells Reservation. One such canal runs in a straight line for seventeen miles in a west by southwest direction from Baboquivari Mountain to the vicinity of Vamori, and is dated as functional in the fourteenth century. A site excavated during the winter of 1939-40 shows a short canal about a half mile long, with strong indication of water diversion from a ditch, also evidently in use during the fourteenth century. Clotts[47] states there is evidence of prehistoric irrigation indicated by old ditches and reservoirs at Santa Rosa, and within recent times the Papago have dug irrigation canals in suitable places to conduct water to their fields. About 1914 they constructed at Cocklebur a canal three miles long with a base width of fifteen feet and a depth of four feet; at Kowlic, nine miles south of Sells, about twenty-five years ago they built a canal fifteen feet wide, three feet deep and a half mile long to take water from the wash for irrigation. Also at Quajote water is taken for irrigation from Copperosity Wash. Lands were irrigated by the Papago from the large fissure spring at Quitobaquito on the Mexican boundary as well as at San Marcelo de Sonoita, at Caborca and Quitobac.[48]

In the western canyons and foothills of the Baboquivari Mountains lie fourteen winter villages, or Wells, at an altitude of about three thousand feet. Of these Fresnal is a very large village, the houses extending about four miles up Fresnal Canyon. The old Baboquivari Valley village was Komalik, with its ancient winter well at Comobabi, in Sonora. However, nearer winter villages have developed in the Baboquivari Mountains, the most important of which is Fresnal.[49]

[46] Emil W. Haury, Personal conversation, April 26, 1940.

[47] Clotts, *Nomadic Papago Surveys*, p. 82.

[48] Bryan, *Papago*, pp. 324, 407; Clotts, *op. cit.*, pp. 44, 49, 75; Davis, *The Papago Ceremony of Vikita*, p. 164.

[49] Hoover, *Generic Descent of the Papago Villages*, p. 261.

Mange[50] wrote of a flowing stream near a high, square *peñasco,* visible for eighteen leagues, which he and Kino visited in 1699, and Bryan is of the opinion that Mange's description seems to apply to no other locality. Here many Papagos lived during the dry season, some remaining throughout the year. In 1915 there were in this canyon small enclosed gardens totaling thirty-five acres, planted to beans, melons, chili, tomatoes and corn. There are no permanently running streams, Fresnal Creek being one of the best, and it runs only for a short time after heavy rain. Part of this acreage was irrigated by water drawn from shallow wells, which up to 1915 were dug by the Indians themselves, and the rest of it was planted to early crops, matured by rainfall alone. There is no evidence of aboriginal dams, wells or other irrigation activity.[51] It is very doubtful, therefore, whether any of the irrigation in Fresnal Canyon represents an aboriginal condition.

Irrigation aboriginally was carried on at San Xavier, the only anciently irrigated village now on the Papago reservation. In Kino's day this was occupied by Sobaipuri who, during the eighteenth century, seem to have died out from some contagious disease, and the Papago have gradually moved in and cultivated their fields. Irrigated agriculture was pursued by utilizing water from springs and, later at least, the flow of the Santa Cruz. One of the sources, a spring issuing near the village and known as the Agua de la Misión, was destroyed by an earthquake in 1883, which forced this flow to the surface farther up the valley. It is now located 1.7 miles south and 0.8 miles east of the mission. The second source of water for irrigation, known as the Acequia de la Punta de Agua, is first mentioned in a Mexican grant of 1851, in which it is related that José Martínez first developed and brought water

50 Mange, *op. cit.,* p. 67; Bolton, *Kino,* I, 193.

51 Clotts, *op. cit.,* pp. 52-3; H. V. Clotts, Personal correspondence, July 17, 1941.

upon his land.[52] This would indicate construction of an acequia, or ditch, which probably tapped seepage water at a shallow depth, and this method was continued by the digging of additional surface ditches until a large channel was cut through the level plain, making it impossible for the Indians to secure water any longer by this means. This gradually became so serious that, by 1912, the installation of pumping plants was initiated. Our one informant at San Xavier said that formerly the Papago cultivated only small patches here, that there were two springs and the water from them combined to form a stream about three feet wide and three deep, which at times filled up with grass and weeds and had to be cleaned out.

Thus aboriginal irrigation at San Xavier seems to have been carried on partly with spring water, the indication being that the Indians utilized small springs or seeps. These were supplemented by the natural flooding of the Santa Cruz, and this valley was covered with grass and mesquite as late as 1873. There was formerly no definite river channel, except probably above the dykes, and during annual floods the water spread out in a thin sheet over the valley. Hence, as rain did not run off quickly and floods were not so great in volume as later, their main effect was that of a thorough irrigation rather than of erosion and destruction.[53] Diversion of the flow of this river in flood season by means of a brush dam evidently has been a development within historic time.

It is difficult to understand Kino's statement in 1689 that at San Xavier "The fields and lands for sowing were so extensive and supplied with so many irrigation ditches that the father visitor said they were sufficient for another city like Mexico,"[54] for there is no reason to believe the cultivated

52 Olberg and Schanck, op. cit., p. 110; Clotts, History of the Papago Indians, etc.

53 Olberg and Schanck, op. cit., pp. 5, 7.

54 Bolton, op. cit., p. 205.

area was very large.[55]   J. M. Berger,[56] Farmer in Charge at
San Xavier, in his special report, August 14, 1900, wrote that
the Indians there had fully four times as many acres of land
under cultivation as they had fifteen or twenty years earlier,
although with a very much smaller water supply than was ever
known to exist. The land under cultivation was given in
Berger's several annual reports as 800 acres in 1890 (Olberg
and Schanck[57] state 1,580), 950 in 1897, 1,040 in 1899, and
1,200 in 1902. After wells and pumps were installed, beginning in 1912, the following acreages are listed: in 1915, 500;
in 1917, 500; in 1919, 1,500; and in 1920, 1,121 acres. On
this basis the amount of land under cultivation in 1880 was
approximately 250 acres, and this estimate is given credence
by McDowell.[58] Our informant at San Xavier advised there
is now much more land under cultivation than formerly.

The first European stimulus to increased irrigation at
San Xavier occurred with the arrival of Kino at the close of
the seventeenth century, but there is no indication that extensive areas were cultivated or greatly improved methods
used. It was not until the more prosperous periods from
1768 to 1822 that there was any considerable development of
irrigation at favorable points along the Santa Cruz near the
mission of San Xavier and the Spanish presidios of Tubac
and Tucson.[59]

Several factors have contributed materially toward deepening the river channel, thus rendering it increasingly difficult to utilize the water for irrigation. One is the introduction of numerous cattle into the area during the last quarter
of the nineteenth century, the resultant overgrazing con-
tributing toward erosion in the valley. As ranching became

[55] Velasco, in his *Geografía y Descripción Universal de las Indias* covering 1571-74, p. 189, reported that at that time there were three thousand Spaniards and thirty thousand houses of Indians *(Casas de Indias)* in Mexico City.
[56] Clotts, *op. cit.*, p. 65.
[57] *Ibid.*
[58] *Report of the Board of Indian Commissioners* for 1919, pp. 67, 75, 77.
[59] Olberg and Schanck, *op. cit.*, pp. 7-8.

more common, attempts were made to develop ground water at several points. The underground-water development which brought about the greatest damage was made by the whites about 1890, six miles below Tucson, when they opened trenches to intercept ground water. By 1912 the channel had eroded upstream eighteen miles to a point three miles inside the reservation, resulting in the destruction of about one hundred acres of Indian farm lands. A third factor was the improper methods used for securing water for irrigation during the second half of the nineteenth century. For example, development of the water source known as the Agua de la Misión caused a channel one to two hundred feet wide by fifteen to twenty feet in depth, extending about two miles up the valley. To collect the water, an earth dam was thrown across the channel, but this washed out at every flood. In 1912 practically all the irrigable land under cultivation (about five hundred acres) lay on the west side of this channel, about half of it being irrigated from a canal heading at the dam.[60]

In constructing the Acequia de la Punta de Agua a channel resulted extending from sixty to one hundred feet wide and six to twenty feet deep, and came to be known as the west-side barranca. In 1912 a ditch leading from the lower end irrigated the remainder of the five hundred acres. At that time this channel extended upstream for approximately two miles, at which point it was about twenty feet deep, and there encountered a deposit of caliche which checked erosion. In 1912 there were four canals in the vicinity of San Xavier, providing an uncertain supply of water.[61] The entire irrigation system, extant in 1912 as well as that proposed, is shown in a map in Olberg and Schanck's paper.

For some years the Santa Cruz has been a swollen flood at San Xavier during the rainy season of July and August, covering farm lands and causing much destruction, but for the

60 *Ibid.*
61 *Ibid.*

rest of the year it has been a shallow, uncertain stream meandering between high banks, or at times completely dry.

The deepening of the river channel and consequent lowering of the water table, with its decrease of available water for irrigation, beginning about 1890, gradually became worse, and, in 1908, agitation was begun to alleviate the situation. In the fall of 1912 the channel of the Santa Cruz was completely choked with sand, and a temporary pumping plant was installed two and one-half miles above the Agency to supply land on the east side of the river. The only available water other than that developed at the pumping plant was a flow from the east channel of the river, making a total sufficient to irrigate 750 acres.

During the heavy floods of 1914 and 1915 the erosion of reservation land by flood water of the Santa Cruz became so pronounced that immediate action was necessary to preserve the Indian fields. Therefore, in 1915, a long levee was thrown up, a number of wells drilled and pumping stations installed to supply the necessary water for irrigation. In 1916 the largest crop ever grown on the reservation up to that time was harvested.

As to Papago living on the Maricopa Indian Reservation just south of Maricopa, Arizona, little can be said. J. J. Grenville, Superintendent of Irrigation, in his report of April 20, 1911, makes mention of about one hundred Papagos near Maricopa who were on the verge of starvation owing to two successive dry seasons, when their crops were a total failure, although they had under irrigation one hundred acres at the time of his report.

At Akchin, about three miles southwest of Maricopa, is a settlement of approximately 120 Indians who came there about 1874 from Maricopa Wells, eight miles northwest of Maricopa; their fields at Maricopa Wells had been irrigated by flood waters of the Santa Cruz, and were so impregnated with salts as to be unproductive. At the new location they supplied about 180 acres with flood water from the Akchin

Wash, although the uncertainty of the source rendered cultivation precarious, especially in years of drought. Therefore.
in 1914-15, the Federal Government drilled a number of
wells, and now water for irrigation is supplied by pumping.[62]

Flood-water Irrigation Among the Desert Papago

Bryan[63] has pointed out that the usually clear distinction
between irrigated and unirrigated farm land is not valid in its
application to marginal lands irrigated by flood water, there
being, in some instances, a complete transition. The Papago
practiced an incipient sort of irrigation to the extent that
their desert environment permitted. (For other aspects of
Papago flood-water farming see Chapter III.) In their country the run-off of the mountain areas collected in streams
with well-defined channels, which, on reaching the large un-
dissected alluvial basins, lost their momentum and spread
out in broad sheets over the level land for a square mile or
more. Places where this spreading occurred were known to
the Papago as Akchin, "arroyo mouth." These were favorite
locations for flood-water fields, and at least six once-inhabited
villages in the Papago country of southern Arizona and
Sonora are named Akchin or some modification of it. In
many cases shallow ditches and dykes, or wings, were constructed starting a mile or more from the fields in order to
collect the surface run-off for the few acres on which they
converged. Low embankments, small brush dikes and short
shallow ditches were used where necessary to control, divert,
distribute and retain water. At times embankments were
disposed as levees, somewhat after the manner of borders
around a field, to retain water until it could soak into the
soil, but this was not common. For some fields water was led
out from the arroyo by ditches, a deliberate effort thus being
made to conduct the flood water to the fields. At present
earth dikes,[64] protected in front by brush supported by stakes,

62 Clotts, *op. cit.*, pp. 83-7.
63 Bryan, *Flood-water Farming*, pp. 444, 449.
64 *Ibid.*

are often thrown across washes to divert flood water, but there is no indication that this was an ancient practice. Ditches from the wash to fields usually ended somewhere in the middle of the field, an effort being made to construct such ditches over the higher portions so the water would cover the entire plot. If there were several fields, a main ditch with several laterals was employed. A certain amount of leveling of fields resulted from the deposition of sediment by flood waters, but the bulk of it was done by carrying dirt in baskets from high to low spots or off the field entirely. As there was an abundance of water during the short time it ran, there was no need to regulate the size of ditches, hence no reservoirs or flood gates were used. Care had to be exercised to locate fields so that each flood would give them a good irrigation but not wash out the crop during heavier floods, although this always could not be avoided. Each man looked after the ditches and dikes serving his own land, but if these supplied the fields of several families the men concerned worked on them jointly. Most Papago farming villages were quite permanent, but the area cultivated might vary slightly from year to year due to erosion. However, informants said there was little of this anciently, but if there were signs of erosion in a field immediate steps were taken to stop it. Within the last thirty years the Federal Government has installed on this reservation a number of pumps to supply water for irrigation.

Excellent examples of primitive flood-water farming are to be seen at Hardimui and Pisinemo; examples of large cultivated areas are found at Big Fields, the Santa Rosa Valley (Santa Rosa, Anegam and Akchin), Ko-opke, Topawa, San Miguel and Vamori.

At present, a method of irrigation from a *balsa* is employed in several places among the desert Papago. This *balsa* is a sort of embanked reservoir, supplied through a gate which allows water to enter from an arroyo. When filled to overflowing, a depth of about two and one-half feet, the water is allowed to go into a ditch through a gate on to the land, and it is possible to raise a crop from the water of a single filling of the *balsa*. In 1939, a planting of teparies, soybeans and cowpeas was made August 26 at Sells, under *balsa* irrigation, and a good crop resulted. Papago native corn, a milo maize, wheat and Sacaton June corn (for fodder only) have also been matured in this way. The original cost of irrigating on this basis is about one hundred dollars per acre. A modification of this system has been found among the Sand Papago, who lived in northwestern Sonora, near mountains where the reservoir was supplied from permanent springs. A ditch leading from the reservoir completely surrounded the fields, and laterals crossed them at intervals. Water collected in the reservoir during winter and early spring was released in June, before the rains began, in order to make an early planting possible. The reservoir might be filled and emptied several times during the season. The *balsa* is not aboriginal, but it has not been possible to determine whether the arrangement used by the Sand Papago is native.

Number of Irrigations

Among the Pima, planting customarily was done only after the ground had first been irrigated, or if already moist from rains. After irrigation, the soil was allowed to dry out for six or seven days, then planting began.

The Pima did not irrigate crops any specific number of times but carefully watched the condition of plants and soil, then irrigated accordingly providing water was available. In general, three to five irrigations were necessary to mature a crop, although because of water shortage it often happened that the heavy irrigation preparatory to planting was all the crop received. It was possible to produce fairly substantial yields of the Pima native soft varieties and Santan Yellow flint corn with only one irrigation, due to their short period of maturity and low moisture requirements. In no case, however, was a crop irrigated until it was well started and up out

of the ground, otherwise the plants turned yellow or would
even die. It was considered advisable to keep crops well
watered while making their most rapid growth and until they
began to set fruit, after which they needed less.

Papago informants said crops had to have three floodings
in order to produce a good yield, two being the minimum,
and that if corn, for example, did not receive two good floodings, plants on the higher parts of a field would produce no
ears. Teparies were very hardy and gave a satisfactory yield
with only two floodings, but pink beans were less drought
resistant and required more moisture, although they would
not tolerate an excessive amount. Water requirements for
the various crops were seen nicely in a field belonging to
Bernabé López at San Pedro village. On one high spot where
it was difficult to get flood water he could produce a good crop
of teparies and pink beans; these turned yellow if planted
in the low spots with the corn and pumpkins.

Pima corn needed more water than teparies. Pumpkins
were usually irrigated twice before setting of fruit, after
which plants were never watered heavily, as a certain fungus
would attack them, causing stem rot and fruit decay. (This
we observed in our own irrigated plantings of Pima pumpkins in the Río Grande Valley at Albuquerque.) Care also
had to be taken with young pumpkins. When fruit was about
the size of a baseball each one was raised off the ground and
supported by a piece of brush, stones etc., before irrigating,
to prevent rotting from too much moisture. Although teparies were quite hardy and gave a good yield with two floodings, three or four produced a better yield with earlier maturity, and while quite drought resistant they would tolerate
considerable moisture. Pink beans had a higher water requirement than teparies but would not withstand frequent
floodings. They did not do well if water covered the plants
and left a mud deposit on the leaves. Teparies tolerated more
drought than maize, kidney beans or lentils, and maize
required less moisture than pumpkins, more than water-

melons. Informants were aware that, although chili requires considerable moisture, it usually dies when planted on flat irrigated ground, hence it was sowed on the sides of raised field borders in hills about eight inches apart. Pima and Papago grew chick peas as a winter crop, planting from November 1 to early December. Papago awaited the winter rains before sowing, while the Pima heavily irrigated the soil before planting and gave the plants comparatively little water afterwards. In no case were they irrigated after blooming began. Garden peas needed frequent watering and could be grown only where there was a permanent source. Wheat was usually irrigated about four times.

Neither Pima nor Papago carried water to plants (other than gourds, which were sometimes watered by hand) to tide over periods of drought, although informants had heard that the Maricopa did so.

Neither tribe had any ritual for irrigation. One Papago informant said getting water on the fields was not a matter of ceremony but of brain work.

SOIL FERTILITY AND CROP ROTATION

Fertilization of the soil was not practiced aboriginally by either Pima or Papago, yet soil depletion to the extent of necessitating abandonment of fields was extremely rare. Pima land was continually replenished with mineral and organic materials deposited by the river in times of overflow; similarly, Papago fields were naturally fertilized by flash floods. The fact that many of the Piman fields have been under cultivation for hundreds of years, producing sustained crop yields without the addition of manures or other fertilizers, is evidence that considerable plant nutrients were carried by the waters used for irrigation in the Gila Basin. Allowing fields to lie fallow in order to build them up was unknown, although it was recognized that new ground produced larger yields than the old.

Neither did these people anciently rotate crops to conserve soil fertility. Today, however, it is known that crops such as small grains and sorghums soon deplete the land and result in reduced yields if grown on the same soil repeatedly, so for a number of decades the Pimans have planted crops of maize, beans, pumpkins, melons etc. on ground from which the wheat was harvested in May or June.

CULTIVATION

Four being the Piman ritual number, it was supposed to take maize four days to germinate and all informants insisted maize, teparies, pumpkins, watermelons and black-eyed beans were up in four days, that pink beans and lentils required five to six, wheat ten days. If the surface of the ground caked, seedlings other than maize with its pointed shoot had some difficulty in breaking through, and in such cases they were usually assisted by removing or pulverizing the clumps of soil around them. One Papago informant said that in farming *everything had to be taken care of,* even to the extent of aiding plants to break through the ground if necessary. Another stated it was not the purpose of the Papago to let plants grow by themselves but that all cultivated plants have to be taken care of and be helped by human hands, and one can not take things for granted. Informants advised that there was no ritual for cultivation since there was nothing could be done in a field to secure good crops except cultivate, and that if this were not done, poor crops would result. Another perspective on Papago industry and outlook was given by Chico Bailey, who, upon being asked whether the Papago ever abandoned fields because of erosion, said the proper thing for the farmer in a dry-farming area to do is stay on his land, work it and not abandon it; that there was nothing to be gained by moving elsewhere.

The soil was worked customarily at planting time and again when crops were cultivated, also a third time if conditions necessitated. A few late weeds in a crop, especially in a field of maize, were not considered injurious. All informants were very definite in their opinion that anciently weeds were much less abundant than at present; that the Pimans kept their fields more free of them then than now. This may well be true when we take into consideration the numerous weeds which have been introduced and the rank growths of Bermuda and Johnson grass in the Gila Valley.

The Piman conception of the necessity for cultivation was primarily to remove weeds which competed with the crops. Time for the first cultivation was closely related to the frequency of rains and irrigation, as these aided the growth of weeds. In some cases it might have to be done soon after the plants were up; in others, when rains were delayed, the growth of weeds was retarded, hence there was little need for it. In general, however, maize was fifteen to eighteen inches high when first cultivated. The second, and last, took place when plants were about four feet high—when the ears began to show well. Pumpkins were first cultivated when plants were about a foot high and again after they began to spread out, but this was discontinued after the vines had begun to run well. Teparies were usually about six inches tall at the first cultivation, and were beginning to vine out at the second. Wheat was cultivated only once since it attained much of its growth during the cool months when weeds did not thrive so well; this consisted of working the soil between hills and rows and pulling out the large weeds, both being done when the wheat was about six inches high. Chili was cultivated twice, first when about six inches high, then again when about a foot tall.

Cultivation or hoeing was always done anciently with the weeding hoe. The operator held the implement by both hands in a more or less horizontal position. A right-handed man held the left palm against the lower side of the handle, his fingers clasping the upper side; the right hand was clasped, palm downward, over the blade about a foot from its terminus. He crawled about on his knees, striking with quick, somewhat diagonal thrusts of the weeder made toward himself from left to right, thus loosening and turning up the weeds. The hills themselves were rather free of weeds since that soil had been worked at planting time. The same type of movements were made in loosening the soil, and all aboriginal crops were cultivated in this manner. These Indians liked to do their hoeing before the weeds reached a height of about six inches. The larger ones were pulled by hand or roots cut with the weeder below ground level to prevent the plants from sprouting again; the smaller ones were simply cut down in stride while working the ground. All soil between the hills was loosened or scratched to a depth of approximately one inch, even though it had no weeds at the time and regardless of the kind of crop (except wheat) . This was done chiefly to discourage the subsequent growth of weeds, but as well to preserve moisture and keep the ground from cracking. Weeds were always allowed to remain on the ground. Informants said teparies would climb if they had support, and unless weeds were kept out there would be no crop. In hilling, the operator worked in a standing position, pushing the soil around each plant to a height of about eight inches for maize, a little less for teparies, kidney beans and pumpkins; the diameter of each worked hill was approximately twelve inches. Hilling was done during the first hoeing and did not constitute a separate job. However, when dirt in the hills began to dry after flooding and packed somewhat, it was customary to loosen the soil in each hill although the intervening ground was not hoed at this time. Informants said the reason for hilling was to keep soil from cracking, also it prevented dirt from drying out around the roots so quickly and aided in producing larger and better plants and crops. Maize was hilled higher than other crops to anchor it against wind and flood waters.

Like planting, cultivating was acknowledged as men's work although women might assist if they cared to; practically, it was a family enterprise and all able members of the family worked more or less together. A few families worked reciprocally in cultivating.

Thinning out of crops was never done; in fact, it was not necessary since the planter was always careful not to put more seeds in a hill than the number of plants desired, the ideal number per hill being three to five. It was well known that if plants were too thick in the hill they did not do well because of competition for food, water and space, and that corn, for example, under such conditions produced thin stalks with poor ears or none at all. Ends of pumpkin and melon vines were sometimes broken off to increase the production of fruits, but this was probably not an aboriginal practice.

Ceremonial copulation in the fields to increase their productivity was unknown.

CONTROL OF CROP PESTS

Young plants were not protected from animals and wind by branches from shrubs or trees as was done by some tribes. Pieces of cloth were sometimes placed on sticks and set up in the fields to scare birds away, and crude scarecrows were also made, although it is doubtful that this practice was aboriginal.

Anciently, as now, the Pimans were bothered by various pests. Grasshoppers at times caused considerable damage and one Papago informant had distinct remembrance of two different occasions when the grasshoppers completely destroyed his grandfather's tepary crop. Little was done by way of control other than an attempt to drive them out of the fields with weeds of various kinds attached to arrowweed branches and set afire, thus making considerable smoke. After the Pima began to grow wheat, the stubble was sometimes burned in an attempt to rid the fields of pests. Locusts were reported in 1897[65] as having eaten almost all the crops that had been

[65] *Report of the Commissioner of Indian Affairs* for 1897, p. 110.

planted at San Xavier. Squash bugs were fairly common but the only attempt at control was sprinkling ashes on the vines, probably not an aboriginal practice. Cut worms gave little trouble, so nothing was done about them. Rabbits usually came at night and caused some damage; at times the Pima attempted to drive them out of the fields with arrowweed fire-brands, but with indifferent success. Papago usually planted their chick peas and lentils in the middle of a wheat field to protect them against rabbits, otherwise these were damaged considerably. When corn began to come up, birds, especially blackbirds and doves, ate the young seedlings, so boys and girls were sent into the fields to drive them away, usually in the morning and evening. There was no watcher's stage. Children protected plants particularly when they were coming up and again when the crop was ripening. On the Gila, quail have caused considerable damage to pink beans by eating the blossoms, although the desert Papago were little bothered in this respect. Various birds ate the young pods of cowpeas. After the coming of the Spaniards, an interesting method of controlling birds that were especially annoying in digging out planted corn grains or seedlings was to tie one end of a horse hair to an earthworm, the other to a stick. When the bird swallowed the worm it found itself unable to escape, was captured and killed.

Pima and Papago native maize was, and still is, little troubled with corn smut. Rust on wheat and barley sometimes was observed; Pima informants knew it was not spread as the result of irrigation, but often became worse in rainy, cloudy periods. There was little remedy for this except to pull up badly infected plants or burn the stubble to prevent spreading. Rusty wheat was cleaned of much of its rust just before using by washing in watertight baskets. The grain was placed in the basket with water and rubbed by hand, the water being changed when dirty. This was woman's work. Aphis was an annoying pest on watermelons and muskmelons. Ants, too, did considerable damage to young wheat plants, particularly after irrigation. Gophers were said to like watermelon roots better than any other food. They were killed with bow and arrow.

Within recent times Johnson grass and Bermuda grass have become established in Pima fields and in those of the Papago at San Xavier, and have constituted a definite annoyance in cultivation.

Chili, which was rather immune to pests, was damaged chiefly by excess moisture which promoted fungal attack of the roots and bases of stems, and by the excessive heat of summer causing blossoms to drop off.

The various fungi attacking crops were regarded as natural agencies. Among neither people was there any ritual or ceremony for cultivation or ridding fields of pests.

CHAPTER VIII

HARVEST, STORAGE AND SEED SELECTION

TIME OF HARVEST

The time to harvest a crop was never determined by the position of the sun, moon or constellations, but by the condition of the crop itself. In other words, each family harvested its crop when ripe, and there was no set common harvest date as among the Pueblos.

Anciently the Pima had two general planting seasons (see section on *Time and Number of Plantings* in Chapter VII). The first sowing, from late March to mid-April, was harvested in late June, just before the sahuaro harvest; the second, made in July immediately after sahuaro harvest, was ripe in October. This is confirmed by Russell's[1] observation. In this connection Emory,[2] writing under date of November 11, 1846, asserts that all Pima crops had already been gathered.

The Papago made a single planting, after the rains began, which was usually in July, although at times delayed until August, and these crops were ready for harvest in October or early November. Among both peoples, introduced wheat and barley were planted from November to February and harvested in May or early June, while the commercial growing of cotton and other crops has resulted in extending the Pima harvest season until mid-November or even later.

There was no established or fixed sequence in harvesting the several crops. Usually, maize, being the major crop, was harvested first, followed by teparies then pumpkins, since a little frost was not considered harmful to them. Teparies could not remain in the field too long, due to the danger of

[1] Russell, *Pima*, p. 90.
[2] Emory, *Notes*, p. 83.

injury from rain. Cotton and gourds were usually gathered after all other crops had been taken in, although if corn were late in ripening it might be harvested last.

DIVISION OF LABOR

Planting, cultivating and irrigating Piman crops were regarded as men's work, in which women played a minor role. Quite the reverse was true with harvest, for it was regarded as essentially women's responsibility and men did only the heaviest of the labor, but both might work together in the field. However, with the introduction of wheat culture, some modification occurred, for the harvesting of wheat fell largely to the men, although assisted by women. Harvesting anciently was often done reciprocally, several families within a geographic area helping each other. To invite relatives to assist with harvest was regarded as favoring them. For their labor they were asked to help themselves to a share of the produce, but what they took was governed by what they considered they could repay in turn. When widows assisted, they were given a portion of the crop in payment.

* * *

MAIZE

Gathering, Roasting, Drying and Storing

The Papago planted a single crop of maize, which they harvested in October; the Pima grew two crops, the first maturing in late June, the second in October. In no case was there any difference in the types of corn grown at the two plantings, nor was there any difference in the purpose for which the two crops were used.

Corn was considered mature and ready to harvest when most of the stalks and husks were thoroughly dry. It was then time to begin even though some ears were still green. The variety of native corn that had been planted first would be ready to harvest first, regardless of color, for no one variety ripened more quickly than any other.

Anciently the Piman method of harvesting maize was to pull up the entire plant, or, in some cases, break it off at the ground, and throw it in piles, care being taken to keep separate the several colors of corn, since they had been planted in different plots; this was man's work. One reason for pulling up and removing the stalks was to have the field cleared for the next season. After Spanish contact, plants were sometimes cut off at the ground with an iron implement. Another historic development associated with turning stock into the field to eat the stalks was to husk the corn directly off the standing plant, the stalk being allowed to remain. The individual first ran a sharpened, hard stick of creosote bush or mesquite through the husk, then broke the ear out and threw it on a pile. In any event, harvesting was begun at a convenient place in the field, and did not proceed by designated direction as among some of the Pueblos. There was no ceremonial restriction against burning the husks, cobs or stalks. Cobs were used as fuel, particularly in cooking, and some stalks might be used in building the walls of a new structure. Saving purple husks to be used as a source of dye was unknown.

The plants were piled in one or more heaps, depending upon the size of the field, and women and older children usually gathered around the piles to remove unhusked ears from the stalks and throw them in piles. These ears were then carried to the dwelling in burden baskets (figured by Densmore[3]) by the women.

Although the Pimans husked some of their maize, particularly in selecting ears for seed, it was the common practice to partially roast their corn in unhusked ears by placing it in piles and covering with brush; this was set afire, green mesquite branches being used to stir and turn the ears, and, after several minutes of roasting, to throw them out on a bed of grass. During the roasting process much of the husk was burned away. These ears were dried on top of the house for

3 Densmore, *Papago Music*, pl. 10.

about ten days. Should rain come while the corn was drying, no special effort was made to protect it, as it was considered the corn would soon dry out uninjured, particularly if the ears were rearranged. One informant said the best way to determine whether corn was dry enough to be stored without molding was to test a few kernels by crushing with the teeth. Another said his method was to take a small handful of grains and shake them, the sound being an indicator of their dryness. Many of the Pima and Papago continue the roasting practice, and it is still not uncommon to find among both peoples storehouses in which partially roasted maize has been stored away unhusked. In some cases the process differed to the extent that the fire was made in an open pit and, when it had burned down, the ears were thrown on the embers to roast. It was considered that such partial roasting improved the keeping qualities and facilitated the grinding of corn.

A less frequent procedure, practiced mainly by the Papago, was to husk some of the ears and remove the grains, then parch and dry them on a sotol mat on the roof.

Shelling

Pima and Papago corn was regularly shelled before storing. After thoroughly drying, the unhusked, partially roasted corn might be shelled in any of three ways. The first, used with small quantities, was to remove a few grains at one end of the ear, then knock off the rest with the butt end of a cob. The second was to remove one or two rows of kernels the length of the ear with the aid of a stone scraper or a sharpened piece of creosote bush wood, then finish by twisting the ear with the hands. Finally, and most common, if one had a considerable amount of corn to be shelled it was placed on a sotol mat or cotton cloth and beaten with a club, then grains remaining on the ears were removed by hand. Unlike some of the Pueblos, there was no difference in the way seed and food corn were shelled. This was woman's acknowledged work in which the man seldom participated, and after corn was shelled it was woman's work alone to care for it. At present many of the Pima and Papago have mechanical shellers. Shelled corn was placed on a mat or cloth and again allowed to dry for two to three days. Grains were then winnowed in a large basket by tossing into the air to remove chaff. Or this might be done by tilting the basket about four feet above ground and allowing the kernels to fall gradually on a sotol mat or cotton cloth. Corn was always shelled before being stored, then was ground into meal as needed.

Storing Food Corn

Crops were never hidden by the Pima for protection from enemies. These Indians usually stored their corn, after shelling, in large cylindrical nest-like bins, or granaries, made of crudely coiled, thick bunches of arrowweed, which were very durable and lasted for years. They needed no base, since the roof or platform upon which they rested served this purpose, although a layer of arrowweed was spread on the spot where they were to stand. Over this granary was a low, cone-shaped roof of arrowweed extending beyond the rim, and covered with dirt. A cotton cloth was sometimes placed beneath the roof and over the contents of each bin. Varying considerably in size, the average bin was about eighteen inches tall by three feet in diameter. Their manufacture has been described in detail and figured by Kissell.[4]

These Pima granaries were usually placed on the roof, less commonly in groups on a platform of logs to keep them above the ground. Small sticks were placed across these logs and covered with arrowweed branches, which also served as a base for the bottomless bins. In post-Spanish times, groups of such granaries on a platform were enclosed by a low fence for protection against stock. In this connection, the reader is referred to Emory, Russell, Clark and Kissell.[5]

[4] Kissell, *Basketry of the Papago and Pima*, pp. 173-90.
[5] Russell, *op. cit.*, fig. 4; Clark, *Lessons from Southwestern Indian Agriculture*, fig. 12; Kissell, *op. cit.*, figs. 29, 30; Emory, *op. cit.*, p. 85.

Pima nest-shaped granaries were not used by the Papago. The very few storage baskets made by them were shaped like a hive, or a barrel, with incurving top, therefore of smaller diameter at the neck, and were about four feet in diameter and three high. The sides were usually crude coiling of twisted grass sewed together with mesquite bark, since arrow-weed is rarely to be found in their territory. These granaries usually were not placed on tops of buildings, but outdoors on stones or boards. Since, unlike the Pima granary, they had no roof, the opening was covered with an old flat basket or a broken olla. Being constantly exposed to the weather, Papago storage bins lasted only about two years.

However, Papago preferred to hide their food, and the usual expedient was to use jars rather than baskets. The most common jar was an old olla which had lost its porosity and no longer kept water cool. But special jars for storage purposes were made, as well as traded. The lid consisted of a piece of broken olla weighted with dirt or a stone.

Formerly the Papago also made temporary enclosures of sotol mats to store their grain.

A patriarchal Papago family stored its crops in several different places. A large supply was kept in the storehouse close to the village, while a few granary baskets might rest on stones near the dwelling, or, rarely, on the roof. A supplementary storage place was located in the flats not far from the base of the mountains, within easy reach of the winter camp. This was often a pit, deep enough to hold jars and baskets, and covered with brush or dirt. Here the baskets were protected with branches of the very spiny cholla, *Opuntia Bigelovii*. During their winter travels, the family sent a man back to the storehouse now and then to get food, but they tried to leave the supply at the village untouched until spring, the period of food scarcity, and it was not drawn upon until absolutely necessary.

A second type of Pima storage container was of coarse coil, used to store maize, beans, wheat, wild seeds etc., and was more carefully constructed than the arrowweed bin. The largest of these were globular in form among both peoples and might be as much as six feet tall and almost as wide. The smaller ones were rather bell-shaped among the Pima, and more or less barrel-shaped with the Papago. They were covered with a lid (usually the bottom of an old basket) and sealed with mud.[6]

After the introduction of wheat, the Pima made such baskets of a foundation of wheat straw bound together with strips of willow bark *(Salix nigra)*, mesquite or catclaw *(Acacia Greggii)*. Papago foundation elements were beargrass *(Nolina)*, ocotillo or wheat straw, the binding material of yucca or mesquite bark. This is the type of basket which Bartlett[7] observed among the Pima, and described as large vase-like baskets made of wheat straw ropes as thick as a man's arm, coiled into graceful forms and sewed together. He asserted that these held from ten to fifteen bushels and were filled with wheat and shelled corn. We have been unable to satisfy ourselves that this type of storage basket, figured and described by Russell[8] and Kissell,[9] is aboriginal. These were kept in a small storage house, never on roofs nor outdoors on platforms. This house is comparatively modern and of the same type as that described by Bartlett[10] in 1852. It was eight or nine feet high, rectangular in outline, with walls made of stakes of ocotillo or sahuaro ribs set close together, and provided with a dirt-covered roof. Although customarily left open for free circulation of air, at times they were covered with a layer of mud.

At present neither Pima nor Papago shell their corn to any great extent before storing. Much of it is simply thrown on top of an ocotillo *ramada* and dried without husking, then shelled as needed.

6 Kissell, *op. cit.*, pp. 179-85.
7 Bartlett, *Narrative*, II, 234-36.
8 Russell, *op. cit.*, pp. 88, 143-48.
9 Kissell, *loc. cit.*
10 Bartlett, *loc. cit.*

It was, of course, impossible to store different colors of corn separately, for cross pollination naturally resulted in considerable mixture. However, this was done to the limits of practicability and ears of similar colors were placed together in separate piles when husking.

Seed Selection

Informants had little knowledge of the hereditary background of crop plants. Both Pima and Papago thought good crops resulted from good culture and that good qualities did not reside "in the blood." These Indians were not interested in the "sports" for they were regarded as freaks. Selection of seed corn was done by women largely, since they were the ones who did whatever husking was done, although this was not their special prerogative. While husking, good ears were put to one side and saved, or, in some cases, ears for seed were selected out when husked ears were being shelled. In no case were ears selected from the plants while standing in the field. The chief criteria were well-developed, mature, plump, clean, large grains, and little attention was paid to size or shape of the ear, or whether the grains were in regular rows. Ears badly worm-eaten were never selected for seed. All grains on a good seed ear were planted, for it was believed the ones at tip and butt were as good as those in the middle. However, the practice has now been modified in that tip and butt grains are not used for seed. Care was always exercised to keep seed corn pure as to color, so it was always taken from ears of unmixed solid colors.

It was not considered advisable to use corn that was more than two years old for seed, as it would not germinate well. Fresh seed was always planted if possible; however, seed left over in any year might be saved for planting the next.

Storing Seed Corn

Even with considerable care, rats, mice and weevils sometimes got into maize stored in baskets. Hence, when shelled and dried seed corn was to be stored it was mixed with wood ashes and placed in ollas. Among the Pima, a cotton cloth was then placed over the top of the olla and sealed with mud made of saline soil, while the Papago usually sealed such ollas by applying mud mixed with grass to the improvised lid. All the seed placed in an olla was of a single color and type, and there was never any mixture. Seed corn was eaten only in case of emergency. No seed or food crop was ever stored in hides.

In some cases seed ears were braided together in clusters by means of their husks, hung outdoors until dried, then suspended from the ceiling in the house.

There was no storage ritual for either food or seed corn.

Utilization of Corn

Informants said blue corn was used mostly for parching, white regarded as best for pinole and yellow as most suitable for tortillas, although these categories were not always maintained. The Pimans utilized a good deal of green corn for food, but in no case was a special planting made for this purpose, such ears simply being removed from regular crops. Several informants said it took a little more than "two rounds of the moon" from time of planting to get good roasting ears —about nine to ten weeks. This conforms with our own observation that native Pima and Papago corns produce silks and tassels within fifty to sixty days after planting. One way of determining its suitability for this purpose was by the condition of the silk, selection being made before the silk became entirely dry; another by judging the hardness of grains through the husk. It was eaten in a variety of ways; for example, directly off the ear after roasting unhusked on the embers of a mesquite brush fire, or such roasted corn was dried, then the grains cut from the ear and stored in ollas or shallow baskets; sometimes the grains were scraped from the ear, placed inside several corn husks, wrapped and tied at the ends with shreds of husks, resembling a tamale, and boiled.

Paper bread was unknown to the Pimans. Corn pollen was never utilized, even ceremonially. One informant said that, as a boy, he used to see people putting ears heavily infested with corn smut on coals to roast, then taking off the smut and eating it without other preparation. The standard Pima meal consisted largely of cornmeal gruel.

PUMPKINS

Time of Harvest

As indicated earlier in this chapter, the Papago made one planting of pumpkins—when the rains began in July, and this was harvested in October; the Pima made two plantings—the first when mesquite began to leaf out in spring, the second immediately after sahuaro harvest in July. The first sowing was harvested in late June, the second in October. All their varieties of pumpkins were sowed at the first planting, only cushaws in the second. Piman pumpkins were usually harvested after maize and teparies had been put away, for many were still unripe at the maize harvest. Color of the fruit indicated whether they were mature enough to be gathered, the cushaw type usually ripening first, the cheese pumpkin last. It was known that light frosts would do them no damage, so it was not necessary to bring them in before that time.

Method of Harvest

Anciently it was woman's work to gather the pumpkins. Varieties were sorted into separate piles in the field to avoid a second handling, then carried to the house in a burden basket. Neither Papago nor Pima left a portion of the vine attached to the fruit, as was done by some tribes, but in severing pumpkins from the vines care was taken not to break the fruit stalk away from the pumpkin itself, otherwise it would rot readily.

Storing

The average family had a crop of sixty to one hundred pumpkins, which were stored immediately after gathering.

They might be placed in a pile outdoors and covered with corn stalks, particularly if the crop were large, but more commonly were piled up in the storehouse with or without a covering of corn stalks. They could be kept at least until February, and in some cases as late as April. Cheese pumpkins kept best and longest, while the cushaws were recognized as poor keepers. If a pumpkin was seen to be rotting in storage it was sliced, then dried, in the manner described below for storing dried pumpkins; if disintegrated, it was discarded.

Anciently, each Pima home was provided with a single storehouse, generally an oval pit about eight feet long and two feet deep, covered by a gable roof of willow branches thatched with arrowweed. A forked pole of mesquite was set at each end of the oval and a beam placed lengthwise of the pit set in the forks of the poles. Willow branches were stuck into the ground along the brink of the pit and leaned against the beam. This storage house was used for pumpkins and, in historic times, watermelons and the like. It was practically identical with that described in detail by Spier[11] for the Maricopa. The same structure, with modifications, is still to be seen among the Pima. It is a cubical pit about three feet deep and as wide and long as required for the supply, now used exclusively for storing pumpkins. The floor of the pit is a layer of poles or logs covered with corn stalks on which the pumpkins are piled. In each corner is an erect forked pole, with cross beams of sahuaro ribs, and a rough arrowweed or cornstalk roof, and finally the whole covered with dirt.

Utilization of Pumpkins

When frost came, many pumpkins were still unripe and in various stages of development. These, particularly the cushaw type, were never discarded, but the skin removed by scraping, the flesh cut into pieces, cooked, usually with mesquite beans, and eaten immediately. At times, small immature pumpkins were gathered during summer and cooked

11 Spier, *Yuman Tribes*, pp. 89-90.

as a green vegetable, either whole or in pieces. Often they were cooked with rabbit meat. Immature pumpkins were also sliced thin and dried, and were said to be like fresh slices when soaked in warm water; these were boiled and eaten. Informants stated the first small green fruit was ready for use within five weeks after planting.

Ripe pumpkins, chiefly cushaws, were stored, then utilized throughout the winter as needed. They were simply cut into two-inch cubes and cooked in an olla, sometimes with mesquite beans, until soft and mushy, or into large pieces and roasted. The cheese pumpkin was regarded as having the best flavor of all Piman varieties, but the cushaw was the only one used to any great extent without drying.

The customary method of drying ripe cheese pumpkins for winter use was to remove the seed through an opening made by cutting out the fruit stalk. After peeling, the pumpkin was allowed to dry for about two days in the sun, then cut into one or more spiral strips about an inch wide, and hung on poles, or laid on top of the house in the sun for about six days. These were twisted into hanks, dried thoroughly and stored in baskets or ollas. When needed they were broken into pieces and boiled, usually with cornmeal.

Soft-shelled pumpkins were best for making strips and drying, and the cheese pumpkin therefore was regarded as most desirable for this purpose. Hard-shelled varieties, chiefly the cushaws, were best for roasting and were the only ones used to any great extent in this way; their only variety of *Cucurbita Pepo* was regarded as good for roasting but not for drying in strips, and for this reason was not more extensively grown. Pumpkins were roasted by burying the halves in the hot ashes of a corncob fire, a whole day being required.

Pima informants said that, at times, the flesh was scooped out of a greenish black variety of cushaw and the hard shell used as a storage container.

Pumpkin flowers also were eaten by both Papago and Pima, but usually only the male flowers since they did not develop into fruits. A quantity was gathered early in the morning and, after removing the calyx, dried in the sun on a mat or cotton cloth for about three days, then stored in a sealed olla. When used they were cooked with mesquite beans. At times, they were mixed with cornmeal and boiled, the mixture spread out on grass or a cloth to dry for about three days, and stored in ollas. This was again boiled when utilized. Twisted flowers, after removal of the green calyx, were also boiled and eaten with pinole.

Papago and Pima regarded pumpkin seeds as a delicacy. These were parched by placing in a piece of olla with live coals, stirring until done, and eaten much as we eat peanuts; or at times these seeds were parched with corn.

Seed Selection

Pumpkin seed was selected in a general way (by either the man or woman) by simply taking those from the largest pumpkins, size being the most important criterion. Or, if a pumpkin proved to be especially sweet, the seed was saved. This was placed in a small olla with others of the same variety and, when sowing time came, a quantity was taken from the olla and planted without culling out individual seeds.

TEPARIES AND COMMON PINK BEANS

Time of Harvest

The Papago made only one planting of teparies—in July, and harvested in October. The Pima made two; their first planting, as mentioned earlier in this chapter, was made when mesquite began to leaf out, the second soon after sahuaro harvest. The first was mature in late June, the second in October.

Informants said if maize and teparies were planted at the same time the maize would be ready to harvest before the teparies, which required a minimum of ten weeks under favorable moisture conditions. They invariably matured less quickly than pink beans. However, they were not allowed to remain long in the field after ripening, due to possible damage by rain.

Method of Harvesting and Storing

The entire process of harvesting teparies and kidney beans, from pulling the vines out of the ground to sealing the seeds in ollas for storage, was regarded as women's work, although men might help if not otherwise engaged.

Brown and white teparies and pink beans were planted in separate plots and harvested separately. The plants were grasped just above the ground line, pulled up, roots and all, and placed in piles. They were then taken to the threshing floor and allowed to dry for from three to six days. The threshing floor was prepared either in the field or near the house by removing weeds from a designated area, then leveling. After it was swept clean it was hardened by tamping with the feet; if dry the soil was first moistened. All tepary vines of one variety, or the pink bean vines, were placed on this threshing ground in a pile and beaten with a pole (five or six feet long and about one and one-half inches thick) so as to knock the ripe pods off the vines. Vines were removed to one side of the floor and allowed to remain for several days to permit drying of pods not fully mature, then beaten a second time.

Pods were placed in small piles on a mat or cloth and beaten with a short stick, about two feet long, to release seeds from the hulls. Many hulls were blown out by the wind, and most of the remaining ones scraped away with the fingers. Final winnowing was done at the threshing floor by allowing the beans to fall gradually from a large shallow basket, held about four feet in the air, to a sotol mat or cotton cloth, most of the chaff meanwhile blowing away with the wind.

Pink beans were harvested in the same manner as teparies. They were said to be ripe when "the moon had gone around twice" after planting. At the home of informant

Gerónimo we observed his wife threshing pink beans in the field on a floor thirty-five feet in diameter. This floor was hard and somewhat depressed because of continued use over a period of years, and there was a pole in the middle to which horses were tied at the time of wheat threshing. Several piles of pink bean, as well as of tepary, vines were on the floor. She sat in front of one of the piles of pink bean vines and flailed it heartily with a stick about five feet long and one and one-half inches thick. After beating for a time she removed some of the vines, then beat again, and finally removed all vines from the pile to the edge of the floor. These vines, even after heavy beating, retained some immature pods, and were dried further before receiving a final threshing. Before she had finished her work for the day it began to rain, so the beans and pods were carried in flat baskets and cotton cloths into the house, the vines being left on the threshing floor.

Both winnowed teparies and pink beans were laid in the sun on a mat or cotton cloth for several days to dry fully, after which, among the Pima, they were stored in close-coiled baskets in the manner described for corn, or in ollas sealed with saline soil. All beans, regardless of kind, were sealed to protect them from mice, etc. Among the Papago, such baskets or ollas were covered with an old flat basket, or a piece of broken olla shaped to conform roughly to the opening, and sealed over with mud mixed with crushed mescal stalks or grass. Both peoples segregated, and stored in separate baskets or ollas, the different colors of tepary (usually only white and brown were grown) , as well as common pink beans.

Yield

Teparies are very drought resistant, although they respond well to additional moisture. In periods of drought they often produce a good crop while common pink beans, or *frijoles,* under the same conditions, are a total failure. Teparies are also much more resistant to insect attacks than are pink beans. That they bear a considerably larger number of pods than do *frijoles* is reported by Freeman,[12] whose experiments showed teparies yielded 450 to 700 pounds per acre by dry farming, compared with 800 to 1500 pounds when grown under irrigation; also that under all conditions teparies outyielded *frijoles* often as much as four to one. There was no difference in the yield of different kinds of teparies.

Utilization

Dry teparies were customarily cooked by themselves and eaten, or cooked with roasted corn. Pink beans were not considered good unless cooked with meat, preferably fat, and, since this was not always available, their use was somewhat limited. Formerly, in times of food scarcity, women would go out into the field prior to the general harvest and gather such teparies as had already matured, but these were never cooked as green beans (i.e., both pods and seeds). *Frijoles* were usually gathered only when ripe, then dried and stored, but on occasions of need were picked in the pod before ripe, and boiled.

All Pimans seem to prefer the taste and quality of the white tepary to that of the brown. However, there is a great deal of variability among individuals as regards preference between teparies and pink beans. There is little difference in the nutritive value of the two, although the tepary markedly surpasses the latter in rate and degree of swelling and of absorptive power when soaked in water; also the seed coat of the pink bean is heavier than that of the tepary.

Anciently there was little use for tepary and pink bean vines, although if building a house a person might place some on the roof and cover with dirt. Hulls were never utilized. At present the vines and hulls serve as fodder for cattle and horses.

[12] Freeman, *Southwestern Beans and Teparies.*

Seed Selection

There was no seed selection of teparies or pink beans. Seed to be planted was simply taken out of the general stored supply at planting time.

COWPEAS (BLACK-EYED BEANS) AND LIMA BEANS

With the coming of the Spaniards, cowpeas, which, despite their name, are more closely related to the beans than peas, were introduced among the Pimans. Planted by the Papago in July, and by the Pima in late March or early April and in some cases again after sahuaro harvest in July, the pods were harvested progressively as they ripened, since plants would grow indefinitely as long as weather conditions permitted, although quite susceptible to frost. Informants said one could begin picking the long pods about eight weeks after planting, those near the base ripening first. At the time of general harvest, the pods remaining on vines were still somewhat green, so the vines were piled and allowed to dry for a week or more before being threshed. Threshing was done by beating with a stick or, if the quantity were small, by hand.

Like black-eyed beans, the single sowing of lima beans (made by the Pima in late March or early April and by the Papago in July) was harvested progressively throughout the growing season as the pods ripened, and the growth of plants was terminated only by frost or lack of moisture. Among the Pima, whenever plants began to fall off in production of pods they were irrigated, whereupon a new crop began to set. The first pods were ready to pick when mesquite beans were fully ripe. Although limas stand drought well, their yield is closely associated with the amount of water they receive, hence, at present they are more extensively grown in the Pima than in the Papago country. Usually women picked the pods and shelled them by hand. However, when families grew a considerable quantity they were placed on the ground on a large cotton cloth and trampled out by foot. The empty pods were then removed by hand and seeds winnowed to remove chaff. The Pima now plant limas in June or July and they yield better if not irrigated too heavily.

Limas and black-eyed beans were usually planted in smaller amounts than teparies and pink beans, hence the quantity of seeds secured at any one picking was small.

As with teparies and pink beans, the harvesting of limas and black-eyed beans was accepted as woman's work.

Seed Selection

There was practically no selection of seed for limas or cowpeas, and seed to be planted was simply taken out of the general supply with no discrimination other than discarding shriveled ones. Informants said one never got poor seed of these crops unless it was immature as the result of injury by early frost. The only precaution was to use fresh seed, for it was known that these beans lost viability rather quickly.

CHICK PEAS AND LENTILS

Both chick peas and lentils were recognized by the Pimans as introduced crops. Pima and Papago grew chick peas, or *garbanzos,* to only a small extent, and lentils even less, although both were regarded as very nutritious. The chick pea is well adapted to arid and semi-arid regions and matures in about ninety days. Both Pima and Papago made a single planting, sowing them as a winter crop from November first to February and harvesting in April or May, consequently they required little moisture. It has been reported that *garbanzos* will endure a temperature of 13° F. without being injured. People began to harvest chick peas when mesquite beans were about ripe, and picked them progressively. The first pods to ripen were simply rubbed by hand. When the plants began to dry up, tops were cut off with a sickle or pulled up, piled and dried for a few days, then threshed by beating with a stick or trampling. They were then winnowed, dried further and stored in a sealed large gourd or olla. On good soil a yield of one thousand pounds of chick peas per acre was not unusual.

Pima and Papago planted lentils as early as February, and they were ready to harvest in April or early May. Pima frequently made two plantings of lentils, the Papago but one; this second sowing was after sahuaro harvest. Like chick peas, they were fairly drought resistant. Lentils were harvested and stored in the same manner as teparies, and were reported as returning a yield of tenfold.

COTTON

Time of Harvest

Both Pima and Papago anciently made a single planting of cotton. Among the Pima this was done from late March to mid-April; the Papago planting was made as soon as the summer rains began, usually in July but at times later. Cotton took at least eleven weeks to mature but need not be picked until all other crops were out of the way, usually in late October or early November.

Method of Harvest and Storage

Anciently it was customary for the Pimans to gather their cotton and pile it in the boll on tops of houses, sheds or *ramadas* for drying. In this connection Emory[13] wrote, under date of November 11, 1846, that "The cotton has been picked, and stacked for drying on the tops of sheds." More recently, in harvesting Pima cotton, two ends of a cotton cloth have been tied over the shoulder, the cloth thus hanging at one side of the body constituting a sort of sack, and in this the bolls were placed as they were picked. They were then taken to the house and spread out on a cloth on the floor in one corner of a room. Only if the season were getting late and frost might kill plants were the stalks removed before bolls matured. Stalks were broken or cut off at ground level then placed on top of the house or a shed and the bolls allowed to

13 Emory, *Notes*, p. 83.

ripen before being picked. Of course, at present, with the commercial growing of cotton, Pima pick the cotton from the open bolls directly off the plants in the field.

Cotton seed was stored in sealed ollas in exactly the same manner as were teparies. There was no selection; seed for planting was simply taken from the general supply stored for food.

Utilization of Cotton

Cotton was grown for both lint and seeds. The lint was used for cordage, cloth, garments and tinder. Tinder was prepared from a cotton rope about one-half inch thick, several inches long and frayed at one end, used especially for lighting cigarettes. Sparks made by pounding two pieces of flint together ignited the fiber. Its use as tinder may be a Spanish introduction.

Cotton seed was parched and eaten much like we use pop corn. The seeds were placed in an olla with embers of mesquite wood on top. The olla was continually shaken and the live coals soon parched the seed. Another way of utilizing the seed was in combination with mesquite or cornmeal. Mesquite pods were pounded fine with a wooden mortar and pestle, seeds removed, and the flour mixed with that secured by pounding parched cotton seeds in a mortar. The two were then mixed and molded into a sort of cake-like tortilla, baked in ashes and eaten. A combination of cotton meal and cornmeal was utilized in the same way. Informants said either mixture tasted like, and had the texture of, tallow. From the pounded seeds Papago and Pima made a kind of bread which was baked in hot ashes. At times, water was added to pounded cottonseed meal, strained, and the liquid used as seasoning in cooking. The strained meal residue was sucked in order to remove the nutriment, and the pulp discarded.

Papago informants stated cotton was used ceremonially on their prayer sticks to symbolize clouds, and thereby invite rain. Pimas preferred eagle down for this purpose.

Ginning, Plucking, Spinning and Weaving

It was woman's work to gather cotton, but weaving was an old man's art although women might help at times. Weaving of cotton was a practice common to both Pima and Papago.

One method of ginning cotton was to turn upside down a thick pottery vessel about fifteen inches in diameter made specifically for the purpose. A mat of cotton bolls was stretched over the bottom of the vessel and a smooth arrow-weed stick (about eighteen inches long and three-fourths of an inch wide), from which the bark had been peeled, was rolled over the cotton, working the seeds out of the lint and toward the edge of the mat, where they dropped over the side of the bowl. This was continued until all seeds were removed.

After ginning, the cotton was spread on a cleaned smooth spot on the ground and plucked with the plucking bow in the same manner as that described by Spier[14] for the Maricopa. This was a scraped stick of arrowweed two to three inches long, strung taut to form a small bow. The bowstring was held close to a mat of cotton and plucked, the string thereby catching up the cotton fibers which were wrapped into a tight roll around the string due to its vibration. When pulled off the string, it was rolled into a loose yarn on the thigh, and was then ready for spinning. One Pima informant insisted that ginning was also done with the plucking bow, the fiber gradually being plucked away, leaving the seeds. In all probability the plucking bow was not aboriginal among these Indians.

Spinning was done by women on a simple spindle, and this process was described by Emory[15] in 1846. Although weaving was not highly developed among the Pimans, it was done on a loom, by old men, in a manner described for the Pima in 1852 by Bartlett. Such a loom, as well as a spindle, is figured and described by Russell.[16]

14 Spier, *Yuman Tribes*, p. 113.
15 Emory, *op. cit.*, p. 85.
16 Bartlett, *Narrative*, II, 255; Russell, *Pima*, p. 148-51.

Dyeing

Cotton was dyed buff by dipping in a dark buff ocher high in ferric oxide, but this was used only for the selvage thread. Cotton fiber dipped into a decoction made from the roots of curly dock *(Rumex crispus)*, an introduced species, as well as other species of this genus, took on a yellow color, and these roots were said to yield a darker color when the plant was in flower. Informants said roots of the native *cañaigre (Rumex hymenosepalus)*, from which all dirt had been removed, were crushed, then boiled to yield a yellowish dye solution for cotton. Fresh mesquite gum was boiled with this dye to make it fast.

GOURDS

Time and Method of Harvest and Storage

Pima and Papago made a single planting of gourds. Ordinarily it was man's task to plant, but woman's to cultivate, carry water for them if necessary and harvest gourds when ripe, although men might assist in any of these stages. This single planting was made by both peoples—by the Pima in late March or early April, the Papago in July. A little more than three months was required for them to ripen.

Gourds were all gathered at once rather than progressively, and this while the plants were still green. Women gathered and carried them to the dwelling in a burden basket or cloth, cutting each one off the vine with a sharp stone. Care had to be exercised in handling them until dried lest they become bruised. When harvested, they were laid away to dry throughly before being prepared for use, usually being placed in a pile and covered with weeds or grass. They were selected by shape according to the purpose for which they were to be utilized.

There was no selection of seed from specific shapes of gourd to propagate particular types, although formerly it was customary to bind a piece of bark or cloth around them while growing in order to secure certain shapes.

Preparation for Use as Vessels and Rattles

Gourds were prepared for use as follows: First they were dried thoroughly, otherwise decay would occur in the process of preparation. The bitterness was drawn out by filling with water through an opening cut at the stem end, then allowing it to stand for three days so that the fleshy interior might decay. Most of the pulp was removed by working with a stick, then the gourd refilled and again allowed to stand for three days, after which as much of the remaining pulp as possible was scraped out. This process was repeated as often as necessary, or until the vessel ceased to impart any taste of bitterness to the water allowed to stand in it. Finally, the vessel was thoroughly rinsed with water several times and was ready for use.

Sometimes gourds which had been prepared as above were baked in live embers for two or three days to harden the shell, as this made them more durable when used as containers. It also gave them a glossy appearance since the outer surface peeled off.

Gourds or their seeds were never eaten. They were used for canteens, dippers, containers, storage vessels, ceremonial rattles and masks. For storing seeds, the hole made at the end of the neck was plugged with a stick. To prepare a gourd for use as a rattle the end of the neck was cut off, then cleaned as described above, and the gourd partly filled with pebbles taken from an ant hill. A wooden handle was fitted into the opening and secured with the gummy secretion of creosote bush or arrowweed. Gourds to be used as dippers or dishes were cut lengthwise by making a continuous row of holes with an awl the whole length of the fruit, then snapping it in two.

DEVIL'S CLAW

A single sowing of Devil's claw, or unicorn plant *(Martynia louisiana),* was made by both Papago and Pima, after sahuaro harvest, and the pods gathered before frost. This was woman's work, as was the cultivation and harvesting. Plants were quite drought resistant.

Only the white-seeded form was grown, as its pods had longer, finer-grained and deeper black strips of epidermal tissue, and therefore more suitable for use in basketry. They were planted in hills about six feet apart with four or five seeds to the hill, in holes about six inches deep, although the seeds were covered to a depth of only two inches.

Pods were gathered as they matured, about the time maize was ripening, but all must be gathered before frost to prevent the black color of the pod from fading. Fruits were ready to harvest when the dry epidermis peeled off readily. The ripe pods were gathered and laid out in piles in the field to dry, and informants said they had seen their mothers spread wood ashes over such piles. When thoroughly dry the pods were hooked together to form large clumps or balls, and stored in a rain-proof building, since weathering affected their color.

Before removing the strips of epidermis for use in basketry, the pods were buried in moistened ground over night to facilitate the stripping. However, more recently some merely plunge the pods in boiling water to aid in removing this tissue. These strips were tied in bundles and stored in baskets or ollas. The process of preparing and utilizing *Martynia* in basketry has been discussed in detail by Kissell.[17]

Seeds of the unicorn plant were sometimes eaten but were of little importance as food. They were removed from the pods at the time the strands of epidermis were stripped, and were dried and stored in a small sealed olla.

WHEAT

Time of Harvest

Pima and Papago planted wheat any time from November to February, and harvested in May or early June. However, late sowings usually produced small plants and a poor yield.

17 Kissell, *Basketry of the Papago and Pima*, p. 202.

Informants said the best crop was obtained when planted about the first of January, as there was then little danger from frost injury when plants were coming into head in April. However, at the Sacaton Experiment Station, November plantings of the principal varieties of wheat for twenty-two years usually have given higher yields than later plantings, and in only two seasons did they suffer any freezing damage after heading. At present it is customary for the Pima to turn cattle into the fields to pasture on the green wheat plants, then irrigate in January, after which the wheat tillers well (puts forth new shoots around the base of the original stalk) and is ready to harvest about the last week in May. Barley can be pastured three or four times and still give a crop, wheat only once, so it is considered superior to wheat for this purpose. Both are first pastured when about a foot high. Pima like to plant their barley in late October and harvest in late May, as there is little danger of frost damage to this crop.

As indicated in an earlier chapter, until recent years large numbers of Papago visited the Gila Pima to take part in the wheat harvest, and the Pima paid them for their labor in wheat. Informants reported that some Pimas became so dependent on the Papago harvest help that the wheat crop would shatter from overripeness if their special Papago families were late in arriving or failed to come at all.

Method of Harvest

Harvesting wheat was usually done by both men and women working together, and reciprocal help at wheat harvest was formerly quite common. If a relative or friend assisted in planting he was given only his meals during the period of his labor, but if he helped with harvest he was invariably given a share of the crop. Since the same spot was used for threshing year after year, the threshing floor was repaired before cutting the crop. For such a floor, a low dike was thrown around an area about thirty-five feet in diameter which did not flood in time of heavy rain and where the soil would cake. All weeds were removed and the ground flooded, or at least moistened, and allowed to dry out until hard enough to support the weight of a man without making depressions in the soil. It was then tamped by foot, or, in later days, with poles four feet high and about four inches thick at the base, or blocks of wood each bearing a handle. A stout pole ten to fifteen feet tall was erected in the center of the prepared area. Among the Papago the threshing floor belonged to the patriarchal family in common.

When wheat was first grown, in early Spanish days, the plants were pulled out by the roots in harvesting; later they were cut off just above the ground with a knife made of ironwood, or with a sickle. This was ordinarily done by both men and women.

Formerly wheat was not sowed as thickly as at present. While this held for the days when it was planted in hills and later in rows, it also applied to broadcast sowing, hence the crop was not as large per given area as at present. There was no selection of seed wheat. Grain to be planted was simply taken out of the general supply used for food.

Threshing

Regardless of how wheat was harvested, it was placed in small piles to be gathered up, usually by women, and carried —formerly in burden baskets, later in a cotton cloth or on their heads—to the threshing floor. At present these piles are gathered and hauled by wagon. Formerly there was no central pole and the wheat was placed on the floor in small piles, allowed to dry several days; then women trampled the grain by foot or threshed it with ocotillo poles, about five feet long and one and one-half inches thick, first beating each pile, then removing the coarser straw, and flailing again. More recently, the wheat has been piled on the threshing floor and leveled. Then three or four horses were tied abreast, with the inside animal tied to the pole by a long rope. A person mounted on another horse, or at times afoot, drove the animals around and over the wheat continuously for seven or eight hours, thus trampling out the grain. One man kept the wheat raked evenly over the floor.

When the task of threshing had been completed, a certain amount of winnowing was done by throwing the straw into the air, formerly by hand, then with improvised forks, and later with steel ones. Women, on their hands and knees, used branches of creosote bush for brushing up, gathering and carrying the coarse straw from the floor. Formerly most of this was burned although a small amount of the straw was saved for making baskets, etc. Small amounts of wheat, too green to be included in the general threshing, were put to one side, allowed to dry further, and flailed later.

Winnowing and Storing

Women then gathered the remaining grain and chaff into shallow winnowing baskets, about three feet across, held them at arm's length in the air and allowed the contents to fall gradually to the ground, the wind meanwhile blowing away the chaff. The grain was then placed in cotton cloths (later in sacks) and carried to the house for further winnowing on some windy day by dropping it from shallow baskets on to sotol mats or cotton cloths. The wheat was finally dried on these mats in the sun for two or three days, remaining bits of straw picked out by hand, then stored in baskets three or four feet high, usually made of grass after the fashion described under the storing of maize. The average Papago family had a crop of about two bushels.

Utilization of Wheat

When flour was needed the grain was pounded in a wooden mortar with a stone pestle, after being softened with a little water. At present, the grain, before being ground into flour on the metate, is dried thoroughly in the sun, then shaken in a basket until the hulls are blown away.

Papago informants said often in earlier days food was

scarce when May came around, and it was common to gather matured heads of wheat, beat out the grains and eat them before the general harvesting was begun.

WATERMELONS AND MUSKMELONS

Time and Method of Harvest

The Pimans were very fond of watermelons, moderately so of muskmelons. The Pima usually made two plantings of both, the first ready for harvesting in late June, the second in October, although muskmelons were a little later in maturing than were watermelons. The single Papago planting ripened in October. Watermelons were tested for ripeness by their sound when thumped; also they were considered mature when the tendril on the stem of the melon dried and curled up. However, they often were eaten before completely ripe. Ripening of muskmelons was determined by their odor and resistance to pressure. Pima informants said when the first planting of watermelons had matured the fruit was picked, then the vines irrigated and in about six weeks there was a second, although smaller, crop.

Either men or women picked the melons when harvesting, and put them in a pile. A few melons at a time were placed on a mat or cotton cloth laid on the ground, and carried to the house or storage pit, this usually being done by the men.

Storage

The Pimans stored a goodly supply of watermelons for winter use, but did not bury them in sand as did the lower Colorado River tribes, although informants had heard of the Yuma and Maricopa doing so. Formerly they were stored in the oval pit with gable roof as described under "Storage of Pumpkins," but more recently Pimans have used a cubical underground pit about four feet in each dimension, slanting inward at the bottom on all sides and built on a hill if possible. Poles were placed on the bottom of the pit and covered with cornstalks, on which were placed alternate

layers of wheat straw or bean vines, and watermelons. Sides
of the pit were not lined. For a roof, poles were laid across
the opening and a layer of arrowweed covered with dirt over
all. Earth at one end of the pit was dug away to allow a
vertical entrance about three feet high, which was covered
with a framework of slender poles. Watermelons thus stored
kept well for as much as three to four months. Informants
said they kept better if a six-inch section of the vine was left
attached to the fruit at the time of picking.

Watermelon and muskmelon seed for planting was always
selected on the basis of size and quality of fruits, thus from
the largest and sweetest specimens.

Utilization

Fruits when ripe, particularly watermelons, were commonly eaten fresh in great quantities, although at times
preserves were made from the rind by cooking without
sweetening. Watermelons were never dried. Muskmelons
did not store well so had to be eaten relatively soon after
maturity, or dried for future use.

The method for drying muskmelons was similar to that
described for pumpkins, except that the melon was peeled
and cut lengthwise, the soft pulp and seeds scraped away.
Only thoroughly ripened fruits were used in this manner.
The short straight strips were then dried on top of the house
or *ramada* for several days, or until they could be worked
well. A number of strips were placed side by side and tied
into bundles, dried further on a shed, twisted into hanks and
stored in baskets, or in ollas with a cloth over the contents,
covered with a piece of broken olla, then sealed with mud.
In spring they were eaten dry without boiling or preparation
of any kind unless they had become quite hard, in which case
they were boiled and eaten with pinole. At times the dried
melon was toasted over a fire to soften, then eaten by alter-
nately taking pieces of melon and drinking pinole. This
practice is very rare today. Unlike pumpkins, such dried

melons did not constitute a staple but were considered more of a delicacy, being sweet and very palatable.

CHILI

Chili *(Capsicum annuum)* is an introduced crop among the Pimans and is recognized by them as such, but its cultivation was not taken over nearly as extensively as among the Pueblo Indians, for example; only a few of the Pimas grew it and even at present it is not cultivated to any extent, for most of them purchase their supply. The chief variety grown today is Anaheim. Chili is grown by the Papago only in very favorable places, since it requires a more reliable source of water than is ordinarily found in Papago territory. These people continue to depend upon the wild *chiltepiquin* (see Chapter IV).

Pima made a single planting of chili, and this when mesquite began to leaf out in late March or early April. It was sowed in small vegetable gardens and harvested in early November. The ripe pods were pulled off by hand and the green ones allowed to remain if weather conditions indicated they might still ripen. However, if frost were indicated, the plants were cut off at the base and piled in the field, and many of the green pods would ripen there. Green fruits were often roasted, then peeled and eaten. At times these dried roasted fruits were stored in sealed ollas and when utilized were steeped in hot water to soften. Those that had not dried readily were tied into strings and hung outdoors, then stored in ollas when dry. Another way of preparing the unripe fruits was to roast and peel them, then pound in a mortar and shape into a large cake, which was dried for future use. When needed, a piece of the mass was broken off and utilized as seasoning.

Ripe fruits were spread on a cotton cloth on the ground or on a layer of sticks and allowed to dry for four or five days, being stirred occasionally to facilitate the process. When fully dry they were placed in a basket or olla, a cloth placed over them, and the lid of the container sealed with mud.

Men looked after the growing of chili, but it was women's task to harvest, dry and store it.

There was practically no seed selection for chili—it was simply removed from ripe pods and stored. Seed for planting was never taken from the unripe pods.

CHAPTER IX

CULTIVATION AND UTILIZATION OF TOBACCO —A CEREMONIAL CROP[1]

The growing of tobacco must be looked upon as ceremonial agriculture, and the smoking of it as an essentially ceremonial practice. It is, therefore, impossible to understand the cultivation of tobacco without taking this ritualistic aspect into consideration, and for this reason it is here considered apart from the growing of other crops.

Among both Papago and Pima, tobacco was regularly grown only by old, rather than young, men although any man had the presumptive right to grow it if he knew its culture and the song. There were two reasons for this limitation to old men—first, a man ordinarily had to be fully grown before he could use tobacco, second, having less to do, the old men had time to grow it.

THE TRADITIONAL ORIGIN OF TOBACCO

Bernabé López[2] gave the following account of the origin of tobacco:

There was once an old woman who had a grandson and she told him that when she died he should take her out where the ground was soft, fertile, and where the water came down, and bury her, but not to let anyone see where he had buried her. He should then go back to the burial spot at the end of four days and he would see a small plant coming up on her grave. This he did, and again visited the spot at the end of another four days and found the plant had grown to a nice

---

[1] For the botanical aspects of Piman tobacco see Chaper IV.

[2] Bernabé López pointed out that his account of the origin, cultivation and smoking of tobacco applied to San Pedro and Coyote Papago villages, and that if we should get accounts from informants at other villages these would be slightly different in certain respects. Informants in general agreed that such inter-village differences existed.

large one. He broke off one leaf and made a cigarette, which he smoked, and thought his mind was clearer after smoking it.

López said tobacco is like a person. After people had used it for a long time, some of them said it was no good, so Tobacco became angry and disappeared, hence people could no longer smoke. She went to the west and the people did not know just where she had gone but they began looking everywhere and finally a man found her. He came back and told the people about it, then went back and tried to persuade her to return. She refused, but did give him one seed pod of tobacco, which he brought back and planted, thus starting it again, and it turned out to be the same kind of tobacco that had originally come up where the old woman was buried, namely "under-the-creosote-bush tobacco" *(N. Tabacum)*. (Another informant said tobacco was not a woman but a man.)

This account of the origin of tobacco is essentially the same as that given by other Papago and Pima informants. Russell's brief account of the myth, as well as that of Densmore,[3] is similar in essence.

PRACTICAL ASPECTS OF TOBACCO CULTIVATION

The Papago always planted their tobacco in a desert wash where the soil was silty, never among other crops in their fields, and took very good care of it. The patch might vary in size from eight feet to eight yards square, and this held true for the Pima as well. The Papago method in some villages was to dig ten to twelve holes, each about eighteen inches in diameter and eight inches deep, place seed in the holes and cover with about one-half inch of soil, leaving a depression. (In one village it was customary to fill the holes with fine silt sifted through the hands.) Only two seeds (one informant said four) were placed in each hole, as otherwise the plants became too crowded and produced small leaves. In the village of one informant it was customary to loosen

---

[3] Russell, *Pima*, pp. 224, 248; Densmore, *Papago Music*, pp. 29-30.

the soil of the entire plot with a planting stick, after which the tobacco seed was placed on the palm of the hand and blown over the plot, and the seed then covered by brushing the ground with a branch of creosote bush.

Among the Pima, tobacco was always grown on irrigated land just like any other crop, preferably in sandy loam, never in saline soil as it would not do well. The ground was first loosened with the digging stick, then leveled. Tobacco seed was planted by an old Pima man holding it in the palm of his hand, placing the tongue in contact with a portion and more or less spitting or blowing it over the soil. Another man followed and covered the seed by brushing the soil with a branch of saltbush *(Atriplex)*.

The Papago said that, unlike other crops, tobacco was planted "in the month when the weather begins to warm up," or late March to early April in our calendar; the Pima planted it when the mesquite trees began to leaf, which corresponded with late March to late April. Both tribes made but one planting. Germination was said to require four days (undoubtedly a reflection of their ritual number of four).

Pima tobacco was irrigated from a ditch like other crops; holes at each corner of the field, and a brush barrier at the point where the ditch entered the field, trapped any debris brought in by the water. Papago plants, however, were never artificially watered, dependence being entirely on rainfall and resulting flood water.

Pima and Papago plants were not thinned out as they were too precious for this; nor were they ever transplanted. Pima tobacco was hoed, but not cultivated as much as other crops, and then only shallowly, since it had not been planted deeply. Weeds were either pulled out or cut off at the level of the ground with a knife about eight inches long, made of mesquite or ironwood, charred somewhat in a fire and sharpened on both edges with a stone. (It must here be remembered that the growing of tobacco was not aboriginal.) Weeding was done once or twice during the growing season. The

Papago did not hoe their tobacco, although in one village it was said to be a customary procedure. However, each time the grower visited his patch, he removed the protecting branches, loosened the dirt and hilled it around the plants by hand before replacing the branches.

It was the common Papago practice to keep animals out by building a fence around the patch, usually of creosote bush or mesquite posts, with thorny cholla cactus between, although in one village we visited the spot was not enclosed. The Pima never specifically fenced their tobacco, but if the plot were in the corner of a field planted to another crop, the entire field might be fenced. When Papago plants had come up, creosote bush branches were stuck in the ground around them for protection and shading, but when the young plants were partly grown the branches were removed. As nearly as could be determined this tobacco was called "under-the-creosote-bush tobacco" because it was always grown in a place where creosote bush was abundant; it was not planted in ashes by either Papago or Pima, as was done by some tribes. The same plot was used by the Papago for growing tobacco year after year, as long as it did well there. When it ceased to do so a new plot was selected. Pima practice was the reverse, for tobacco was rotated. Manuel Lowe said no volunteer plants came up, but this would be unusual if *N. rustica* were always the species grown. The soil was never fertilized by either people.

Both Papago and Pima knew that leaves on the plant were mature when they began to turn yellow or brown, and picked them progressively as they ripened. Among the Papago, the first leaves ripened and were gathered before sahuaro harvest, and the rest would be left until after the sahuaro season. Pima tobacco required about ten weeks to produce the first mature leaves, and the patch as a whole was not harvested until after the sahuaro fruit was gathered. Leaves of the first picking were larger, but not of better quality, than those of later ones. The mature leaves were

dried by the Papago in the sun on a sotol mat outside the
house, or on a piece of ground swept clean for the purpose,
and were regarded as ready for smoking when about half
dried and very bitter. Leaves were usually dried by the Pima
on a cotton blanket, either in the sun or the house, and
stirred occasionally with a stick to facilitate this process. If a
Papago wanted to use the tobacco before it was fully dried,
some leaves would be toasted on a piece of olla over hot
coals. However, customarily the leaves were fully dried in
the sun and stored without breaking, or first rolled into balls
before they were fully dried. They were then placed in an
olla or gourd, covered with a piece of broken olla, and sealed
with mud mixed with "sticky grass." This dried tobacco
might be stored in real bird nests kept in the house, but often
in a cavity made by the red-shafted flicker *(Colaptes cafer
collaris)* in a sahuaro tree. The Pima knew that leaves dried
more rapidly in the sun, but those dried indoors were stronger
and made better smoking, as the leaves curled somewhat and
seemed thicker than the sun-dried ones; they were rolled and
pressed into an olla and a cotton cloth tied over the top, or
sealed by placing a shaped piece of broken olla over the
opening and securing it with mud. This was for the purpose
of keeping out moisture and insects. Neither in drying the
leaves nor in putting them into the olla was any particular
care taken to keep the leaves unbroken. The olla was stored
in the brush house. When a quantity was wanted for smoking, the olla cover was removed, a few handfuls placed in a
buckskin (or in later times canvas) pouch, then the olla
resealed. This tobacco was very strong.

Among both Papago and Pima, the seeds, pods and flowers
were not smoked, but occasionally if a man's supply were low
he might crush and mix pieces of small stems with the leaves.

The Pima, after harvesting the ripe leaves, pulled up the
plants at the end of the season, and tied them in bundles for
storage. Leaves left on these plants matured more or less,
were called "third tobacco," and were also smoked. The

naked plants were placed on top of the house, never thrown away or burned, for tobacco was regarded as a man. When time came for making "wine" from sahuaro fruit, these stems were placed on top of dead ashes on the ground and the wine pots set upon them. Finally the stems were disposed of by burying in a pile of ashes.

After the Papago had gathered all leaves from the plants, a number of pods were gathered for seed, leaving the stalks standing. Pods were dried in an olla and stored in a gourd, sealed with mud mixed with "sticky grass," and kept in the house; or the seed might be stored in a hole in a giant cactus made by the red-shafted flicker. The Papago did not select their tobacco seed, because they usually needed to gather all available. But among the Pima, seed was selected from those plants which were tallest and had the largest pods. Late seed might also be gathered, but if so it was planted by itself because it did not do as well. The seed was cleaned and placed in a gourd, which was sealed with the gummy secretion from the creosote bush, then stored in the ground. Occasionally, however, among these Pima whole plants bearing seed pods were pulled up, dried and hung up indoors, this constituting the seed supply. Tobacco seed was considered by both tribes as very valuable and sometimes given as gifts.

Ritualistic Aspects of Tobacco Cultivation

Unlike some tribes, neither Papago nor Pima considered that other crops grown with tobacco would be injured. However, the Papago never grew tobacco in their fields, for it must be grown in secret and a man must be in the right spirit when planting. One who planted it must not let anyone see him do so, and, when visiting his tobacco patch which was out of sight of all the other fields, took a circuitous route so that no one would suspect or learn where he was going. If someone discovered the patch and saw the young plants, they would dry up. After plants were grown there was no objection to others seeing them, as no damage could result.

Also, if one should see a person planting, and knew he was planting tobacco seed, it would not come up. If a man who had ill thoughts came near the tobacco it might not come up, or if it did would not be any good.

The Pima practice differed somewhat. They, too, grew tobacco in an isolated portion of a field where no one else would see it, and for the same reason, but a man could never do the planting by himself. He must always have one or more old men accompany and help him, or at least watch him plant it. The men who assisted were paid in tobacco which the grower had previously raised. The same man did not plant tobacco every year, since he raised enough in one year for two or more years' supply. Several old men worked together to harvest the crop just as they did in planting it.

Papago and Pima tobacco had to be planted by older men who knew how to "talk" to it when planting, since it was regarded as a person, saying about as follows: "Now I place you here; may you come up well, grow strong and ripen so that my friends will come here and use you," or "I am a tobacco man and I plant you." The Papago planter then sang the tobacco planting song four times and finally placed the seed in the ground. Each time he came back to see the plants, at required intervals of four days, he sang the same song to the tobacco four times, believing that this gave it more strength (four is the ritual number among both the Papago and the Pima). After the eighth obligatory visit, he need no longer sing the song unless he wished to do so.

Piman women were not allowed to see tobacco growing, and if a menstruating woman were to see the plants they would shrivel up. In planting, tobacco seed must not be called by its real name, else it would not come up, and plants should not be watched too much while growing lest they be dwarfed. All ritualistic aspects of tobacco cultivation were regarded fully as necessary as the practical ones in producing a crop.

SMOKING

Pima usually carried tobacco in a special buckskin or foxskin pouch, decorated with sun symbols in bright colors and rattles, sometimes fringed, and closed with a flap folding over the top or occasionally with a drawstring. The simplest Papago pouches were a circular piece of dressed buckskin with a fringe around the entire edge, and tied up with a thong. Others were made of rabbit, or sometimes fox, skin with the fur left on. All present-day Papago pouches are of buckskin, dyed red with the root of *Krameria glandulosa*. They are made of two semi-circular pieces sewed together with fringe around the seam and a flap fastened by a knot or thong serving as a button.[4]

Papago and Pima had no true pipes, a fact mentioned by Lloyd[5] in 1911. Cigarettes for smoking tobacco were made usually from tubular stem sections of pigweed, or *bledo* (*Amaranthus Palmeri*). These were from one-fourth to nearly an inch across, and six to eight inches long, cut when the plants were mature, dried and the pith bored out. After coating with a layer of gummy secretion from the mesquite tree, they were ready for use. A Papago informant said the *Amaranthus* stems were being used for smoking when he was a boy, but that reed grass (*Phragmites communis*) stems had been utilized at an earlier time and had fallen into disuse due to scarcity and consequent difficulty in finding them. This reed grass does not occur in southern Arizona (except along the Colorado), but is found along streams in Apache, Navaho and Coconino counties.[6] Russell[7] states that it was formerly common along the Gila. Rolled cigarettes, made by wrapping tobacco in inner corn husks, seem to have been a later development among both peoples. Any special gathering for the good of the tribe or ceremonial occasion demanded

[4] Castetter and Underhill, *Ethnobiology of the Papago Indians*, p. 50.
[5] Lloyd, *Aw-aw-tam Indian Nights*, p. 89.
[6] J. J. Thornber, Personal correspondence, Feb. 13, 1940.
[7] Russell, *op. cit.*, p. 134.

that smoking be done only with the reed grass cigarette, never with corn husks. This was true for both Papago and Pima. Lloyd[8] observed that the ceremonial pipes of reed grass had bunches of small bird feathers tied to them. Corn husks to be used for cigarettes were selected when the corn was being shucked, and by each man for himself; only the soft, white inner husks were saved, and these stored in an arrowweed basket. These cigarettes were six to eight inches long and tied at both ends with shreds of corn husk. Often the cigarette was not all smoked at one time, as tobacco was scarce.

Smoking was practically universal among older Papago and Pima men, but less common among women and practically forbidden for young men. By both tribes it was considered injurious to young men, weakening them, causing a cough, making them lazy and fat, or unable to stand cold and preventing them from being alert. They did not believe it injured old men in any way. A father's usual reply to his son who requested permission to smoke was, "I will let you smoke after you have killed a coyote." In modern times, this restriction as regards smoking by young men largely has broken down, particularly among the Pima.

Tobacco was not chewed nor used as an emetic by either Papago or Pima.

To both tribes, smoking was essentially a ceremonial performance, and it had to be tobacco (*Nicotiana*) that was smoked, for it was regarded as having power and no other plant possessed equal efficacy.

Ceremonial smoking in a circuit, using only the reed grass cigarette, was fundamentally similar among Pima and Papago, although differing in detail. It was done only on a few special occasions, such as a party preparing for war, deciding on going on a hunt, having a race with another village, or, in fact, a discussion of any tribal problem, and was regarded as an aid in securing supernatural guidance at

8 Lloyd, *loc. cit.*

such times. When either tribe had such council meetings to settle common problems, the men first talked for a while, then the one in charge of the meeting (usually the chief) took a hollow section of *Amaranthus Palmeri* or *Phragmites communis* stem, filled it with tobacco and lighted it. After taking the ritual number of four puffs he handed it on to the man at his right, always counter-clockwise. In warrior circles, it was moved along near the ground, with the words, "It is traveling low—sneaking like a warrior." Each man took four puffs and similarly passed it to his right, and so on until the cigarette had gone around the entire circle. As each moved the cigarette along to the next, he called him by his kinship term, such as brother, uncle, cousin etc., this conveying the expression of friendly feeling. On its return to the one who lighted it, it was stuck into a small pile of ashes at his side. The men (among both tribes) then discussed the topic of the evening for a time, and when all had agreed on the issue in question, the chief relighted the cigarette and passed it around the circle just as before; or, if the problem were a knotty one requiring lengthy discussion, the cigarette might be relighted and again go the rounds. The main reason for all smoking the same cigarette at the meeting was, in the view of these Indians, to develop a unity of thought, spirit and purpose.

In ceremonies or meetings, each man blew the smoke upward to a Spirit in the heavens, upon whom he was calling for help or guidance in making decisions. Some informants, particularly among the Pima, asserted that the great power called upon was the sun. Smoking, both group and individual, was regarded as a sort of prayer—a medium of communication between the smoker and the Great Spirit, while the smoke itself was a means of gaining an audience, as well as the bearer of messages. Procedures and sequences in this ritual circuit smoking were always in fours, but smoke was not blown in the several directions as was customary among some tribes.

When smoking individually, a man might do so merely for pleasure or to communicate with the Great Spirit. Thus, while out walking somewhere, he might sit down to smoke and blow the smoke upward as a kind of unexpressed or incipient prayer, meanwhile talking to the tobacco or the smoke. But, in such cases, he must always finish the cigarette; that is, smoke it to a short stub, then roll it into a ball and gently place it on, or stick it into, the ground. A Papago, while smoking, must talk to the smoke which carried his prayer, else it would have no virtue. A man in trouble always smoked, and it was customary to do so before engaging in any endeavor, either personal or collective, for this was looked upon as a great help. It was done either to obtain aid for specific things or for the general welfare, such as planting, seeking rain, securing good crops, curing, health, preparing for warfare, sports etc. In planting or otherwise caring for his crops, a man, while smoking, blew smoke over the field, asking the Great Spirit that his crop grow well, that he have a good crop and that his relatives might benefit thereby. A man planning to run a race against someone from another village might blow smoke toward that village. In this case he would not talk to the Spirit but would say to his opponent, "You are not a great runner, I can beat you." He might also blow smoke toward the Apache when preparing to go to war against them, or toward the Gulf of Mexico when preparing for a salt expedition. One could talk to the Spirit without smoking, but smoking was thought to be an aid.

Pima informants said that to them everything was mysterious, and for this reason prayed to the darkness. At night a Pima would smoke and blow the smoke on his breast saying, "Kind darkness, give me good rest and good dreams and may nothing harm me." They also had great respect for the sun, well-nigh amounting to worship. In the morning the Pima would blow his smoke toward the sun saying, "Oh kind traveling sun, pity me. Give me the strength that whatever work I undertake I may accomplish easily through your power."

Both Papago and Pima regarded tobacco smoke as a purifying agent possessing definite curative properties, and smoking was believed to clear one's mind so that he could think better. The shaman, while singing for a patient to ascertain the cause of illness, paused at regular intervals to smoke and puff it over the patient as a means of cleansing or driving out the causative agent, the idea of prayer also being associated with the smoking. The shaman did not grow tobacco for himself; he either hunted wild tobacco or it was given to him, as the Pimans held their shamans in high regard. A Papago man who had come into contact with the supernatural by killing an enemy or an eagle, or by joining the salt pilgrimage, needed to be purified by a period of segregation and fasting. When this period was ended, older men who had gone through the same experience sang a series of ritual songs. Then each separately approached the novice and blew tobacco smoke over him, this portending success for his future.[9]

Smoking was essential while holding the ceremony for rain, and this was done by shamans, whose special task it was to see that the ceremony was held once a year (see fig. 5). They got together for four days and smoked, and their helpers danced. While smoking, these men searched for rain clouds and called on them to come. It was the office of this class of shamans to make it rain, and rainmaking was not a function of the general population.

[9] Castetter and Underhill, *op. cit.*, pp. 76-7.

CHAPTER X

GENERAL CEREMONIAL ASPECTS OF PIMAN AGRICULTURE

Ceremonialism was feebly developed among the Pimans as compared with the Pueblos. Underhill[1] has pointed out that the native line of division among the Papago is along a north and south line, the more advanced groups being to the east, and the more primitive ones to the west. Thus the Archie group retains many of the old ceremonies abandoned elsewhere, such as the important ceremony of the Vikita. Although the Pima formerly had as much or more ritualism than did the Papago, it is much better preserved and more easily and completely obtainable from the Papago.

The Piman conception was that ritual was just as important as actual cultivation in producing a crop, and no crop could be expected without it, consequently there existed a variety of individual and collective magical practices associated with the various stages of cultivation.

There was no formal group planting ceremony, the planting ritual consisting largely of singing individual songs of invocation and praise, maize, teparies, pumpkins and tobacco being planted with an individual invocation, which centered around maize as the principal crop. Also, with the Papago, the chief in each village got the people together just before planting time and exhorted them, saying it was now about time to plant crops, and that they should plant and industriously care for them. The day before planting started people began singing planting songs and continued until their repertoire was exhausted. During the summer, various nights of group singing were held to encourage the growth of crops. The most common of the various magical

1 Underhill, *Papago*, pp. 60, 234-35.

222

practices in parts of the Papago territory, to insure a good yield of both wild and cultivated crops, was to make effigies of the desired fruits and plant them in the gathering grounds after a night of ritual singing; or merely an ironwood stake would be planted instead of an effigy. In general the Papago did not ask for things directly, but in their rituals made statements to the Great Spirit and assumed their needs would be taken care of.

In addition to individual or personal ritualism, the Pimans had certain group ceremonies. After the crops had been put away, inter-village rejoicing often took place, at which games and races were held; this was occasion for jollification, as food was plentiful. People from other villages who helped in the observance were given meals and, at times, such products as corn to take home as a reward for their services. This celebration was held reciprocally from year to year, but always at a village which had harvested a good crop.

A characteristic and important Papago ritual was the green corn ceremony, held when the plants were about three feet high and just before the grain began to set, usually in September. Men gathered ocotillo poles and sang songs over them, then went to the fields and stuck an ocotillo rod at the base of certain corn plants, as well as representatives of each of the several kinds of crops. The object was to invoke the plant to grow strong like ocotillo and bear fruit. This ceremony was a combination of solicitation for a good crop and thanksgiving for those already received.

A regular ritual, practiced by both Papago and Pima, was the rain ceremony held at the time of giant cactus harvest (see fig. 5). This celebrated the beginning of the Piman New Year, and was the occasion when the fruit of sahuaro was fermented to yield an alcoholic beverage, which was drunk in quantity. This was performed specifically to bring rain, and, formerly, planting was never begun until after the first rain ceremony had been held. This was not because it was taboo, but due to dryness of the soil. Any village which found it convenient held the first ceremony and "caused the rain," then other villages in succession held celebrations during the summer to insure the continuation of rains. One custom was to erect two poles outdoors, about fifteen feet apart, and stretch a rope between them; on this shamans tied eagle feathers, symbolical of clouds, and all danced around these ceremonial objects.

Pima informants spoke of a "rain calling" ceremony in which certain groups of people got together in the council house for the purpose of bringing rain. Runners were sent out into every part of the village to secure all available sotol mats, then four posts were erected in a square and the mats arranged around these to form an enclosure, leaving an entrance at the east. Large baskets were placed upside down around the wall, inside the enclosure. Three shamans sat near the west wall, facing the east, with singers behind the baskets. Before each shaman was placed a large bowl containing eagle down, symbolic of clouds, and laid beside the bowls were tail feathers of an eagle. Using notched wooden rasping sticks, the musicians made a peculiar noise by drawing these over the baskets, and all joined in the singing. This was done four times. At certain stages each shaman took all the eagle down from the bowl in front of him, grasped it tightly in his left hand, rubbed it with his right hand and held it to the west, rubbed it again and held it toward the east, and so on in all directions. Then, changing the feathers to his right hand, he moved around in front of the baskets shaking the feathers toward the singers.

This ceremony was carried on during the entire night, and, at its close, the shamans revealed what they had "seen" during the night and prophesied how many days would elapse before it rained.

This is doubtless the "rain-calling" ceremony referred to

Fig. 5. Papago Rain Dance. (Reproduced from Underhill, *The Papago Indians of Arizona and their Relatives the Pima*, through the permission and courtesy of Dr. Willard W. Beatty, Director of Education, U. S. Office of Indian Affairs.)

by Hrdlicka,[2] held by the Pima during the long dry spell ending in the spring of 1905, in which notched sticks of greasewood *(Sarcobatus vermiculatus)* were rubbed along smaller plain sticks.

A modification of the above was the performance of a growing season ritual, held just before crop plants began to set fruit. Singers lined up along the edges of a field, each equipped with a notched rasping stick of creosote which he drew over a plain, slender creosote stick. Starting at the western end of the field, the singers, led by a shaman, moved around its edge until they arrived at the eastern end, meanwhile accompanying noise of the rasps with singing. They used no other ceremonial equipment, and the purpose of the performance was to call upon higher powers to give the people a good crop of well-developed fruits.

Informants said that formerly there was more rain in the Papago and Pima country; the reason for this was that the world was then newer and had greater power, also that more rigid observance of the ceremonies increased the rain.

One of the important Papago group ceremonies was the harvest festival. The Papago villages in the Santa Rosa Valley held this ceremony of Vikita jointly at the end of November or in early December, presumably every fourth year (in the southern part of Papaguería every year). However, its actual occurrence at Santa Rosa depended largely upon a successful harvest rather than the passing of any stated interval. This festival has been described in some detail by Lumholtz, Mason and Davis,[3] although the ceremony discussed by Davis, held in August at Quitobaquito, in Sonora, was accompanied by the drinking of much sahuaro wine, a feature obviously missing in early winter at Santa Rosa. The purpose of this ceremony was to invoke the higher power to give the people a good crop, to bring rain, free

2 Hrdlicka, *Notes on the Pima of Arizona,* p. 41.
3 Lumholtz, *New Trails,* pp. 92-8; Mason, *The Papago Harvest Festival;* Davis, *The Papago Ceremony of Vikita.*

crops from disease and to insure good health and long life. The paraphernalia used consisted of effigies representing clouds, corn, sahuaros, chollas, mesquite beans, deer etc., and were carried in a procession by masked singers. Every man in each village made some such effigy out of twigs and colored cotton, and this he carried to the scene of activity. Painted prayer sticks, adorned with fine turkey or eagle feathers, and the bull-roarer symbolized growing corn, lightning, thunder, clouds and the sound of rain. A group of clowns performed a variety of activities, such as carrying long poles to represent those with which sahuaro fruit is gathered, gourd rattles, portraying giant cactus trees, and wearing turkey feathers on their heads to symbolize the fruit. There were also representations of the sun and moon. They went through the motions of shooting at men disguised as deer, or at imaginary jackrabbits, antelope and other game. A replica of a field was made by each village, and sand brought from the arroyo was placed nearby to portray the mouth of the arroyo close to the field. Clowns in proper costume investigated to see if these "fields" were in proper condition, and imitated people working in fields by cleaning the "ditches" and burning "weeds." Shamans sprinkled cornmeal on the breasts of everyone, thus preventing sickness and bringing them long life, and, according to Davis,[4] such meal was made only from branched or twin ears of corn. Representatives from each village sang their cycle of eight songs, repeating as often as necessary, for singing continued all night. Just before dawn, the singers disrobed and painted themselves in a spotted fashion to depict multicolored ears of corn, principally blue, red and white. Girls carried ears of blue and white corn, and in each village group there were two men who represented yellow corn. Invariably the best specimens of corn, pumpkins and teparies were used in this ceremony. Content of the songs represented a description of the appearance of clouds, the occurrence of thunder, light-

4 *Ibid.*

ning, of rain and water running in the arroyos, of corn growing and fruiting. The purpose was to assist in producing a plentiful harvest and to give thanks for favors already bestowed.

Pima informants said that in earlier years their people had taken over from the Papago, in a half-hearted way, the ceremony of Vikita, but that it soon died out. However, in 1906, Brown[5] described a Pima-Maricopa harvest festival formerly held south of the village of Blackwater on the Gila, and, though known as a harvest festival, it might be performed on one or more important occasions each year. Here a group of musicians beat drums of carefully burned out cottonwood logs, a piece of half-tanned deerskin stretched across each end. Others drew bone rasps over the bottoms of upturned baskets, which had been spread with a layer of the gummy secretion of the mesquite tree. An unusual feature of this celebration was that the performers carried wooden and stone phalli, which were doubtless symbolic of fertility. Also, they carried long wands, evidently prayer sticks, tipped with feathers of wild turkey.

Some ceremonial practices and beliefs similar to those found among the Pueblos were also to be observed among the Pimans. One of these was color-direction association. The Piman ceremonial number is four, and four directions are recognized, associated with ceremonial colors. As applied to maize, one Pima informant at Sweetwater volunteered the information that white corn is east; red corn, west; blue corn is north; yellow corn, south. In addition, variegated corn was said to represent "up," while "down" corn was nearly black. This informant was asked on a number of different occasions to repeat the relation between directions and colors of corn and the results were invariably the same; we found it impossible to confuse him. Although this color direction does not check exactly with that given by Parsons,[6] who has listed a

[5] Brown, *A Pima-Maricopa Ceremony.*
[6] Parsons, *Notes on the Pima,* p. 459.

number of comparisons between the Pima and the Pueblos, or
by Underhill or Whiting,[7] the general situation has its counterpart among the Pueblo Indians.

Another Pueblo resemblance is seen in the assertion of
some Pima informants that, if a man accidentally cut off a
stalk of corn while hoeing, it was buried in the field, or
tucked under his belt and carried home at night. He felt very
badly about the experience for corn was his very life. It was
just like "killing his own life," or injuring a friend. Papago
had no such outlook. When a Papago cut off a stalk of corn
he too felt badly, but this was due purely to economic considerations. However, one informant said that, if the hoes
of two persons struck together while hoeing, it was an omen
that enemies were coming, so the workers quit and prepared
for them. This, too, has its Pueblo counterpart. Still another Pueblo resemblance is seen in the statement of one
Pima informant that planting was always started in the east of
the field and proceeded toward the west.

It is customary among the Pueblos for the people of a
village to prepare, plant, hoe, irrigate and harvest the
cacique's field, which in reality is a community field. Among
the Pimans, it was not uncommon for the people in a village
to take care of the chief's or headman's field, although this was
never out of ritualistic considerations as among the Pueblos,
but for purely practical reasons. Their view was that if the
chief were too busily engaged with tribal matters to look after
his farming it was only fair for his people to assist. It was in
no sense compulsory.

Pimans, particularly younger women, carefully avoided
branched or twin ears of corn, but these were commonly used
to provide cornmeal for ceremonies. Informants said that
women refrained from eating such ears because they feared
having twins, which were regarded as an ill omen.

There was no ceremonial sexual restriction at harvest or

[7] Underhill, *op. cit.*, p. 124; Whiting, *Ethnobotany of the Hopi*, p. 45.

any other period in the cultivation of crops, nor was there ceremonial copulation in the fields to increase fertility.

A magical practice common to Pima and Papago was performed for the purpose of increasing the productivity of crops, particularly pumpkins, watermelons and muskmelons. When these plants began to flower their owner sought a set of female twins whom he took into the fields. Each twin gathered tips of four pumpkins or melon vines, and walked through the patch chewing them and blowing her breath over the plants. The twins advised the owner to stay out of the field four or five days, then come back and he would see that numerous pumpkins and melons had set.

BIBLIOGRAPHY

ALEGRE, FRANCISCO JAVIER. *Historia de la Compañia de Jesús en Nueva España.* 3 vols. México, 1841-42.

ALEXANDER, HUBERT G. and PAUL REITER. *Report on the Excavation of Jemez Cave, New Mexico.* Bull., Univ. New Mexico, Monograph Ser., Vol. 1, No. 3. 1935.

ANONYMOUS. *Documentos para la Historia de México.* 20 vols. in 4 ser. Ser. 3 in four parts referred to as vols. México, 1853-57.

————. *Rudo Ensayo,* 1763. Trans. by Eusebio Guitéras. Records, Amer. Catholic Hist. Soc. of Philadelphia, Vol. 5, No. 2. 1894.

AUDUBON, JOHN W. and MARIA R. AUDUBON. *Audubon's Western Journal: 1849-50.* Cleveland, 1906.

BAILEY, L. H. *Manual of Cultivated Plants.* New York, 1938 (1924).

BAILEY, VERNON. *The Wild Cotton Plant (Thurberia thespesioides) in Arizona.* Bull., Torrey Bot. Club, *41*:301-06. 1914.

BALDWIN, GORDON C. *Dates from Kinishba Pueblo.* Tree Ring Bull. *1* (4) : 30. 1935.

BANCROFT, HUBERT HOWE. *The Native Races.* Vol. 1, *Wild Tribes.* San Francisco, 1883.

BANDELIER, A. F. *Final Report of Investigations among the Indians of the Southwestern United States* ... 1880-1885. Papers, Archaeol. Inst. of Amer., Amer. Ser., Nos. 3, 4. Cambridge, Mass., 1890-92.

BARTLETT, JOHN RUSSELL. *Personal Narrative of Explorations and Incidents in Texas, New Mexico, California, Sonora, and Chihuahua, etc.* 2 vols. London, New York, 1854.

BEALS, RALPH L. *The Comparative Ethnology of Northern Mexico before 1750.* Ibero-Americana, No. 2. Berkeley, 1932.

BOLTON, HERBERT EUGENE. *Kino's Historical Memoir of Pimeria Alta.* 2 vols. Cleveland, 1919.

————. *Anza's California Expeditions.* 5 vols. Berkeley, 1930.

————. *Rim of Christendom.* New York, 1936.

BRAND, DONALD D. *Notes to Accompany a Vegetation Map of Northwest Mexico.* Bull., Univ. New Mexico, Biol. Ser., Vol. 4, No. 4. 1936.

BROWN, HERBERT. *A Pima-Maricopa Ceremony.* Amer. Anthropol. *8*:688-90. 1906.

BROWNE, J. ROSS. *Adventures in the Apache Country, etc.* New York, 1874 (1869).

BRYAN, KIRK. *The Papago Country, Arizona.* Water-Supply Paper, U. S. Geol. Survey, No. 499. 1925.

————. *Pre-Columbian Agriculture in the Southwest, as Conditioned by Periods of Alluviation.* Annals, Assoc. of Amer. Geographers, *31*:219-42. 1941.

BUKASOV, S. M. *The Cultivated Plants of Mexico, Guatemala and Colombia.* Bull. Applied Bot., Genet. and Plant Breed., Suppl. 47; English summary pp. 470-553. Leningrad, 1930.

231

CASTETTER, EDWARD F. and RUTH M. UNDERHILL. *The Ethnobiology of the Papago Indians.* Ethnobiol. Studies in the Amer. Southwest II. Bull., Univ. New Mexico, Biol. Ser., Vol. 4, No. 3. 1935.

CLARK, S. P. *Lessons from Southwestern Indian Agriculture.* Bull., Univ. Arizona Agric. Exper. Sta., No. 125. 1928.

CLOTTS, HERBERT V. *Report on Nomadic Papago Surveys,* to C. R. Olberg, Supt. of Irrig., U. S. Indian Service, Pts. 1, 2 (Manuscript). 1915.

————. *History of the Papago Indians and History of Irrigation on Indian Reservations.* Dept. of the Interior, U. S. Indian Service (Manuscript). 1917.

COUES, ELLIOTT. *On the Trail of a Spanish Pioneer. The Diary and Itinerary of Francisco Garcés, etc., 1775-1776.* 2 vols. New York, 1900.

CURTIS, EDWARD S. *The North American Indian,* Vol. 2. Cambridge, Mass., 1908.

DARLING, F. FRASER. *A Herd of Red Deer.* London, 1937.

DAVIS, EDWARD H. *The Papago Ceremony of Vikita.* Indian Notes and Monographs, Vol. 3, No. 4. 1920.

DAVIS, HORACE. *California Breadstuffs.* (Reprinted from the Journal of Political Economy, No. 2.) Chicago, 1894.

DENSMORE, FRANCES. *Papago Music.* Bull., Bur. Amer. Ethnol., No. 90. 1929.

DICE, LEE R. *The Sonoran Biotic Province.* Ecology 20:118-29. 1939.

DRUCKER, PHILIP. *Culture Element Distributions: XVII, Yuman-Piman.* Anthropol. Records, Vol. 6, No. 3. 1941.

EMORY, W. H. *Notes of a Military Reconnoissance from Fort Leavenworth, in Missouri, to San Diego, in California.* Senate Ex. Doc. No. 7, 30th Cong., 1st Sess. Washington, 1848.

————. *Report on the U. S. and Mexican Boundary Survey.* Ex. Doc. No. 108, 34th Cong., 1st Sess., Vol. 1. Washington, 1857.

ERWIN, A. T. *A Rare Specimen of Zea Mays var. saccharata.* Science 79:589. 1934.

FEWKES, J. WALTER, *Casa Grande, Arizona.* 28th Ann. Report, Bur. Amer. Ethnol., pp. 25-179. 1912.

FORBES, R. H. *Irrigation and Agricultural Practice in Arizona.* Bull., Univ. Arizona Agric. Exper. Sta., No. 63. 1911.

FORDE, C. DARYLL. *Ethnography of the Yuma Indians.* Univ. California Pubs. in Amer. Archaeol. and Ethnol. 28:83-278. 1931.

FREEMAN, GEORGE F. *Southwestern Beans and Teparies.* Bull., Univ. Arizona Agric. Exper. Sta., No. 68. 1918 (1912).

————. *The Tepary, a New Cultivated Legume from the Southwest.* Bot. Gazette 56:395-417. 1913.

————. *Papago Sweet Corn, a New Variety.* Bull., Univ. Arizona Agric. Exper. Sta., No. 75. 1915.

FULTON, J. F. *Hopi Cotton, a Variable Species.* Jour. Agric. Research 56:333-36. 1938.

GAILLARD, D. D. *The Papago of Arizona and Sonora.* Amer. Anthropol., o. s. 7:293-96. 1894.

GIFFORD, E. W. *The Cocopa.* Univ. California Pubs. in Amer. Archaeol. and Ethnol. 31:257-334. 1933.

GLADWIN, H. S. *Excavations at Casa Grande, Arizona.* Southwest Mus. Papers, No. 2. 1928.

————. *Excavations at Snaketown II. Comparisons and Theories.* Medallion Papers, No. 26. Globe, 1937.

GLADWIN, H. S., E. W. HAURY, E. B. SAYLES and NORA GLADWIN. *Excavations at Snaketown. Material Culture.* Medallion Papers, No. 25. Globe, 1937.

GLADWIN, W. J. and H. S. GLADWIN. *The Red-on-Buff Culture of the Gila Basin.* Medallion Papers, No. 3. Globe, 1929.

————. *The Eastern Range of the Red-on-Buff Culture.* Medallion Papers, No. 16. Globe, 1935.

GRAY, ASA. *Planta Wrightianae Texana—Neo-Mexicanae: an Account of a Collection of Plants Made by Charles Wright, A. M., in an Expedition from Texas to New Mexico, in . . . 1849, etc.*, Pts. 1, 2. Pub. by Smithson. Inst. as Smithson. Contribs. to Knowledge; Pt. 1 as vol. 3, art. 5; Pt. 2 as vol. 5, art. 6. Washington, 1852-53.

————. *Synoptical Flora of North America,* Vol. 2, Pt. 1. New York, 1878.

Grossmann, F. E. *The Pima Indians of Arizona.* Ann. Report, Smithson. Inst., for 1871, pp. 407-19. Washington, 1873.

HALSETH, ODD S. *Prehistoric Irrigation in the Salt River Valley. Symposium on Prehistoric Agriculture.* Bull., Univ. New Mexico, Anthropol. Ser., Vol. 1, No. 5, pp. 42-7. 1936.

HAMMOND, G. P. *Don Juan de Oñate and the Founding of New Mexico.* Pubs. in History, Hist. Soc. of New Mexico, Vol. 2. Santa Fe, 1927.

HANSON, HERBERT C. *Distribution of Arizona Wild Cotton (Thurberia thespesioides).* Tech. Bull., Univ. Arizona Agric. Exper. Sta., No. 3. 1923.

HARDENBURG, E. V. *Bean Culture.* New York, 1927.

HAURY, EMIL W. *Roosevelt: 9:6, a Hohokam Site of the Colonial Period.* Medallion Papers, No. 11. Globe, 1932.

————. *The Canyon Creek Ruin and the Cliff Dwellings of the Sierra Ancha.* Medallion Papers, No. 14. Globe, 1934.

HENDRY, GEORGE W. *The Adobe Brick as a Historical Source.* Agric. Hist. 5:110-27. 1931.

HILL, W. W., *Notes on Pima Land Law and Tenure.* Amer. Anthropol. 38:586-89. 1936.

————. *The Agricultural and Hunting Methods of the Navaho Indians.* Pubs. in Anthropol., Yale Univ., No. 18. 1938.

HINSDALE, W. B. *Distribution of the Aboriginal Population of Michigan.* Occasional Contribs., Mus. of Anthropol., Univ. Michigan, No. 2. 1932.

HODGE, F. W. *Prehistoric Irrigation in Arizona.* Amer. Anthropol. o. s. 6:323-30. 1893.

HOOVER, J. W. *The Indian Country of Southern Arizona.* Geog. Rev. 19:38-60. 1929.

————. *Generic Descent of the Papago Villages.* Amer. Anthropol. 37:257-64. 1935.

HORNADAY, WILLIAM T. *Camp-fires on Desert and Lava.* New York, 1914.

HOUGH, WALTER. *The Hopi in Relation to their Plant Environment.* Amer. Anthropol., o. s. 10:33-44. 1897.

——. *Culture of the Ancient Pueblos of the Upper Gila Region, New Mexico and Arizona.* Bull., U. S. Nat. Mus., No. 87. 1914.

HRDLICKA, ALES. *Notes on the Pima of Arizona.* Amer. Anthropol. *8*:39-46. 1906.

——. *Physiological and Medical Observations among the Indians of Southwestern United States and Northern Mexico.* Bull., Bur. Amer. Ethnol., No. 34. 1908.

JONES, VOLNEY H. *Ceremonial Cigarettes.* Southwestern Monuments, Monthly Report, Suppl., Oct., 1935, pp. 287-91 (Mimeographed).

——. *A Summary of Data on Aboriginal Cotton of the Southwest. Symposium on Prehistoric Agriculture.* Bull., Univ. New Mexico, Anthropol. Ser., Vol. 1, No. 5, pp. 51-64. 1936.

KIDDER, ALFRED VINCENT and SAMUEL J. GUERNSEY. *Archeological Explorations in Northeastern Arizona.* Bull., Bur. Amer. Ethnol., No. 65. 1919.

KING, C. J. *Crop Tests at the Cooperative Testing Station, Sacaton, Ariz.* Circular, U. S. Dept. Agric., No. 277. 1923.

KING, C. J. and A. R. LEDING. *Agricultural Investigations at the United States Field Station, Sacaton, Ariz., 1922, 1923, and 1924.* Circular, U. S. Dept. Agric., No. 372. 1926.

KING, C. J. and H. F. LOOMIS. *Agricultural Investigations at the United States Field Station, Sacaton, Ariz., 1925-1930.* Circular, U. S. Dept. Agric., No. 206. 1932.

KING, C. J., R. E. BECKETT and ORLAN PARKER. *Agricultural Investigations at the United States Field Station, Sacaton, Ariz., 1931-35.* Circular, U. S. Dept. Agric., No. 479. 1938.

KISSELL, MARY L. *Basketry of the Papago and Pima.* Anthropol. Papers, Amer. Mus. Nat. Hist., Vol. 17, Pt. 1. 1916.

KROEBER, A. L. *Handbook of the Indians of California.* Bull., Bur. Amer. Ethnol., No. 78. 1925.

——. *Cultural and Natural Areas of Native North America.* Berkeley, 1939.

LEE, W. T. *The Underground Waters of Gila Valley, Arizona.* Water-Supply and Irrigation Paper, U. S. Geol. Survey, No. 104. 1904.

LEWTON, F. L. *The Cotton of the Hopi Indians: a New Species of Gossypium.* Smithson. Miscellaneous Collecs., Vol. 60, No. 6. 1912.

LIPPINCOTT, J. B. *Storage of Water on Gila River, Arizona.* Water-Supply and Irrigation Paper, U. S. Geol. Survey, No. 33. 1900.

LLOYD, J. WILLIAM. *Aw-aw-tam Indian Nights.* Westfield, N. J., 1911.

LUMHOLTZ, CARL. *New Trails in Mexico.* New York, 1912.

MALLERY, T. D. *Rainfall Records for the Sonoran Desert.* Ecology *17*:110-21. 1936.

——. *Rainfall Records for the Sonoran Desert II.* Ecology *17*:212-15. 1936.

MANGE, JUAN M. *Luz de Tierra Incógnita en la América Septentrional y Diario de las Exploraciones en Sonora.* Publicaciones del Archivo General de la Nación, tomo X. México, 1926.

MASON, J. ALDEN. *The Papago Harvest Festival.* Amer. Anthropol. *22*:13-25. 1920.

McGREGOR, JOHN C. *Winona and Ridge Ruin, Part I. Architecture and Material Culture.* Plant Material by Volney H. Jones. Bull., Mus. N. Arizona, No. 18. Flagstaff, 1941.

NICHOL, A. A. *The Natural Vegetation of Arizona.* Bull., Univ. Arizona Agric. Exper. Sta., No. 68. 1937.

[OBREGÓN, BALTHASAR DE.] *Obregón's History of 16th Century Explorations in Western America, Entitled Chronicle Commentary or Relation of Ancient and Modern Discoveries in New Spain and New Mexico.* Trans. and ed. by G. P. Hammond and Agapito Rey. Los Angeles, 1928.

OLBERG, C. R. and F. R. SCHANCK. *Special Report on Irrigation and Flood Protection, Papago Indian Reservation.* Senate Ex. Doc., Vol. 24. 62nd Cong., 3rd Sess. Washington, 1913.

PARSONS, ELSIE CLEWS. *Notes on the Pima, 1926.* Amer. Anthropol., *30*:445-64. 1928.

PÉREZ DE RIBAS, ANDRÉS. *Historia de los Triumphos de Novestra Santa Fee, en las Missiones de la Provincia de Nueva España.* Madrid, 1645.

PFEFFERKORN, IGNAZ. *Beschreibung der Landschaft Sonora.* 2 vols. Köln, 1794-95.

PIPER, C. V. *Studies in American Phaseolineae.* Contribs., U. S. Nat. Herb., 22:663-701. 1926.

REED, E. K. and J. W. BREWER. *Excavations of Room 7, Wupatki.* Southwestern Monuments, Special Report No. 13 (Mimeographed). 1937.

Report of the Commissioner of Indian Affairs for 1858. Washington, 1859; *ibid.* for 1863. Washington, 1863; *ibid.* for 1864. Washington, 1864; *ibid.* for 1865. Washington, 1865; *ibid.* for 1869. Washington, 1869; *ibid.* for 1871. Washington, 1872; *ibid.* for 1875. Washington, 1875; *ibid.* for 1878. Washington, 1878; *ibid.* for 1883. Washington, 1883; *ibid.* for 1887. Washington, 1887; *ibid.* for 1891. Washington, 1891; *ibid.* for 1897. Washington, 1897; *ibid.* for 1898. Washington, 1898; *ibid.* for 1899. Washington, 1899; *ibid.* for 1904. Washington, 1905; *ibid.* for 1914. Washington, 1915; *ibid.* for 1919. Washington, 1919.

ROSS, CLYDE P. *The Lower Gila Region, Arizona.* Water-Supply Paper, U. S. Geol. Survey, No. 498. 1923.

RUSSELL, FRANK. *The Pima Indians.* 26th Ann. Report, Bur. Amer. Ethnol., pp. 3-389. 1908.

SAUER, CARL. *The Road to Cibola.* Ibero-Americana, No. 3. Berkeley, 1932.

———. *The Distribution of Aboriginal Tribes and Languages in Northwestern Mexico.* Ibero-Americana, No. 5. Berkeley, 1934.

———. *Aboriginal Population of Northwestern Mexico.* Ibero-Americana, No. 10. Berkeley, 1935.

SAUER, CARL and DONALD BRAND. *Prehistoric Settlements of Sonora with Special Reference to Cerros de Trincheras.* Pubs. in Geog., Univ. California, *5* (3):67-148. 1931.

[SEDELMAYR, JACOBO.] *Sedelmayr's Relación of 1746.* Trans. and ed. by R. L. Ives. Anthropol. Papers, No. 9, Bull., Bur. Amer. Ethnol., No. 123. 1939.

SETCHELL, WILLIAM ALBERT. *Aboriginal Tobaccos.* Amer. Anthropol. 23:397-414. 1921.

SHREVE, FORREST. *The Plant Life of the Sonoran Desert.* Scien. Monthly *42*:195-213. 1936.

SMITH, H. V. *The Climate of Arizona.* Bull., Univ. Arizona Agric. Exper. Sta., No. 130. 1930.

SOUTHWORTH, C. H. *A History of Irrigation on the Gila River Indian Reservation* (Manuscript). 1916.

SPIER, LESLIE. *Havasupai Ethnography.* Anthropol. Papers, Amer. Mus. Nat. Hist., *29*:83-392. 1928.

———. *Yuman Tribes of the Gila River.* Chicago, 1933.

———. *Cultural Relations of the Gila River and Lower Colorado Tribes.* Pubs. in Anthropol., Yale Univ., No. 3. 1936.

STEEN, CHARLIE R. *The Upper Tonto Ruins.* The Kiva *6* (5). 1941.

STEEN, CHARLIE R. and VOLNEY H. JONES. *Prehistoric Lima Beans in the Southwest.* El Palacio *48*:197-203. 1941.

SYKES, GODFREY. *The Camino del Diablo: with Notes on a Journey in 1925.* Geog. Rev. *17*:62-74. 1927.

———. *Rainfall Investigations in Arizona and Sonora by Means of Long-period Rain Gauges.* Geog. Rev. *21*:229-33. 1931.

THWAITES, R. G. *The Personal Narrative of James O. Pattie.* Early Western Travels, 1748-1846, Vol. 18. Cincinnati, 1831.

TURNAGE, WILLIAM V. and T. D. MALLERY. *An Analysis of Rainfall in the Sonoran Desert and Adjacent Territory.* Pubs., Carnegie Inst. of Washington, No. 529. 1941.

TURNEY, OMAR A. *The Land of the Stone Hoe.* Phoenix, 1924.

———. *Prehistoric Irrigation in Arizona.* Phoenix, 1929.

UNDERHILL, RUTH M. *A Papago Calendar Record.* Bull., Univ. New Mexico, Anthropol. Ser., Vol. 2, No. 5. 1938.

———. *Social Organization of the Papago Indians.* New York, 1939.

———. *The Papago Indians of Arizona and their Relatives the Pimas.* Sherman Pamphlets, U. S. Office of Indian Affairs, No. 3. Haskell Inst., Lawrence, Kan., 1940.

VAVILOV, N. I. *Botanical-Geographic Principles of Selection.* Lenin Acad. of Agric. Sciences of the Inst. of Plant Breed. of the U. S. S. R. Leningrad, 1935.

VELASCO, JUAN LÓPEZ DE. *Geografía y Descripción Universal de las Indias recopilada por el cosmógrafocronista [Juan Lopez de Velasco] desde el año de 1571 al de 1574.* Madrid, 1894.

VOEGELIN, ERMINE WHEELER. *The Place of Agriculture in the Subsistence Economy of the Shawnee.* Papers, Michigan Acad. of Sci., Arts, and Letters *26*:513-20. 1941.

WHIPPLE, A. W. *Official Report of the Survey of the River Gila,* 1852; in Bartlett, *Personal Narrative,* Vol. 2, appendix D, pp. 597-602. 1854.

WHITING, ALFRED F. *Ethnobotany of the Hopi.* Bull., Mus. N. Arizona, No. 15. 1939.

WHITTEMORE, ISAAC T. in *Among the Pimas or the Mission to the Pima and Maricopa Indians.* Albany, N. Y., 1893.

WILSON, GILBERT LIVINGSTONE. *Agriculture of the Hidatsa Indians, an Indian Interpretation.* Bull., Univ. Minnesota, Studies in the Soc. Sciences, No. 9. 1917.

WOODWARD, ARTHUR. *The Grewe Site.* Occasional Papers, Los Angeles Mus. of Hist., Sci. and Art, No. 1 (Mimeographed). 1931.

WYLLYS, RUFUS KAY. *Padre Luis Velarde's Relación of Pimería Alta, 1716.* New Mexico Hist. Rev. *6*:111-57. 1931.

INDEX

Sage hen, 30
Sagie Canyon, 93
Sahuaro (giant cactus), 24, 31, 41, 45,
  57, 58, 59, 61, 62, 63, 70, 130, 149,
  185, 189, 214, 215, 223, 227
Salado people, 29, 34
Salt, 220, 221
  pilgrimage, 221
Saltbush, 22, 23, 61, 62, 212
  desert, 22, 24
  brittle, 22
Salt cedar, 23
Salt River, 22
Salvatierra, Juan María, 75
San Agustín de Oiaur, 103, 119
San Angelo del Bótum (Cocklebur),
  118, 162
San Bernardino, 4
San Cayetano del Tumacácori, 115, 117
San Gabriel, 69
San Ignacio River, 5, 41
San Juan, 4
San Juan Basin, 97
San Luis Bertrando, 59
San Miguel, 169
San Miguel del Tupo, 74
San Miguel Valley, 4, 5
San Pedro River, 5, 8, 14, 21, 22, 24,
  37, 65, 103, 146, 156
San Pedro Village, 111, 171, 210
San Rafael del Actúm Grande, 44, 45
San Valentín, 115
San Xavier del Bac, 4, 5, 49, 52, 65,
  71, 78, 103, 110, 117, 118, 145, 149,
  163, 164, 166, 177, 178
Sand Papago (Areneños), 6-7, 11, 62,
  70, 170
Sand root, 58, 60, 61, 62, 64
Santa Catalina Mountains, 24, 27
Santa Cruz River, 5, 6, 8, 14, 21, 22, 23,
  36, 103, 145, 156, 163, 164, 165,
  166, 167
Santa Eulalia, 60
Santa María de Bugota, 103
Santa Rosa, 37, 162, 226
Santa Rosa Valley, 24, 169
Santa Viviana, 60
Santo Domingo, 62
Saracachi, 107
Sauer, Carl, 2, 3, 4, 6, 9
Sayal, 41
Schanck, F. R., 164, 165, 166
Screwbean, 22, 31, 57, 58, 62, 63, 64, 70,
  134, 136
Sedelmayr, Jacobo, 103
Seed selection, 186, 191, 195, 196, 198,
  200, 204, 207, 209, 215

Seeds,
  number per hill, 153-54, 176
  soaking, 155
Seepwillow, 23
Selection, knowledge of, 186, 191, 195,
  196
Seri Indians, 1, 2
Setchell, William Albert, 108, 111
Shaman, 221, 224, 227
Shawnee Indians, 55
Sheep, 39, 75
Shellfish, 70
Short planting, 149
Shovel, 137
Shreve, Forrest, 12, 21
Sierra del Alamo, 67
Sierra del Viejo, 67
Sierra Madre, 1
Sierra Maricopa, 158
Size of Piman farms, 51-7, 132
Skunkbush, 22
Smith, H. V., 14, 19, 20, 145
Smoking, 214, 217-21
Snakes, 70
Snaketown Canal, 17, 156, 157
Snaketown Period, 31
Snaketown site, 103
Soapberry, 26
Soba, 2, 5, 9, 65
Sobaipuri, 2, 3, 5, 8, 9, 11, 37, 43, 49,
  65, 71, 72, 73, 103, 156, 163
Soil,
  fertility, 172-73, 213
  quality of, 122-25
  saline, 122-25
Somerton, 6
Sonoita, Río de, 6, 7, 25, 48, 49, 62
Sonoita, San Marcelo de, 7, 48, 145, 162
Sonora, 1, 4, 6, 37, 59, 60, 61, 66, 67,
  70, 74, 104, 118, 150, 162, 226
Sonora, Río de, 1, 5
Sonoran Biotic Province, 12
Sonoran Desert, 12, 19, 20, 29
Sorghums, grain, 77, 78
Sotol, 205, 214, 224
Southworth, C. H., 15, 18, 54, 157
Soybeans, 170
Spanish missionaries, 2, 3, 4, 10
Spier, Leslie, 5, 6, 8, 38, 58, 68, 73, 81,
  107, 109, 110, 111, 113, 127, 189, 199
Spinach, 78
Spinning, 199
Squash bugs, 177
Squawberry, 22, 25
Squirrel, ground, 30
Star lore, 143
Steen, Charlie R., 34, 35, 90, 113
Stone Cabin Canyon, 94

THE AUTHORS

EDWARD FRANKLIN CASTETTER: born Shamokin, Pa., 1896; Ph.D. Iowa State College, 1924; Graduate Fellow in Botany, Pennsylvania State College, 1919-20; Assistant Professor of Biology, Southern Methodist University, 1920-21; Instructor, Assistant Professor, Associate Professor of Botany, Iowa State College, 1921-28; Professor and Head, Department of Biology, University of New Mexico, since 1928. Author: *Ethnobiological Studies in the American Southwest*, I-VII (II with Ruth M. Underhill, III with M. E. Opler, IV-VII with W. H. Bell), University of New Mexico Biology Series, 1935-41; and other contributions in the field of botany.

WILLIS HARVEY BELL: born North Washington, Pa., 1908; Ph.D. University of Chicago, 1932; Assistant Principal, Concord Township High School, 1927-28; Instructor in Botany, Duke University, 1928-29; Assistant Professor, Associate Professor of Biology, University of New Mexico, since 1931. Author: *Ethnobiological Studies in the American Southwest*, vols. IV-VII (with Castetter; see above); *Description and Botanical Relationships of Important Range Plants Regions 7 (New Mexico) and 9 (Arizona)*, U. S. Department of the Interior, Washington, 1938; and other articles on botanical subjects.

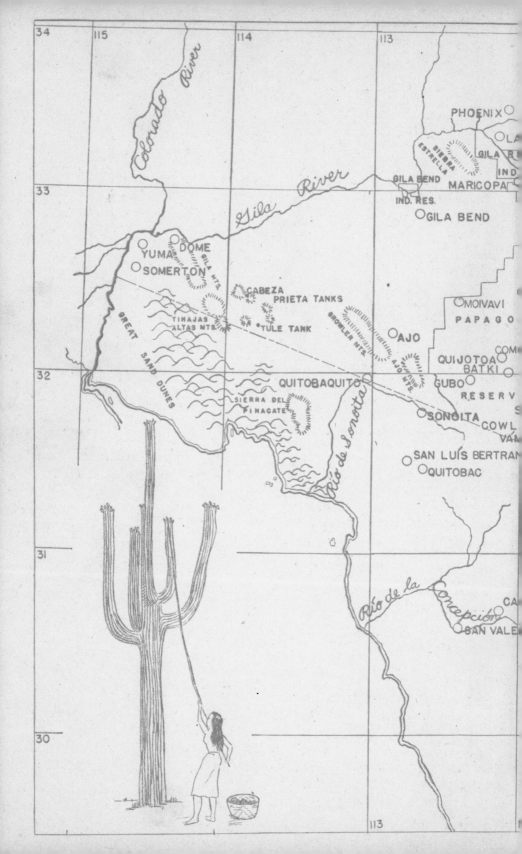